WELCOME TO OUR WORLD

CORWIN
PRESS

The Corwin Press logo—a raven striding across an open book —represents the happy union of courage and learning. We are a professional-level publisher of books and journals for K–12 educators, and we are committed to creating and providing resources that embody these qualities. Corwin's motto is "Success for All Learners."

WELCOME TO OUR WORLD

Realities of High School Students

Robert N. Gilbert
Mike Robins

Artist/Illustrator: Joey Depakakibo

CORWIN PRESS, INC.
A Sage Publications Company
Thousand Oaks, California

For information:

Corwin Press, Inc.
A Sage Publications Company
2455 Teller Road
Thousand Oaks, California 91320
E-mail: order@corwin.sagepub.com

SAGE Publications Ltd.
6 Bonhill Street
London EC2A 4PU
United Kingdom

SAGE Publications India Pvt. Ltd.
M-32 Market
Greater Kailash I
New Delhi 110 048 India

Printed in the United States of America

Library of Congress Cataloging-in-Publication Data

Gilbert, Robert N.
    Welcome to our world : Realities of high school students / Robert N. Gilbert, Mike Robins.
        p.   cm.
    Includes bibliographical references.
    ISBN 0-8039-6679-2 (cloth : acid-free paper). — ISBN 0-8039-6680-6 (pbk. : acid-free paper)
        1. High school students—Illinois—Conduct of life—Case studies. 2. High school students—Illinois—Attitudes—Case studies. 3. High schools—Illinois—Public opinion—Case studies. 4. Public opinion—Illinois—Case studies. 5. High schools—Illinois—Sociological aspects—Case studies.   I. Robins, Mike.   II. Title.
LA229.G54 1998
373.18'0973—dc21   97-33766

This book is printed on acid-free paper.

98   99   00   01   02   03   10   9   8   7   6   5   4   3   2   1

Production Editor: S. Marlene Head
Editorial Assistant: Kristen L. Gibson
Typesetters: Laura A. and William C. E. Lawrie
Cover Designer: Marcia M. Rosenburg
Artist/Illustrator: Joey Depakakibo

Contents

Preface

Despite the overwhelming attention paid to the crisis of education, rarely is there inclusion of the student perspective. The purpose of this book is to introduce students as intelligent, fully vested partners in the vital debate on school reform.

If the goal of educators is to make sound education policy in the real world, then educators would benefit from understanding the realities in which students operate daily. If education policy is to deliver the impact intended, then it stands to reason that educators would benefit from understanding the dynamics of its impact. Students, as recipients of policy, are well positioned to offer insight as to the potential impact of policy. Indeed, we argue student input should be directly related to the degree policy potentially affects students.

Today's students will inherit tomorrow. They must succeed! Students have a vested interest as fully participating partners to make certain their schools do succeed. Students can complement the efforts of administrators and teachers working to remedy the problems facing our schools.

Chapter 1 suggests that administrators, teachers, and students all live in different realities. Administrators must successfully manage a large, diverse body of teachers and students while still answering to the larger community. Teachers try to personalize lessons for tests that are increasingly standardized. They strive for commonality within increasingly diverse classrooms. Students want to learn but often cannot fit into the standardized roles in which teachers and administrators wish they would fit. We suggest that the gap between these various realities results in a battle that students are more likely to lose.

Chapters 2 through 6 include what is truly special about this book. Students, from a middle-class suburban high school outside Chicago, explain in their own written words the issues that concern them most. The essays, originally written for this book, are powerful and profound. These are not spur-of-the-moment, off-handed remarks spoken into a tape recorder, but rather meaningful compositions about the issues that students deal with every day. Students chose their own topics. They address academics, sports, extracurricular activities, working, family, and larger societal issues with thoughtfulness and insight. The essays were submitted on disk, put through Grammatik, a grammar-checking program, and returned unchanged to the students. Students then made only those changes they wished. Although the compositions vary in tone, maturity, and length, few editorial changes have been made in order to preserve the voice of each student.

The essays included here were chosen from a group of more than 100. A panel consisting of one current student and two alumni chose the essays for the book. Each essay was rated on a scale of 1-5 in two categories: content and style. The panel worked carefully to include essays that represented the entire student body and not only the most gifted writers. In turn, originality of ideas and significance of the message outweighed the importance of composition skills. All of the students' ideas are equally relevant. Their articles impressively represent the great diversity of the school and the community in which they originated.

Most striking throughout these chapters, however, is the extreme intensity of many of the contributions. From a predominantly white, affluent, upper-middle-class suburb, students shock us with the number of "adult" issues they face in their young lives. Even the more sensitive and caring teachers and administrators may have no idea what is actually going on in the lives of their students:

- The "rich" student who must work three jobs (more than 50 hours per week) in addition to attending school full-time to help mom make the mortgage payments
- The seemingly happy, outgoing honors student who goes home to the pain of an alcoholic father each night
- The nervous, terrified student who cannot concentrate because she is being stalked by a former boyfriend
- The student who learns at age 15 that he is an illegal immigrant and subject to deportation and separation from his family
- The student who is BD (Behavioral Disordered) at school but not at home and not at work
- The honors student who ditches school in order to complete homework assignments
- The gay, lesbian, bisexual, or transgender student who is subjected to gay-bashing, hate, and threats to his or her life in class

Again, these are not the experiences of a lower-middle-class, urban school but those of an affluent suburb. These are the so-called normal kids. Obviously, students bring more to the classroom than a rigidly standardized curriculum can hope to accommodate.

This book should be read by teachers and administrators interested in better understanding the serious diversity and complexity of so-called "normal" students. School social workers may benefit from the wide-reaching psychological and emotional issues raised by students, many of whom they would not normally see. In addition, the book offers a unique perspective to future teachers and can serve as a useful text in college courses that address teacher training, educational psychology, student lore, philosophy of education, or school administration. In a similar fashion, the student reality is relevant to courses in psychology, sociology, anthropology, ethnography, adolescence, and social work. This book will generate much class discussion as students in all of these courses find much to which they can relate.

Our primary goal is to remind all that students are complex, multidimensional, thinking, feeling, unique, and active participants in their education. The student voices here support this point magnificently.

Acknowledgments

I would like to acknowledge James S. Coleman, Professor of Sociology and Professor of Education, the University of Chicago, and President of the American Sociological Association from 1991-1992. James had wanted to write the foreword to this book. He will be greatly missed. Professor Coleman's landmark survey research includes *The Adolescent Society* and *The Coleman Report on Equal Educational Opportunity*. James Coleman personally encouraged the development and publication of this work. Just as I have encouraged my students, Professor Coleman encouraged me. He demonstrated the power of faith in students. He was an educator of educators. From this I have benefited greatly and am most grateful. Professors William H. Schubert and William Ayers of the University of Illinois, Chicago, were early and loving supporters of this work. Their encouragement is much appreciated. My coauthor, Mike Robins, is a most talented and impassioned writer. I have benefited greatly from his intra- and interpersonal gifts and his truly independent thinking. Mike is evidence that teachers can learn much from their current and former students. To Mike, I am most grateful. Thanks are extended to the many amazing, loving, very three-dimensional high school and college students who brought and continue to bring to class a natural love for learning and thinking. Of the many students who had a message and wanted it heard, I regret that not all of them could be accommodated. This book represents the collective genius of the many students I have taught and from whom I have learned so much.

ROBERT N. GILBERT

First and foremost, I must thank Robert Gilbert, teacher and mentor, for the opportunity to be part of such an exciting and worthwhile project. What started as a couple of fascinating discussions about the state of high school quickly became the greatest intellectual pursuit of my life thus far. Bob's dedication to integrity, honesty, and a lively, meaningful classroom should be the model for schools everywhere. However, these traits pale in comparison to his boundless compassion and loyalty as a friend. For that, most of all, I am forever in his debt. My father, Barry Robins, through constant love and support, importantly reminds me that my family is the most precious thing I have. He remains, quite simply, the best parent one could ever hope for. This book could not have been written without him. Michael Riseman, my close friend and intellectual sparring partner, consistently illuminates the world view of those around him. His comments concerning Noam Chomsky and contemporary politics significantly contributed to the present text. Tony Williams, Associate Professor of Cinema Studies in the English Department at Southern Illinois University at Carbondale, serves as a constant source of inspiration. His friendship and professionalism encourage students to write passionately and intelligently. And finally, I cannot begin to thank Tanya Romersa, my wife and best friend, for her unconditional love and respect. She daily reminds me that the world is a place worth fighting for, and I am humbled by the fact that we share the fight together.

MIKE ROBINS

Both authors wish to thank Sean Kopeny '94, who served as Student Editor, and to Garrick Greenblatt '90, who served as Alumni Editor. Together with coauthor Mike Robins '90, Sean and Garrick methodically and judiciously evaluated student and alumni contributions for inclusion. Kathy Betts '93 contributed ideas for illustrations. Joey Depakakibo '94 tirelessly, meticulously, and lovingly illustrated the work. Alice G. Foster, our editor at Corwin, a former high school English teacher, recognized the importance of this work and gave us much support. Her brilliant advice and editorial assistance are much appreciated. Gracia A. Alkema, President, Corwin Press, is a model of style, grace, and substance. She makes us proud to be represented by Corwin.

About the Authors

Robert N. Gilbert earned a B.A. in sociology and a B.S. in administration from the State University of New York at Buffalo in 1972 and an M.A. in sociology from the University of Chicago in 1973. He teaches educational psychology and social sciences at Harold Washington College in Chicago. He taught high school for 20 years. Gilbert is the author of *Doing Survey Research in the Introductory Social Science Course,* published in 1996 by the American Sociological Association, and he is recognized nationally as a leader in social science education. He is an active member of many professional associations, including the American Sociological Association, the American Anthropological Association, the National Council for the Social Studies, and the International Center for Critical Thinking and Moral Critique. He is a frequent presenter at state, national, and international conventions.

Mike Robins is an independent filmmaker and author based in Chicago, Illinois. He graduated from Southern Illinois University at Carbondale in 1994 with a B.A. in cinema and photography and minors in sociology and psychology. He is a member of the British Film Institute, the Film Center of the Art Institute of Chicago, and Illinois Peace Action. In addition, he is president of Dead Birdie Films, an independent film cooperative dedicated to the production of low-budget feature films and documentaries. Currently, Robins is in production as writer-director on his first feature film, *Three Flat.*

Dedicated to Susan L. Leibowitz, an incredible person, teacher, and wife, and a source of inspiration and encouragement. In loving memory of my first teacher—my mother, Marion Gilbert Zalles.

ROBERT N. GILBERT

Dedicated to my dad, Barry Robins, with love.

MIKE ROBINS

1

Living in Different Realities

"The student perspective is a reality. It cannot be denied or ignored, for without it, schools cease to be relevant, real, or the priority for students."

The purpose of this book is to include students as fully vested partners in the national debate on the crisis facing our nation's schools. As the student voices in this book realistically and passionately explain, schools can no longer create curriculums and administer from a position detached from the reality in which students negotiate daily. We must address the realities facing today's teenagers. If we do not, we risk denying an entire generation the opportunity for a prosperous future. This is a risk we cannot afford to take.

The 80 million people born in the United States between 1961 and 1981 (inappropriately dubbed "slackers" or "Generation X") face a future riddled with obstacles unknown by previous generations. As Neil

1

Howe and Bill Strauss point out in *13th GEN* (1993), this generation will be the only one born in the 20th century to "suffer a one-generation backstep in living standards. Compared to their own parents at the same age, the 13ers' poverty rate will be higher, their rate of home ownership lower, their pension and health care benefits skimpier" (p. 220).

The above observation should be no surprise. The National Commission on Excellence in Education, in the well-publicized report *A Nation at Risk: The Full Account* (1984), warned, "For the first time in the history of our country, the educational skills of one generation will not surpass, will not equal, will not even approach, those of their parents."

There are additional grim forecasts. Today's teenagers will have to deal with the AIDS epidemic, a Social Security crisis, a widening gap between rich and poor, resegregation, and increasing environmental hazards. Please do not misunderstand. Every generation faces odds that appear more complex and intimidating than those of previous generations. The difference this time, however, is that we are not creating a generation that will be able to deal with its problems intelligently and effectively.

The industrialization and standardization of schools during the last 15 years are well documented, most recently in Geoffrey T. Holtz's *Welcome to the Jungle* (1995). However, a brief summary will be useful. In sharp reaction to the experimentation of "open" schools in the late 1960s and 1970s, administrators applied a "back to basics" approach throughout the 1980s. Whereas "open" schools had attempted to allow students to develop in an environment less rigid than traditional classrooms where desks were once screwed to the floorboards, the 1980s saw an emphasis on reading, writing, and mathematics skills. The U.S. Department of Education's report, *A Nation at Risk: The Imperative of Educational Reform* (Gardner & Larsen, 1983), reinforced this trend, alleging that declining U.S. test scores compared unfavorably with the achievement of students in other industrialized countries. In order to compete internationally, schools adopted increasing numbers of standardized tests so that students' skills could be measured, evaluated, and compared. By using these tests, administrators hoped to reinforce the importance of basic skills in students, thereby making them more competitive in future economic markets.

At the same time, however, we fear the process of learning may have been lost in the translation. While GPAs, SAT scores, state achievement tests, and other quantitative measures of performance took on greater significance, the primary lesson became "doing well on standardized tests." As David Elkind puts it in *The Hurried Child* (1988, p. 56), "If it is the grade you get rather than what you know that counts, then the most important thing is to get the highest grade."

Many students quickly realize that the things they learn in school may be of little use to them in the "real world." It logically follows that students would then prioritize school *behind* work, activities, and family. Understandably, their performance in class would be shadowed by their performance out of class and out of school. Academic performance would naturally decline. The goal of educators should be to make school relevant once again to students. Educators and administrators must begin to understand the reality of what it means today to be a teenager. They must stop drawing lines between school and the "real world." Teenagers' lives in and out of school are just as real to teenagers as the lives of adults are to adults.

Teenagers live, work, and are subject to realities like everyone else in society. In addition to going to school full-time and putting in overtime on school publications, activities, competitive sports, and studying, many students work on school nights and weekends, often until closing. Some students have reached the limit. There are simply not enough hours in the day to accomplish all that teachers, parents, and society expect from teens. As the cost of college has increased faster than inflation, many parents are less able to contribute as much as they would like to help their children. Many students are working more hours during the school week to help with current living costs and to defray future college expenses. Some parents, dependent on their children to contribute to their living expenses, have an incentive to look away. Educators *must* make it a point *not* to do the same.

This combination of the numbing and ineffective standardization in the schools and the seemingly overwhelming societal forces placed upon students cries for an immediate remedy. That remedy is the inclusion of the student perspective. Since students are the subject of policy, the greater the understanding of student realities, the better and more effective will be the policy created. Teachers and administrators must answer to many constituencies in addition to complex bureaucracies. The realities of students should not be overlooked in the process.

We are not suggesting students should make school policy. First, students do not fund the schools. Second, school boards, democratically elected by the "larger" community, have the legal and moral authority to make school policy. Finally, students do not necessarily have the insight necessary to create a well-rounded curriculum. Nevertheless, there exists a need to recognize the student perspective. Without this input from students, administrators are creating social programs from within a social vacuum. Is it any surprise that some students find their high school experience vacuous? The student perspective is a reality. It cannot be denied or ignored, for without it, schools cease to be relevant, real, or the priority for students.

Recognizing Different Realities

"It is first necessary to recognize student realities. Only then can educators meaningfully examine the reality system from which students view school and within which students learn."

It is important to emphasize that teenagers are not lost in "their own world." Although neither teens nor adults live in what philosophers call "the ultimate reality," teens live in a world as real to them as the adult world is real to adults. Do educators in each school understand the needs of an ever-changing student body? In order to find answers to this question, it is first necessary to recognize student realities. Only then can educators meaningfully examine the reality system from which students view school and within which students learn.

Again, as explained, teenagers live, work, and are subject to realities like everyone else in society. However, although both students and high schools exist in the real world, high schools are administered as if they did not. Increasing standardization in testing and curriculum quickly alerts students to the fact that much of what they "learn" in school will be of little use to them in the real world.

As a result, students give priority to extracurricular and noncurricular activities. Athletics and organizations lead to personal fulfillment, social status, and even college scholarships. Schools often hold assemblies during the academic day to promote sports and celebrate the accomplishments of their athletic teams, apparently applauding sports over scholastic performance. Similarly, part-time jobs offer a source of spending money, college savings, and financial help. Such income sources are especially significant for students from single-parent families. On the job, students and adults interact in a reality meaningful to both. In addition, students often learn practical social and occupational skills not offered in school. On the job, students are more likely to inter-

act in the diverse and multicultural reality than they are in the age- and ability-tracked artificiality better known as school. As a result, the job becomes more meaningful and significant in their lives than ideas encountered in school. In turn, school becomes irrelevant because it just does not match up to the student's perceived reality. Schools must be aware of, understand, and respect the student reality.

The students who contributed to this book have seriously attempted to explain the student reality. They are the students of "Weberville" High School (a pseudonym), located in the suburbs of Chicago. Although not rich, Weberville ranks in the third quartile (above average) for both income and median home value among Chicago suburbs. In 1990, close to one half (51%) of residential units were unattached and single family. Nine percent were attached townhomes. Forty percent were apartments.

There are slightly fewer than 2,000 students, 78% of whom are white. The remainder are Hispanic (11%), African American (5%), and Asian or Pacific Islander (6%). Six percent have limited proficiency in English. Twelve percent receive Special Education services. Twelve percent are from low-income families. Four percent of all students drop out each year.

The school is well funded. Some departments, physical education for example, have an abundance of physical resources. Not including the many outdoor athletic fields and courts, there are eight gymnasiums. There exist a total of six computer labs housing approximately 170 computers. The library offers access to high school-level databases on CD-ROM. Approximately 78% of students indicate that they plan to enroll in college the semester after they graduate. Advanced Placement and "gifted" programs are offered. Over the years, the community has remained steadfast in its support of quality education and facilities. The school is part of a multiple high school district centrally administered.

Weberville has a population of approximately 40,000. One million people pass through the community each day. Many use its shopping, fast-food, and other service-oriented industries. Teenage jobs are plentiful throughout the year. Students report hourly wages significantly above the federal minimum wage. There is much industry. The industrial base is mixed and includes large electronics and other manufacturing facilities.

This book is not intended to praise or criticize a specific school or individuals within. The purpose is strictly to demonstrate a case for attending to the student perspective.

The Institutional Reality

"If the institution is only evaluated by standardized exam scores (and funded according to their results), then it will only emphasize the skills that enhance these scores. In turn, teachers 'teach the test' rather than the skills the tests are supposed to be evaluating."

The school is a social and local community institution that has an institutional life of its own. As new students enter every year and stay for only 4 years, the school must always remain. Although education of students is its mandate, the institution's imperative is self-perpetuation.

An institution as large as a high school district requires a complex and often pervasive bureaucracy for efficiencies created from specialization and the division of labor. Bureaucracies also have a life of their own. Although the primary goal is the education of the students living in the district, this function is often lost in the shuffle between bureaus. In *The McDonaldization of Society*, George Ritzer analyzes the sweeping standardization taking over U.S. culture. His comments on bureaucracy are helpful.

Bureaucracies can, in effect, be seen as large-scale, non-human technologies. These are huge, non-human structures with innumerable rules, regulations, guidelines, positions, lines of command, and hierarchies that are designed to dictate, as much as possible, what people do within the system and how they do it. The consummate bureaucrat thinks little about what is to be done, but simply follows the rules, deals with incoming work, and passes it on to the next step in the hierarchy. (1993, pp. 117-118)

Although Ritzer's ideas intend to describe the current corporate model, they also detail the workings of a high school and the larger

school district. Through standardized tests, administrators and, in the process, teachers often sacrifice the process of learning for high test scores. Since quantity is more easily measured and publicized than quality, quantitative successes become the priority.

For example, because grading the mechanics of writing (spelling, grammar, and organization) is easier than grading content, students are more likely to learn *how to write* than to develop ideas *about which to write*. Hence although students may learn *how* to write, *what* they write is often not worth reading. Lost in the process is the reality of purpose. Rather than learn the joys of writing, the opportunity to express oneself, and the means to inform others, students learn that writing is drudgery. This is the result when *form* is emphasized at the expense of *function*. Function is reality based. The lesson for schools is direct. Quantitative success is good but qualitative success must remain the ultimate goal.

Furthermore, if the institution is evaluated only by standardized exam scores (and funded according to their results), then it will only emphasize the skills that enhance these scores. In turn, teachers "teach the test" rather than the skills the tests are supposed to be evaluating.

This process greatly enhances the public image of a school. In other words, high performance on standardized tests creates the image that the school is doing a "quality" job. Whether these high scores directly relate to success for students in college or in their careers is in serious question.

Obviously, the subjective reality of the teenage high school student differs significantly from that of the high school as a social institution.

Social expectations, motives for participation, sources of status, and definitions of success for students may be at odds with those of teachers or administrators. The confrontation between student and institutional reality systems, then, proves to be quite a battle, and the student generally loses. Besides the obvious scholastic consequences, the student may suffer future economic, social, and psychological harm as a result.

The standardization of curriculum, textbooks, and final exams leads to a compromise and agreement along the least common denominator. Another term for this is mediocrity. *Are we in search of excellence, or are we in search of mediocrity?* By settling for mediocrity, schools encourage all students, whether they are capable or not, to learn the same information in the same way. Brighter students suffer by not being allowed to develop in the most stimulating environment possible. For example, several years ago, Weberville High School offered an English independent study course for accelerated seniors. This was "traded in" by the district for an Advanced Placement (AP) English course. Although the independent study class allowed students to create their own curriculum and develop in areas they felt important, the AP course prepared students for the highly standardized AP exam. The district felt that the trade-off was worthy although many colleges grant Advanced Placement college credit only to those students with scores well within the range considered "passing." Some schools do not recognize the exam at all.

Also, students with less scholastic ability suffer because poor performance on standardized tests can lead to low self-esteem and lack of recognition from teachers and parents. Some students have skills in areas that the school neither encourages nor celebrates. A student who does well in autos class, but poorly in English, is deemed a failure by the school. The student, of course, is not a failure; he merely does not excel in the exact way that the school wants him to excel. A student in this position should be rewarded with the same recognition for *his* or *her* unique talents that is given to the best English student in the school.

More important, standardization of the curriculum poorly prepares students (bright and otherwise) for the dilemmas of the future. Beyond scholastic experiences, the failure to develop critical thinking skills in a standardized environment leaves students unprepared to tackle the economic, social, and political problems of the next century. As Elkind explains,

> The industrialization of our schools is not surprising, for universal schooling in the United States was introduced, in part, to prepare children for the new ways of living and working brought about by the machine age. What is surprising about our schools today is that they continue to follow a factory model at a time

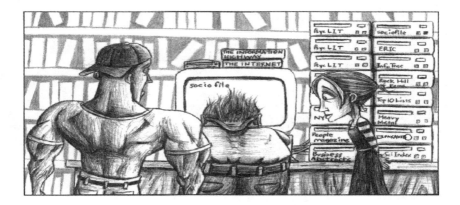

when factory work, as it was once known, is becoming as obsolete as farming without a tractor. (Elkind, 1992, p. 47)

Young people feel cynical about the future because they feel ill-prepared to deal with it. As SAT scores and other quantifiable measures of success fluctuate from year to year, wages, health benefits, and job security steadily decline. Students recognize when they are being taught something that will be of little use to them outside the class-room. In turn, students may see standardized testing as a game of chance. They may participate, play along, or tune out. Often they make extracurricular activities, jobs, and family responsibilities the priority. Either way, many students may find little satisfaction in the academic facets of school. This situation benefits no one.

Although poorly prepared students eventually leave school, they do not leave society. Schools must succeed. As a society, we have no op-tion. Many worry that the current generation of students is not equipped to overcome future hardships of which we are already aware. If this is true, the future social and economic prosperity of our country is seriously threatened.

School institutions, as part of planning, would benefit from con-ducting "reality checks" from the perspective of the different reality systems affected by policies. Because students are generally the subject of school policy, an understanding of the student perspective is needed. Student input is the best means to access student realities. By hearing what students have to say, administrators and teachers could begin to understand the experience of today's teenager. As a result, the curriculum could be written in the best interests of *everyone* involved. As long as a large gap exists between student and institutional realities, the future of a generation, and the country as a whole, remains uncer-tain.

The Learning Realities

"Students have a fundamental need to educate themselves. Education is not something we do to kids. Education is something they have to do for themselves."

Students are always learning. This may be because of or despite the official curriculum. The problem, of course, is they may be learning something other than what teachers want them to learn. The reality is that students learn what they want, when they want, and where they want.

Steve Jobs and Stephen Wozniak dropped out of college because what they wanted to learn was more important to them than what college professors wanted to teach them. When they dropped out, they started Apple Computer. Bill Gates, who started the Microsoft Corporation, dropped out of Harvard when he was 20 for the same reasons. At 37, he is the richest man in the world. His worth is valued beyond $35 billion.

Although perhaps a little extreme, Jobs, Wozniak, and Gates do serve as a reminder that some students are better served out of school than within, precisely because some students need more control over their education.

Most students are better off in school. However, because only *students* can actually do the learning, some degree of control rests with individual students, whether teachers and administrators like it or not. Some students may wish a teacher could "learn me that," but they cannot.

Similarly, teachers need to consider that no matter how fancy a song, dance, or comedy routine they do in class, students individually decide to learn the song, dance, comedy, or the ideas in the lesson.

The student has to agree to learn. It is easier to get meaningful agreement when students sense this control and act upon it. There are two ways of accomplishing this goal. One is cognitive, in which the student consciously agrees that the assignment and lesson are meaningful and hence worth learning. The other is psychological and emotional. The student identifies with or enjoys the instructor or the assigned work. Learning may happen because of unconscious factors. Either approach works.

Educational theorists teach three basic curriculum questions that all involved in education must answer. These questions are

1. What knowledge is most worthwhile?
2. Why is it worthwhile?
3. How is it acquired?

There is no pat answer to the above questions. Scholars, school boards, administrators, teachers, parents, and even state legislatures are asking, and to the dismay of some, trying to impose answers. Although students do not often think of the first and third questions, they daily challenge teachers when they ask the second question in the form as follows: "Why do we have to know this?" Teachers in turn should ask themselves: "Why do students have to learn this?" If teachers cannot think of a convincing answer, they need to find one or dump the lesson.

Students have a fundamental need to educate themselves. Education is not something *we do to* kids. Education is something *kids* have to do for themselves. Emotionally healthy students and students not psychologically damaged by punitive schooling experiences have unencumbered fundamental needs to learn about themselves, their abilities, and their world, and to find the limits of their capabilities. Students have an inherent, innate need to grow physically and mentally. Just as students want to find the limits of their muscles, coordination, and aim, students want to find the limits of their musical, writing, math, creative, and artistic abilities. Students love puzzles and they love to solve problems. Contrary to popular belief, students love to think. In addition, students have a fundamental and innate psychological need to be productive. Problems develop when students are frustrated in their attempts to satisfy their needs, especially needs related to learning. It is the teacher's job to pace students through learning to increase the likelihood of success without frustration. Again, the basic given is that young people want to learn.

What knowledge is most worthwhile is culturally determined. *Which* knowledge is chosen for inclusion in the official curriculum is political. Alan Bloom (1987), in his widely read book *The Closing of the American Mind: How Higher Education Has Failed Democracy and Impoverished the Souls of Today's Students,* argued that not all curricular content is worthwhile. According to Bloom, if all theories and knowledge were accepted in a culturally relativistic framework, our cultural heritage would drown in a curricular and cultural mishmash.

E. D. Hirsch, Jr. (1987), in *Cultural Literacy: What Every American Needs to Know,* another widely read book, went one step further than Bloom and listed more than 5,000 essential names, phrases, dates, and concepts. The list included everything from Hank Aaron to the Adirondack Mountains, back down to Akron, Ohio, Johnny Appleseed, the John Birch Society, and Brutus, as well as Cezanne, Chaplin, Chicago, the Zodiac, and finally Zurich.

The problem is that no student is typical. Each is very much an individual. This fact is especially evident if one argues that students decide what they will notice, what they will learn, and how they will learn it. Because students educate themselves, because they choose what they will remember, there can be no same set of concepts right for any two people, let alone all students or all U.S. citizens. One student's concept of something as basic as a "family" will be different from another's. To make things even more complex, a single student's concept of "family" might change over time. Concepts are mental constructs. They exist in our mind, not necessarily in reality. Even the concept of the elements as listed on the periodic table are theoretical mental constructions subject to change.

Decidedly missing from the education debate is a most basic question: Where does education take place? If one asks students what was their most meaningful lesson during high school or what was the most important thing learned, one is in for a surprise. This was the question asked of students who contributed to this book.

The students suggest that the most meaningful knowledge was not necessarily gained in class. Nor was it necessarily related to an academic subject. Sometimes it was despite what we traditionally think of as school. This fact is particularly surprising because the overwhelming majority of teachers at Weberville High School are dedicated and caring, and give much of themselves in every lesson. Many faculty members are recognized as experts. Many can be seen in the halls helping students with personal crises between, even during, classes.

The purpose of this book is to remind everyone what is meaningful in school. The book offers students a chance to give their perspective. Direct and from the exact point of experience, all from within their locus of control, students graciously have invited the reader to an intimate look at high school, from their hearts and from their minds.

The Reality of Student Control

"The locus of learning is in the mind of each individual student. Hence if educators want to achieve learning experiences, they are going to have to understand school and school experiences from the student's perspective."

Imagine a high school where educators are working hard and thinking of what is best for the students. They come in early for extra meetings in the groggy hours long before students arrive. Some even stay late, busily working on innovations and new programs for students long after students leave. In fact, it seems the best time to create programs for students is before and after school, when the building rests in its quiet, dormant state.

With only the best intentions, plans are carefully made how best to mold and carve students so they fit the new exciting programs meticulously designed for them. Granted, when one is planning for 2,000 kids to conform to new creative and exciting programs, some must be force-fitted, but with a little accommodation, a little hammering, chiseling, and sledging, success is guaranteed. There is bound to be some breakage, but that has to be expected.

If the program does not work, students cannot be blamed, for many reasons. For one thing, they had no say in the design. They were not even consulted. Hence if it does not work, it is not their fault. Then again, how could kids ever be to blame? After all, if they do not shape up to our expectations, it must be the fault of those hired to do the shaping, the hammering, the chiseling, and the sledging. Remember:

Kids are like clay. It is up to teachers to mold them. If they come to school in any other form, if they're hardened from experience, it is up to teachers to pound them, pulverize them, and reshape them. That is what one does to clay and stone.

It would be nice if the above metaphor were pure sarcasm, if none of it had even a ring of truth. Unfortunately, in some of our nation's schools, in some departments within schools, it is the modus operandi.

With all the talk about going back to basics, rarely is it ever mentioned that the individual student is the most basic component of a school. Without students, there would be no schools. The goal of schools is to pass on knowledge, and without students, nothing would be passed on. The individuals who have to do the learning are the students. The locus of the learning is not the school, nor is it the classroom. It is not the student's desk, nor the textbook. Nor is the locus of learning "the students." The locus of the learning is in the mind of each individual student. All learning experiences are received, processed, stored, and output from this location. Hence if educators want to achieve learning experiences, they are going to have to understand school and school experiences from the student's perspective.

School officials may think they are in control. To some extent they are. Central administrators often evaluate building officials on how much control they seem to have over their buildings. They can threaten principals. Principals can threaten teachers. And teachers can threaten students. However, with few exceptions, each individual student is the only one capable of controlling his or her individual behavior.

The problem with the logic in the beginning of this section is the analogy of students to clay. It is a false analogy. Students are not made of clay. Clay is inanimate. It lacks consciousness. It cannot make choices. Clay is an object, like a rock. As philosopher Jean-Paul Sartre espoused, a rock is an effect. A rock is never a cause. A rock is inanimate. People are not rocks. People are not effects. People are the cause. To deny that we are the cause of our actions is to deny our very existence. If we do, we are guilty of bad faith. We must always make choices. We shape our own lives. We decide which factors will affect us. We decide whether to participate. The problem arises when we see students as effects. In the educational jargon, these effects are termed *outcome statements*.

The lesson should be obvious. Whether teachers, administrators, or parents like it or not, students decide whether they will learn. Students decide what they will forget. Students choose to forget what they do not want to remember. It is doubtful any teenager on the way to a party has ever forgotten to pick up his or her date.

Students make choices all of the time. Students choose whether to do their math homework first, later, or not at all. Students decide whether to start their paper when it is assigned, pace themselves through it, or rush it the night before it is due. Students decide if they are going to place more emphasis on schoolwork or an after-school job. Students decide if they will seek belonging, esteem, prestige, and status within or out of school. Students decide if they will do quality work before or after the dismissal bell.

Nothing in this world is inherently boring. And nothing is inherently interesting. Students decide whether a lesson, reading, or course is exciting or boring. Students define, label, categorize, and evaluate reality based on their own perceptions. Anyone who has tried to tell a student how to define something finds out readily that no matter what one tells the student, the student will redefine it for him- or herself. One student may find math exciting. Another may find it boring. Well, which is it? Since excitement and boredom are emotions and emotions take place in the mind of the individual, then it is the individual's perception and interpretation of the experience that determines the type and degree of the emotional response. Excitement and boredom take place at the locus of the experience, the student's mind.

Again, the lesson should be obvious. Administrators, teachers, and students must understand that only the individual student can control his or her behavior as a student. The locus of all control is the individual. We need to empower individual students to make the right choices. We need to stop deluding ourselves that only administrators and teachers can think, design, and build learning environments for students.

The Reality Gap: The Importance of Student Input

"Administrators and teachers who dismiss the importance of student perspective and its corollary, student input, miss the opportunity to create quality programs with students."

In Chapter 3, The Student Reality: Activities and Sports, student Jeremy Ulander, using strong language, criticizes VOLUNTEER, a school program initiated during his senior year requiring students to volunteer in community service agencies. According to Jeremy, such a program requiring "forced volunteering" is "a contradiction in terms." Jeremy, on his own, long before VOLUNTEER, had secured a volunteer position in the emergency room of a major regional hospital. Other students used the phrase "mandatory volunteer program." It was even immortalized in the school's yearbook. Jeremy was not alone in criticizing the program. Another student, upon hearing the requirement that seniors volunteer 20 hours in the community, blurted, "Twenty hours of community service? That's what the judge gave me!" Many other students became cynical and questioned the motives of the school administration.

What may have been motivated solely out of love and affection for students came to be seen as a power grab at the expense of students to "win another award for the school" and "get themselves a pay raise."

At the end of the year, it was found that teachers of senior year students had similar "success" with the program. Although all seniors were required to participate and no exceptions were to be made, approximately one fifth of the school's honors-level students chose to receive a letter grade of F in the program rather than complete the requirements. Approximately one third of the average-level students and two thirds of the lower-level students chose an F. Not all students who failed the program were defiant. Some explained they did not have transportation; for example, their mothers worked and needed the car. Others explained their spirit of volunteerism was abused by the agency, for example, "Basically, I just mopped floors and 20 hours of that sucked. I couldn't stand it. After 7 and a half hours, I quit." Another student could not afford to lose hours from work. Some students found they would lose an entire day of work if they had to volunteer 2 hours during their normal shift.

Why was the student reaction so intense? Why did cynicism and defiance seem to dominate the mood of seniors? Why did so many seniors choose to define volunteering as punishment? Why did these seniors not see the many ways volunteering could benefit them? Why did other seniors define volunteering, whether required or not, as a positive experience and personally rewarding? For example, some gained self-esteem and self-respect, and others developed empathy. Most were quick to add their volunteer experience to college and college scholarship applications. Some found new career options, a job for second semester and college summers. A few gained experience in their future career areas. All learned about their hometown and perhaps came closer to finding the meaning of community and life.

Student input had not been sought. Should it have been? Of what benefit is student input? Philosophically, should students participate in the creation of educational policy and program? In the practical world of an administrator, what are the advantages and disadvantages? At what point in the planning process is student input appropriate? For example, should students be in from the start, at the initial suggestion, or should they be brought in at the implementation stage, after policy has been determined? Can student input be expected to contribute to or distract from classroom instruction? Can student input be representative of a school's varied mix of students?

Please note that we have avoided use of the term *power*. Legally, only the officially elected or appointed school board has power to determine policy in the running of public schools. Included is the power to appoint administrators and hire teachers. Generally, much power is delegated to the superintendent and, in turn, to principals. Principals

assign the tasks and paperwork to assistant principals. Teachers rarely have the opportunity to affect the contents of policy once an idea is suggested from above. Rarely, if ever, do policy ideas start at the student or even teacher level and move upward. In addition, students are generally the last to learn of policies affecting them. Why?

If the goal of educational administrators is to make and execute educational policy that works in the real world, then administrators could only benefit from input from the policy's proposed recipients. Students who live each day in the real world of school can offer a perspective unavailable anywhere else. Indeed, no one could possibly picture, let alone calculate, the daily impact and potential effects of policy on students better than students. In fact, problems are more likely to develop when students are prevented from having input. *Student input on policy should be directly related to the degree that policy affects students.*

Now let us be careful. There are parameters. For example, perhaps the local administrative slogan operandi is "students and parents do not write curriculum." For the sake of discussion, let us agree that students and parents do not write the curriculum. This, however, does not foreclose the opportunity for students to have input. After all, if power to write the curriculum resides with administrators and teachers, an understanding gained from students' ideas about how the curriculum affects students can only be a source of increased power.

Please note we are avoiding another issue: whether a volunteer program such as VOLUNTEER should be part of the academic curriculum, part of the voluntary after-class activity program, or neither. We are trying to keep the issue simple.

Were students not included because they were expected to have no contributions worth making? If so, how was this determined? Were students not included because it was believed their contributions would be contrary to the goals of the administration? If so, this begs the question, for whose needs were these goals intended to meet? If the goals were to satisfy students' needs, how was it determined that students had these needs? Were the needs determined after a discussion with those who would be affected? In other words, were students, parents, teachers, and community officials asked to give their perspectives on how they would be affected by a major new policy? This was no minor policy: It required 450 students individually to apply in person and, if accepted, travel across town or to a nearby town to a local community agency on at least 10 additional occasions. Were any of these groups avoided because potentially they might be in opposition? Was it determined why such groups might be in opposition? Were such points of potential opposition evaluated? Potentially, how could student input have benefited the construction of a program like VOLUNTEER?

In "the real world," in the community, the input of community members is often sought. The official vehicle for community input is the *community hearing*. Hearings on local projects are often required by law. It is part of the democratic process.

"The real world" of students, *as students*, is school. Without factoring in sleeping in class, students spend one half or more of their waking life during the school year at school. School is the location of the experience where teens make friends, learn what is normal, and learn about themselves. School is the real world where students *as students* can meet the five basic needs as defined by Glasser (1990, p. 43): survival, love and belonging, power, fun, and freedom. Students have innate psychological drives to meet these needs. If school does not allow students to meet these needs *in* school, students will be driven to meet them *out* of school.

A quality *student* volunteer program is one that would be viewed from the *student* perspective, with *student* input, and be designed in the *student's* quality world to satisfy *student* needs while helping the community.

One such student need is survival. Volunteering can help a student meet survival needs. Volunteering provides chances to learn skills. These may include interpersonal skills, leadership skills, office skills, occupational skills, and so forth. Student input would have underscored the need for the program to avoid competing with the many demands specific to senior year. Senior year is the busiest year. Some students take difficult Advanced Placement college-level courses. Most are burdened with finding the right college and submitting college, scholarship, and financial aid applications. Most are working many hours to afford the social expenses specific to senior year. Some are able to save for college. Hence student input might have suggested volunteering be made available starting freshman year, include summers, and continue until graduation. Volunteering before the age required for a work permit could have avoided competition with opportunities to work for money.

Most probably, student input would have suggested that the volunteer program be voluntary. Had the program been completely voluntary and had the hours volunteered simply been posted on student transcripts for colleges and scholarship-granting institutions to see, students would have volunteered hundreds of hours without complaint. After all, if two students are similar but one of them has more volunteer efforts documented on a transcript, that person has a distinct advantage.

Volunteering can help prepare students for teen and adult jobs. As noted earlier, Jeremy Ulander discusses the value of volunteering in his essay in Chapter 3, The Student Reality: Activities and Sports. Jeremy gained fabulous preparation for a planned career in emergency medicine. Jeremy's volunteer work helped meet his "survival needs" head on. Bobby B. Roberts, on the other hand, as explained in his essay in Chapter 4, The Student Reality, Working: 3:25 to Closing, was barely meeting his own survival needs and those of his mom. Bobby would have been unable to meet the needs of VOLUNTEER. Another student (who chose not to write for this book) was homeless at the time. His stepfather kicked him out the day he turned 18. This young man worked until 5:30 a.m. at a nearby pancake restaurant to have a place to stay overnight. He had a short fuse. The VOLUNTEER program, when explained, was not well received by this young man. Another student was unable to complete the volunteer requirements because it worked against her survival needs. In Chapter 6, The Student Reality: Facing Society, Valerie Curda explains the effects of stalking.

Students have a need for love and belonging. Feeling welcomed and wanted by those who are less fortunate can satisfy these needs. In Chapter 3, Julie Randazzo explains the benefits of volunteering at a nursing home, and Jeremy Giutini and Kevin True, in separate essays

about the school's football program, explain the sense of belonging developed when an entire team volunteers together.

Like all individuals, students have needs for power. Students who choose to volunteer experience more control over their lives. They develop self-confidence. A volunteer program designed with student input would not have required students to surrender all power, especially the power to change hard-earned grades in academic courses from A to Incomplete to F, as was originally planned. Such a program frustrates rather than satisfies power needs. Such action is a power grab. It suggests the real goal might have been less volunteerism and more the display of power—who has it and who does not.

All power relationships concerning students must be subject to checks and balances. Checks and balances were so essential to the American ethos that they were built into the U.S. Constitution. This fact is required and taught to students in every high school. In the rush to design programs, checks and balances can be forgotten. Student input into program design can provide informal checks and balances.

Students have a need for fun. Learning is inherently fun. We are programmed to learn. Learning results in growth, and growth implies the development of skills. Skills make more things fun, and skills also can give us power. A volunteer program is a chance to learn and have fun. Fun, however, is fragile and can be easily converted to frustration. A program designed without student input can have many turn-offs to students. Rules for the sake of rules and rules for the sake of making others look good can detract from opportunities to have fun. The VOL-UNTEER program had many such rules. For example, the 20 required hours had to be evenly spread over at least 10 volunteer sessions. Students were allowed to count only 2 hours of volunteering a week. Students were not allowed to bunch hours together. As mentioned earlier, this was a problem for many who worked weekends and for those who did not regularly have access to transportation. In addition, some volunteer agencies needed students sporadically and for periods greater than 2 hours at a time.

Had student input been sought, the administration would have learned that many students, before the program began, already were donating their time in the community. Often such efforts were discounted for reasons of program management. Some students went on retreats with their local community church to dig toilets and improve sanitation facilities and village life in countries such as Haiti. Such volunteerism was not counted. These students were told to volunteer additional hours in a school-approved project as soon as they came back. Students wishing to "micro-volunteer"—for example, rake the leaves or mow their elderly neighbor's lawn—would not be counted because they were not in approved programs. Student input would have alerted program designers to such problems prior to the policy being officially approved and sealed from changes.

Finally, students have a need for freedom. Students must have the freedom to work additional responsibilities into an existing schedule without detracting from existing obligations. Only with student input can planners understand the effects on students. Freedom is a prerequisite for anything to be meaningful. A volunteer program should not be built on the ruins of another's freedom. A volunteer program must be the result of freedom.

Administrators and teachers who dismiss the importance of student perspective and its corollary, student input, miss the opportunity to create quality programs with students. Student input is a prerequisite for programs designed to satisfy student needs. One should never underestimate the strength of the drive and the creativity of students to seek and find ways to satisfy the five basic needs: survival, love and belonging, power, fun, and freedom.

2

The Student Reality: 8:10 to 3:25

Students want to be in school, and they want to learn. When students claim school is boring, something is definitely wrong. Students have little difficulty distinguishing between lessons that are relevant and lessons that are a waste of their time. Students are on to the game, and they often tune out from school as a result. The lesson for educators is simple: Make school relevant, respect each student, and make every lesson count.

Students understand that the main priority of high school is to provide an education. Students want to educate themselves. From teachers they seek assistance toward their goal. It must be the goal of teachers and administrators to make school a site promoting intellectual development. This chapter allows students, in their own words, to discuss issues concerning academics. Their conclusions stress the importance of the student perspective.

Kopeny, who served as student editor of this book, insightfully introduces the student perspective. He criticizes teachers who encourage mediocrity by making it easy for students to get by with doing minimal work. The problem cited by Kopeny is not unusual. Indeed, it may be systemic. Teachers, conscious of competition for students in elective courses, often lower standards so as to attract more students. The effect is to seek the lowest common denominator. Instead, the goal of educators should be to expect more and get more.

Radetski, Gribbon, and DiCanio examine the effects of tracking within school. Radetski intelligently compares students labeled "accelerated" with those labeled "average" and finds that there is little difference in student behavior or attitude across academic tracks. Gribbon, a former learning disability student, passionately questions the validity of tracking. He explains that lower-level students often experience low self-esteem and feel left out of mainstream school activities. Finally, DiCanio convincingly argues that all students should be required to take applied technology courses such as woods, applied home maintenance, and building construction. Besides the practical knowledge the courses provide, the entire student body might finally celebrate those students who excel in such classes. On different levels, Radetski, a gifted student; Gribbon, a slow processor but an insightful writer; and DiCanio, a vocational student, demonstrate the quality thinking that too often is allowed to remain dormant.

Haden, Petrusha, Mann, and Suarez argue that teachers have completely lost touch with what it means to be a student. They explain that both the classroom and homework assignments remain consistently boring, unchallenging, and irrelevant. As a result, Haden pronounces, "We are not robots!" and Petrusha begs teachers to realize that there are only 24 hours in the day. Mann explains that while writing papers can be fun, tedious class assignments generally remove all of his enthusiasm and creativity. Suarez suggests that ditching school offers students quality "school" time at home as a replacement for the quality school time not found in school.

Gonnella, Zaben, and Greenblatt search for intellectual meaning within school structures. Upset by a slanted selection process, Gonnella sharply examines the role and institutional function of the National Honor Society. Despite the NHS's prestigious status, she finds it to be a "bogus" group in which elitism weighs more than accomplishment. Zaben provides a similarly scathing review, but of the entire school system. Emotionally, she explains that school drains students of creativity and independent thought as it forces them through a dull, repetitive routine. Schools, according to Zaben, are simply no place for intellectuals. Greenblatt evaluates the quality of the curriculum and pointedly criticizes the school's emphasis on athletics over academics.

Lacey and Lis describe experiences in which rigid policy, difficult teachers, and incorrect medical diagnoses contributed to frustrating and often damaging school experiences. Following his parents' divorce when he was in the fifth grade, Lacey became withdrawn and extremely quiet in school. He was placed in a BD (Behavioral Disorder) class with kids who were hyperactive. He adjusted well to his surroundings. Although not BD at home or at work, in school he remained BD. However, when Lacey wrote the piece, he was no longer BD. In fact, he returned the day after graduation to write his story for this book. Lis, on the other hand, overcame difficult teachers to prosper as a student. Diagnosed with attention deficit disorder, he struggled through uncomfortable class situations and the use of the medication Ritalin to rise above his slow academic beginning. Lis clearly understands that the locus of learning is the student. Inner-directed, motivated, and with a strong sense of self, Lis persevered. The singular goal of educators, far more important than any imaginable content, must be to instill a love for learning. From this all else follows. This must be our priority.

Finally, Lindstrom passionately describes the physical, emotional, and social effects of long-term illness and injury during the school year. Lindstrom's back surgery forced her to reduce her tremendous scholastic and social schedule and depend on others for even the smallest things. She relates the loneliness, jealousy, and depression that followed.

The most striking feature of the student pieces in this chapter (and in the rest of this book) is the complete lack of complaining one might expect from students suddenly allowed to express their views. In fact, the exact opposite occurs. Students describe efforts to learn and grow despite the intimidation of school policy and curriculum. The conclusion is simple. Students have a strong need to learn and grow. They will have this need whether the school wants them to have it or not. Impressively, the student contributors to this book have developed intelligent critical thinking skills despite their scholastic surroundings. Now, teachers and administrators must do the same. Educators must seriously consider the personal experiences of students in classroom assignments. They must recognize the impact of extenuating circumstances (e.g., long-term illness) and make appropriate considerations.

Students are professional learners. They must be treated as such with fairness and respect. They must be encouraged to develop critical and analytical skills that will allow them to assess their role in society and empower them to make it better. The extremely high caliber of student ideas presented makes a convincing case. Imagine the accomplishments of a school that makes this, above all else, its main priority.

Welcome to the Real World
by Sean Kopeny

"'What have they to worry about? They have their whole life ahead of them.' That statement practically answers itself."

Sean Kopeny is a junior at Weberville High School, where he is captain of the Scholastic Bowl team, editor-in-chief of the student social science magazine, and a member of the school newspaper and the Model United Nations Club. He is also a Boy Scout who has achieved life rank. Sean is still pondering his options after high school, though college is a certainty. When not at school or sleeping, he is bagging groceries.

It is constantly said to me that high school is preparation for "the real world." It was not until my experience with this book that I questioned that statement rather than blindly accepted it. I should point out what so few people realize: High school is the real world. Experiences in high school shape the rest of people's lives. The nerd who was bullied can become a shy and withdrawn adult. The star athlete may live a life of nostalgia if his adult career turns out to be less successful than his high school victories. The accelerated student whose girlfriend got pregnant junior year could spend the rest of his life trying to keep up with life rather than getting ahead.

The respect, or lack of it, that a student is shown in high school can greatly shape his or her future perceptions. In my high school, you were assigned an ID number and it was more important to remember than your name; you get the feeling that you are little more than a number on an assembly line. Because the school is mass-producing students, it seems somewhat unimportant if they lose a couple of the many along the way. Although the students are getting a fast-food education (each year there are progressively more people in each of my classes, making it increasingly difficult for the teacher to truly help students), the mediocre nature of the education they are receiving is being lost. The teachers I hold the most respect for are the ones who teach the material in a way that allows the student to learn only if he or she wants to learn. The teacher of my advanced placement English class requires no homework during the semester, and there are only two grades per grading period: two essays that encompass everything that has been covered that semester. There are practice essays during the semester, and if you B.S. or simply do not do them the teacher will not cater to your laziness; she will continue on to the next lesson. Only if students truly want to learn will she slow down to make sure they are able to understand the material.

However, too much of high school is like my psychology class. The teacher is amiable and the coursework is decent, but students are ˎ

pampered along their way to As, Bs, and Cs. It is easy to pass the class while learning only a little about psychology. The grades are based on homework (study guides that many students work on in groups or copy), and the structure and content of the tests are given to a great enough extent that only the lazier students would not be able to ace the test. My purpose is not to belittle the class, but if you are not there to learn about psychology (in other words, if you are there to fulfill a requirement), the teacher will still try to make sure you pass the class with minimal effort.

This is not exclusive to my school and the schools around it— mediocrity is becoming accepted on a national level. The SAT, a common tool used by colleges to evaluate students, recently "adjusted" their scoring scale. The end result was nothing more than giving a higher score for the same number of correct answers. Maybe some people will be fooled when they see the average test score rise and, in time, the nation can probably convince itself that it has improved and the students are learning more. Why not? We have fooled ourselves that the diplomas being handed out actually mean that someone received a good education.

If we stopped patting each other on the back long enough to look around, we would realize that we are creating people who are taught to do the minimal amount of work. In my classes, whenever anyone goes beyond the minimal requirements one or both of two things usually happens: 1) The other students mock that person for being a "brown-nose" (someone who is trying to get in a teacher's favor) or 2) the teacher commends him or her for what should have been seen as a normal task and not something exceptional. There is almost competition between students to see who can get the best grades with the least work. Whenever a paper comes due (such as a research paper I had to do for an English class), people seem to compete to see how long they can wait before starting the paper. In this English class, the students that were most admired by their fellow students were those who had been up the entire night writing the paper and still managed to get an A. The teacher herself said a couple of weeks before assigning it: "I would assign the paper now but I know that nobody will begin until at least 2 weeks before the due date."

High school romance, admittedly, is not a very serious topic for students, much less for their parents. However, for some students, it is a way to salvage their sanity. I used to be irritated when I saw a couple clutching each other before class. It seemed excessive considering they were only going to be separated for the 50-minute class period; later I learned that they were both encountering emotional trauma at home and they were each other's refuge. To some students, classes seem trivial in comparison to the hardships and demands they are facing from the "outside" world. All too often, teachers and administrators get so caught up in the rhythm and rhetoric of the concept of "quality school-ing" that the students get lost in the statistics. What is the significance of a graduation rate if the diplomas are being handed out rather than awarded?

Outsiders do not try to realize that the students are going through many of the same dilemmas they are. Many adults see stress as an af-fliction that high school students do not suffer. "What have they to worry about? They have their whole life ahead of them." That state-ment practically answers itself.

For those who question the reality of high school and the things that students experience, simply look at a sampling of what has happened to me: An acquaintance whose charisma I admired hanged himself, I babysat for a murderer, two fellow classmates (one with whom I had a class) were murdered along with five other people at a local fast-food restaurant, and I was stranded in Indianapolis overnight with no place to stay. If those aren't real enough, look at the situations of some of my classmates: a friend was working more than 80-hour weeks between school and work, an acquaintance pondered suicide and deepened the extent of his drug use when his girlfriend became pregnant, and an-other acquaintance was stalked by her ex-boyfriend. These are just a couple stories of many that are hidden beneath the portrait that high schools paint of themselves.

Problems can be magnified by the social setting of high school. An executive is not going to have to worry about how his parents will pun-ish him if they find out his girlfriend is pregnant. If a working woman gets pregnant, provisions are made so she can temporarily leave her job, and the general reaction of her coworkers is excitement and happi-ness. If the same situation is transplanted to high school, the compas-sion and understanding shown by those around her is far less and the accommodations made for her at her place of work (the school) are fewer.

Two of my favorite movies are *Heathers* and *Say Anything*. *Heathers* is a story about a couple that deals with the pressures of high school in a highly unusual way—they murder fellow classmates. As far-fetched as the movie is, most parts ring true of today's high school. Its portrayal of the malevolent attitude of those who are perceived to be strong toward those seen as weak is an example. In the movie, the "popular" kids ha-rass the "nerds" and "freaks" for the sheer fun of it. This Neanderthal way of treating people is not limited to the movies: One day in gym class I was playing softball and a dispute arose over whether I was out or not. I took my place at first base and had this conversation with the first baseman (an athlete who disliked me solely because I was differ-ent):

"You're out, faggot."

I replied, "Am I supposed to be offended by that?"

"Shut up, fag."

"I'm not a homosexual, and whether I am or am not, why should I be offended when someone talks about my sexual orientation? Maybe you're just afraid of homosexuals because you are insecure in your own sexuality."

His well-thought-out and fact-based reply was, "Fuck you."

I know several people who lack "social skills," and for this they are mocked by people who are supposedly "young adults." One friend of mine (we'll call him John), who was slightly overweight, had a headline and picture taken from a tabloid (it read "167 Pound Baby Born" and had a body with rolls of fat with the head of a baby) and, with the help of computers, the pranksters put his head in the place of the baby's, made copies of it, and passed it around school. Another time, a supposed friend of John's dumped the books out of his book bag and, with the help of someone else, kicked his books, folders, and papers all over the school simply for the fun of it. The worst part of the adolescent's cruelty is the motivation for it: a feeling of superiority and a relative lack of rational reasoning for their actions.

One final example comes from when I went to the prom on a double date; the couple with us went as friends and the man was a known homosexual. All evening we heard that some people were trying to get together a group to beat him up solely because he was gay. Fortunately, nothing ever materialized, but the sheer fact that people were bothered enough simply by his sexual orientation to want to resort to violence shows the extent immaturity can reach in "young adults."

The Anatomy of Tracking
by Joshua Radetski

"Although the class was supposed to be a group of 'gifted,' the only thing in which we were gifted was how to goof off."

Joshua Radetski is a senior. He is on the varsity football team, in every possible school band, and a member of the National Honor Society. Josh will be attending the University of Illinois at Champaign—Urbana. Computers and role-playing games occupy the little free time he has.

They call us the "cream of the crop," the "elite few." After being in the accelerated track since the seventh grade, I have noticed that in some instances, the "normal" track students are the same as or sometimes even better students than the "gifted" students. In terms of mentality and attitude, accelerated and honors-track students are often no different from those in the normal track.

I began my "accelerated" track learning when I was in seventh grade. The high school placement tests placed me into the honors track once in high school. All of my classes have been accelerated, honors, or advanced placement, with the exception of world geography, American history, French, and band. What I have to say is based on personal experiences from my years in these two tracks. The average student and the accelerated student in some respects are the same.

The district and Weberville High School, like most other high schools in this country, offer a three-track system. There is a "remedial" track designed for the slower learners, the mentally disabled, and those who refuse to use their intelligence. The "normal" track is for the average student and for the student who just wants to "get by" in high school. Finally, there is the "honors" or "accelerated" track for those exceptionally bright students or for those who got lucky on their high school entrance placement exams and guessed a large amount correctly. There are also other programs of classes not associated with the tracking system. These include classes for the disabled and work programs for those not planning on continuing their formal education after high school.

In both normal-level and accelerated classes, there have been students who have worked diligently for their A's. There is also the group of students who, no matter what the class, normal or accelerated, do not do any work and do not care what the consequences are. They just do not like school and don't care one way or the other if they get a passing grade. There is a third group of students in both tracks. This group of procrastinators will put off any assignment given to them until the last possible moment, will still get the assignment in, and will get a good grade for the least possible work done.

The normal classes in which I have been involved have been in the social science department. In my American history class last year, every group imaginable was represented. I sat on one side of the room with athletes like myself. Closer to the teacher on my side were the "brains," a group of kids who, like myself, are normally in accelerated classes but either could not fit an accelerated history class into their schedule or did not want their schedules overloaded. In the back of the room sat the females. They could not be put into any subgroup because there were so few of them. The far side of the room had what I would call "the drug group." They spent the entire period every day reading car magazines, comparing who got more drunk over the weekend and who was going to get the most wasted this coming weekend. Occasionally, one of them would show up to class this last period half-drunk. Not all were this way in class. One member of that group, when he did try, usually got one of the highest scores on tests in the class. Unfortunately, most of the time he was paying more attention to the local discussions than to the teacher.

My side of the room wasn't any better. A friend and I spent most of the time talking about football, which we were both in, or ridiculing the other side of the room. Both of us, along with the others on our side of the classroom, are in mostly accelerated classes and therefore we knew we could do as little work as possible and still get a good grade on natural skill alone. My friends and I would even play cards when we had free time to study in class. Near the end of the year, we began to take sheets of graph paper and play battleship while the teacher was lecturing. He put a stop to that, however. Unfortunately, he could not control the other side of the room as easily. Our side was easy to control because we were occasionally willing to learn, whereas the other side, in most cases, refused any type of teaching.

There is a class called "Gifted-Independent Study," nicknamed "Gifted." To get into this class, a student first has to do exceptionally well on the high school entrance exams. Then, after teachers from high school talk to the junior high teachers, a handful of students are selected to take a second exam testing creative and critical thinking skills. After this screening process, we ended up with the most unique kids imaginable. Variety was probably intended. The entire class lasted three semesters: second semester freshman year and both sophomore semesters. We started with about 25 students in the class, ranging from football and track athletes to speech and theater group members to nonactivity students just in school so they can get out. During the break between freshman and sophomore years, a large portion of the original class dropped, leaving 13 students. These students splintered into the same types of groups that were present in the normal-level class. Three of my friends and I formed the "athlete" group; the front of the room had 3 students whom we called the "brown-nose" group; in the rear was the small group of girls; and in the far corner was what could be called the "rebels," a group of 5 kids who did not kiss up to teachers and would not be caught dead in sports.

Although the class was supposed to be a group of "gifted" students, the only thing in which we were gifted was how to goof off. The teacher would give us a project to be done in a week. Not one of the students would do it until the night before. Only the brown-nose group would even attempt to listen to any lectures by the teacher, and often they too would not listen. The whole third semester was supposed to be used to do one project that was to be shown at an expo at the end of the school year. Because we were a "gifted" class, we knew how to blow off the assignment until the last week before this public districtwide event. Our teachers tried to get us to do the projects in parts over the whole semester by pairing us with faculty mentors. Unfortunately, we found ways to get around any check or evaluation. We either faked progress on the sheets or would do one section of the project in class in about 2 minutes. We would use the rest of that week's classes to do homework from other classes or just sit around and talk. The teachers had no control over what we did. Substitute teachers would come to our class and call us the "worst bunch of students they had ever seen" and say that we behaved worse than "normal" students.

Overall, the tracking system does not necessarily have the profound effect intended. Both sets of tracks exhibit the same adolescent behavior in class. Even though accelerated students probably have more difficult homework, the attitude of the "honors" track students promotes procrastination, whereas the normal track students put off assignments because they feel less pressure to do as well.

No matter which track, "normal" or "accelerated," the same student behavior occurs. The same types of groups form in each. The same attitudes about doing homework are present. The only use for tracking is to give "honors" students more with which they can procrastinate.

Challenging Learning Disabilities
by J. T. Gribbon

"Why do you leave us in lower-level classes . . . and out of a lot of your activities?"

J.T. Gribbon is a senior at Weberville High School. Out of school he plays in several types of bands, mostly "death metal." He is active in church and the church group LIFT (Living in Faith Together). In the fall he will attend Northland College in Ashland, Wisconsin and study wildlife management. When not writing for the student social science magazine, J.T. is writing poems or songs for his bands. He enjoys "listening to groups from classical music all the way up to death metal." One of his many jobs has included hanging billboards by the highway.

Somewhere out there, everybody has a problem. Some of us have bigger problems than others, whether it be at home, at work, with friends, or at school. A lot of us have some kind of learning disability, whether it is reading, writing, or maybe taking notes on something.

Learning disabilities are caused by a lot of things like malnutrition, early childhood development, emotional and social problems, brain injury, muscular weakness, and vision impairment. Other times, people may develop a learning disability due to things such as psychogenic amnesia (a disorder in which traumatic events cause lapse of memory), multiple personalities, schizophrenia, etc. They are probably this way because of an early accident or because, at some time in their development, something went wrong.

A lot of people see these kids in the hall and make fun of them and throw stuff in their faces. It's not their fault they were born this way.

Maybe one day we might find out why. But until then, only God knows why, and we don't have a clue.

I personally know a lot of people with learning disabilities or physical handicaps. Ever since I was in third grade, I have been in learning disability classes. This is the first year that I have not been in learning disability classes.

I was in learning disability classes because I could not work as hard or as fast as other students. My problem was that I could not read things and it took me longer to understand than a person in regular or accelerated classes. Some of the people in my classes were dyslexic. This means they read backward instead of forward. Other people had behavioral disorders or personality disorders, or were physically handicapped.

So when you see these kids in the hall, next time don't make fun of them because in a way they are depressed about who they are. They would rather be you than who they are. When you make fun of them you bring them down. And from that one day, they might never come up from that depression. Now try living with that.

But what I would like to know is why do you leave us in lower-level classes and learning disability classes and leave us out of a lot of your activities? It's kind of like saying we're not human, so we can't work with the other students. Yes, it sounds as cold as ice, but that's the way you make us feel.

I know a lot of times we are the kids who fool around in class or come up with excuses on why our homework is not done. We know we are going to pass these special classes, so why bother doing homework? What we need is a challenge instead of being put in the lower-level classes and sitting there feeling stupid. How would you like to be in that predicament?

Why don't you just make classes all one level? After all, God created man equal, so who gives you the right to tell me that I am not as smart as the next person? If you gave us a challenge, you would probably find out that we are just as good as your average students, if not better. And the best judge of that is us, because we know what we can do.

Applied Tech Classes Are Good for All
by Rich DiCanio with assistance from Israel Juarez and Carlos Lopez

"If accelerated students were in my building construction class, I could show them a thing or two. . . . Maybe then we wouldn't have such low self-esteem."

Rich DiCanio's favorite class is building construction, a course in which each year a house is built from scratch. Although he is uncertain about a career, he is

*interested in graphic arts. He enjoys all sports and plays in a softball league
each summer. Rich is a lot of fun. His sense of humor and playfulness enter-
tained all in class.*

Additional training in at least one applied technical class should be
recommended for all to graduate. Whether a student is college-bound
or not, technical classes teach skills that are very useful and beneficial
throughout life for all. It does not matter if it is woods, metals, or autos;
these classes are not meant merely for learning random facts as in most
academic classes, but they also teach students how to develop as people. The final product of any technical class is a lesson in the development of initiative, resourcefulness, flexibility, adaptability, and creativity, as well as tolerance, understanding, and cooperation in group
activities.

Technical classes also have the advantage of learning through
hands-on experience. "A (university) degree no longer guarantees success in the job market," said a U.S. Department of Labor official. With
this statement in mind, a person may need a technical skill to fall back
on.

A technical class will also teach some of the accelerated students that
they are not "brains" in every class. Some students think that just because a student is in an applied tech class, he or she is not as intelligent
as college-bound students. This is not true. Tech students may be just
as intelligent; however, they just choose to use their brains in a different way. I think if tech students applied themselves properly in their
academic courses, they could be just as smart. Even Jesus Christ chose
to be a carpenter, and He had the intelligence to be whatever He
wanted. The educated ones of His time looked down upon Him as the
accelerated students look down upon us.

Accelerated students may be book-wise, but not wise in simple
things. For example, many are not very smart when it comes to little
odd jobs around the house like the proper way of staining, varnishing,
hanging a door, patching a hole in drywall, installing a light fixture,
changing the oil in their car, or even hooking up a VCR or a video game
system. Maybe if accelerated students were in my building construction class, I could show them a thing or two. Maybe then they wouldn't
look down on us. Maybe then we wouldn't have such low self-esteem.

My favorite class is building construction. This class is 2 hours long,
and we actually build a house each year for the school district that they
sell on the open market. It includes everything from the basement to
the roof. How many college-bound students can install windows, sid-
ing, cabinets, woodwork, drywall, a roof, and everything else involved
with completing a house? The reason this class was so much fun and
rewarding is because I gained a lot of experience. I feel this is the most

beneficial and useful class of my 4 years of high school. I wish that others could have experienced just a portion of what I have.

It's unbelievable that some people choose to remain so uneducated in home repair and home improvement skills. I work in the paint department at a hardware store, and it is amazing. Men dressed in suits and ties ask the dumbest questions. These three-piece "suits" were probably accelerated students back when they were in school. For example, one man asked the "brilliant" question, "How do I go about painting the corners of a room when the roller touches the other wall?" Here's another dumb question from the "suits": "What is the difference between flat and gloss paint?" The people who ask these questions will buy anything you tell them is necessary to complete the job. Sometimes they buy things they don't need just because someone told them they'll need it. I also love it when they say that I am too young to know what I am talking about and ask if they could talk to someone older. This annoys me. Little do they know that when the older person comes he's going to say the same exact thing that I just said. When the people look back at me I say, "I may be only 17 but I have already built two houses." Only after I say that will they listen to me.

Another beneficial class is autos. Learning how to repair and maintain a car saves a lot of money and it protects one from being ripped off by a deceitful mechanic. I used to work at a tune-up and brake shop, and I witnessed several customers getting ripped off. For example, in some fuel-injected cars it is very hard to clean the fuel injectors; therefore, we used to spray carb cleaner on the injectors and charge them for a full injection cleaning. Perhaps if these "white collar" customers had taken a few shop classes during their high school career, they wouldn't be so naive. Since most college-bound high school students never take a shop class, they don't get to learn such valuable skills as taking apart an engine and putting it back together. Even in my own school there is a teacher in the math department who twice blew an engine in his Chrysler Caravan. The first time, he thought, "Heck, I am planning on getting gas in a mile, I'll ask a mechanic then." What an idiot! He did not realize that when the oil light goes on you should stop and add oil or let the car cool down before going any farther. The engine light signals low oil pressure—in other words, no oil. You can't run a car without oil! I bet you he was in all college-bound classes in high school. If those accelerated students are going to live in the real world, they ought to take some courses in the real world!

All in all, whether a student is college-bound or not, applied technical classes are just as educational as accelerated classes, and students taking these classes can be just as successful in the job market as any college graduate. Weberville High School should not put so much pressure on students to take all college-bound classes. High school shouldn't be so shortsighted. They shouldn't prepare kids just for college. Life doesn't end when students finish college. High school should prepare students for life after they've finished their schooling.

We Are Not Robots!
by Robert Haden

"Sometimes I perceive teens to live by the rules of a different reality, something teachers often don't recognize."

Rob Haden anxiously awaits graduation after serving his required 4 years in high school. He plans to attend James Madison College of Michigan State University this fall. When not writing papers for school, he's writing hallucinatory prose inspired from the dreams of 10-hour-plus nightly sleeps.

Personally I find it frustrating being a teenager. As a teenager, I have become more aware of my surroundings. Also, I have become aware of many difficulties involving the school system, one of them being a gap of misunderstanding between teacher and student. This fact has gnawed at me for nearly 4 years, and gradually I'm becoming more irritated each time a teacher fails to see the rationale behind my academic behavior. For this reason it is necessary to explore the real side of teens for the sake of teachers. Perhaps, on the chance my teachers read this paper, they will gain a better understanding of me and my fellow teens.

The teacher-student relationship is one in which the teen at first sees the teacher as a threat. Only when the teacher proves his [or her] worth does the teacher attain the label of being "cool." Often a student won't consider the teacher cool unless the class involves little work. Such a class is often termed a "blow-off." The student-teacher relationship is present Monday through Friday in the classroom. In this environment the teacher sees the student and not the troubled teen. It is here that I suffer the trials of education that led me to compose my thoughts on the unseen side of teens that I shall now reveal.

First things first: Teens are confused souls trapped in a whirlpool of troubles. Relationships are the number one facet of teen culture. Included are not just relationships between sweethearts but also relationships with parents, siblings, friends, coworkers, employers, and yes, teachers. To me it seems that teachers never stop to think what a teen does outside the classroom. The last thing teens think about doing in their daily routine (before retiring to bed, of course) is schoolwork. I get upset any time someone within earshot mentions school. I loathe the institution.

I know the necessity of a fine education; therefore I still frequently attend. Keep in mind, dear reader, that I am writing this not for my sake, but for the sake of the teachers who appear so ignorant. Ignorant?

Yes, indeed. I am not slighting teachers, for I owe them my gratitude for many things I've learned. In fact, I deeply respect some of the teachers who had the honor of my presence in the classroom. I mean they are *ignorant* in the respect that they are unaware of the personal side of teens. With only a few observations and a little investigation, a teacher would not have much trouble seeing this side of a pupil.

Dear reader, I get the impression you find me arrogant and feel I show subtle animosity toward my teachers. This is true, and it is partly the reason for my continuation on the subject. Let me continue. As I was saying, teachers do not see the nonstudent side of teens. The side they are missing is quite emotional and filled with vivacity and energy. Most teens are colorful characters, but they are abnormal. I hold the conviction that I am one of the sanest persons I can think of. Everybody my age is screwed up in one way or another. It just comes with being a teen. I hope teachers remember the time of their youth and can relate to the turbulent years of adolescence.

The process of maturation affects the teenage mind a great deal. It has made me arrogant, for I am more self-aware and aware of my potential and what I have to offer to the rest of the world. I know what I am capable of doing and what I am capable of getting away with *not* doing. Hence I make decisions and I consider ramifications. For example, I created my own deadline for the paper that you are now reading. Important decisions present themselves to teens like myself every day. A situation where teens often find themselves under stress, in need of decisive action, is that of peer pressure. Some of these situations may seem comical to adults and teachers, and sometimes myself, but they are taken very seriously by teens.

Did I mention peer pressure? Ah, yes. Peer pressure may lead one to take a hit of marijuana, drink at a party, or have sex. "Teachers are aware that teens experience such situations!" you may say, but teachers may not be aware of the stress produced from them. I experience a drop in my grades occasionally, but it is not a result of sheer laziness on my part. Rather it is more often a result of teen experiences out of school.

After pondering the thought that teachers do not know how I function, it leaves me marked with frustration. I once had a teacher who attributed a decline in the quality of my work to being "in love." To this day I wonder where Mr. Blank came up with that hypothesis. To his credit, he tried to find out what the problem was. When teachers relate to students and make tiny inquiries, students feel more comfortable with the situation. Our school teachers are getting better at understanding teens who sit in the desks before them, mostly because they've opened their ears and eyes a crack. The more teachers see my natural side, the more efficient I can be, simply because it's comforting to know the figure of authority can sympathize.

Teens are in a constant state of disillusionment. Sometimes I perceive teens to live by the rules of a different reality, something teachers often don't recognize. The truth is that teens just "wanna be adored"; so go the lyrics of a song I'm familiar with. I doubt that a single teacher has ever heard the song. Teachers must remember the days of their youth, for empathy sometimes is the best method of understanding, and with the anguish and near insanity teens experience, teens need every bit of help available.

Teachers, Here Are Your Do's and Don'ts
by Amy Petrusha

"They must all get together and plan certain days when something is due in every class."

Amy Petrusha is 18 and plans to attend Northern Illinois University this fall to pursue a career in commercial design. Her favorite pastime is driving to unknown destinations while listening to U2.

Teachers, here is the student point of view. Please don't worry, it's not all bad! "Teachers" is a topic some love to hate. But it is also a topic capable of prompting and motivating students to actually write and enjoy writing. What a concept—enjoyable writing! Yes, teachers, it's true! For only an unbelievable "topic of their choice," a piece of paper, and a pen, you too can receive a great response from your students! This statement leads me to tell the basis and reasoning behind my selection of this topic.

In order to teach, one must have learned, and who better to learn from than your own students? I'm hopeful that each and every word printed on these pages will encourage teachers to take students' thoughts and suggestions into deep consideration. It will make you guys better teachers (not to say most of you aren't good already), which, in turn, makes us better students, which, for most of us, couldn't hurt.

Since the purpose of this book is to bring about a better understanding of what teachers can do to improve their classroom (learning, relations with students, etc.), I think I'll just get right down to it by telling and explaining the "do's and don'ts" from the student view. First off, the number one most important point is to work with and not against students. We realize there are things that have to be taught and learned, but you have to realize that most of us have at least four or five other classes where the same amount of teaching and learning is required. Often students wonder aloud things like the following: "Do they think this is the only class we have?" and "They must all get together and plan certain days when something is due in every class." All we're asking is that you consider that we do have other classes and that you not load up an impossible amount of work on us each night. Please at least spread the work out over a period of time. After all, there are only 24 hours in a day, and not even half of that can be spent doing work. Even if we try, we get penalized for doing the wrong work in the wrong place at the wrong time. Class can be so boring you can't even concentrate on what's being taught!

This leads me to my next point, BOREDOM. Maybe the reason your students aren't working up to potential is because the class, day after day, is so boring and "straight from the book" that they can't concentrate enough to even follow the material. Of course we all expect class to be boring sometimes, with an occasional lecture all period. You know those kinds of lectures, like in chemistry—"the anatomical structure of the carbon monoxide molecule." Yeah, it's boring, and we learn to live with it if it only occurs once in a while, but day after day after day—no, I don't think so. We learn and retain so much more when teachers give examples and tell personal or other stories relating to the topic. Almost everyone also agrees that we learn from "hands-on" experiences. If teachers could just incorporate these things into their curriculum a bit more, students would actually want to come to class ready to learn. You have to realize that the things that are exciting to you aren't always exciting to your students. That's why you have to make it exciting. A good idea that has worked in the past, that cures the boredom we feel listening to endless lectures and actually makes us do our work, is "work day." Whether it be once a week or once every 2 weeks, even if it's just half a period long, let us ask questions and finish homework.

Other ideas that help us get our work done are syllabi and study guides. Make the syllabi for a class as far a time in advance as possible and try to stick to it. That really helps us to stay organized, and when we're organized, that usually improves our attitude about school. Study guides also help us be organized because we understand the points you're trying to get across much more clearly. For the kind of study guides where you have to answer the questions or fill in the blanks, like for a novel, don't grade them. It's a pain for us and a pain for you, too. Just make sure we have most of it done and be sure to go over every question.

You guys have to loosen up a bit. Give us some freedom. It's hard for students to sit in the same desk for a whole period, six or seven periods a day. I'm not saying let us go to the cafeteria every day during class, but maybe sometimes take us outside. At least let us get up out of our seats once in awhile. Let us sit on the floor if we want. It sounds crazy, but we actually listen better if we're comfortable and don't feel as "trapped."

In addition to actual, physical freedom in the classroom, give us freedom in our work and learning process. I think Scantron testing should be eliminated, or at least have an essay test as an option. I honestly think teachers don't believe there are people who are poor test-takers. We know the information, but we get nervous and sometimes the questions aren't clear or we get confused. Maybe even a project could replace a test.

The last, very important point that I need to address is that teachers need to be a little bit more personal and a lot less traditional and "stuffy." We love hearing you guys tell us "stuff" about yourselves—likes, dislikes, stories from your childhood, stories from the present, and especially all the stupid things you did when you were our age. Teachers can give us so much more than just an education. Some students see their teachers more than their own parents. Because of this, our teachers become our role models. Role models give a sense of achievement, self-worth, self-confidence, and just a good, happy, healthy environment in which to be. I'm not saying teachers should also be psychologists, analyzing every student's life and giving out advice and guidance to everyone. We have good people like counselors to do that, but students benefit much more from life if teachers just take a little time out to care about us, our feelings, thoughts, and situations that do and don't relate to school.

The impact teachers have on students is far greater than either of us realize. Though sometimes the effects can be devastating, many teachers really can play a big role in our lives in helping us get through life smoothly. We'd like to thank those of you who have done so.

In conclusion, I hope that all you teachers out there have learned something from and for your students. Keep in touch and in tune with them and their lives. These aren't just things we want. Some of us need these things to help us through school, even life, and our hope is that teachers will soon realize this.

Why I Hate to Write Papers!
by Daniel J. Mann

"When I got to write about wrestling, I hate to say it, but I actually enjoyed it. That just doesn't sound like me, but I did."

Daniel J. Mann is a senior at Weberville High School, where he is captain of the varsity wrestling team. He participates on a wrestling team with the park district each spring. Dan plans to attend the local community college in the fall. When not writing papers, he is either wrestling, playing beach volleyball, or riding his motorcycle.

I hate writing papers. Well, I must make it clear that I don't hate writing all types of papers. Don't get me wrong; I don't like it either. Papers that include research are just a waste of time because I probably won't want to learn about it, let alone write about it. Papers that include no research, where you can just sit down and "freestyle" it, are not that bad but still take up too much time. Instead you could be out with your friends, sleeping, eating, or watching TV. Basically, I would rather be in church listening to a boring sermon than write a paper.

Writing papers is the biggest waste of time. You could be assigned many better things. Nobody in their right mind could have fun researching something about which they don't really care. But you must do it anyway. Why? Because you are so lucky to have a teacher who assigns it. There are a lot of little things that can go wrong. Your teacher might check something that you think is really good but within a matter of seconds, the teacher shoots it down. That just pisses me off; so does missing a deadline when you busted your ass to try to make it. Another little thing is when in class, you just get going, you're writing real well, and then the damn bell rings. This totally messes up your concentration. You try to return to it the next day or at night when you get home, but it's just not the same. If you are on a free hour in school and you go to the computer lab, there may be nowhere to sit or the teacher won't let you in because [he or] she is teaching another class.

Research papers must be the biggest, most boring thing you could ever be assigned. In "expos class" (college prep composition, a one-semester senior-year formal writing course), a course schools should not even have, you have to do way too much work for a paper you don't even care about. In addition, you must meet deadlines that are too soon. First you have to pick out a topic. You look though a sheet of topics and see nothing of interest. You end up getting stuck with something with which you don't want anything to do.

Then you get to do note cards, a minimum of 100! They just suck! You must write a note card for every bit of information you find. This is after you find all your sources. Some libraries don't even have books you can use as a source! Then when you get all your books you get the privilege of looking up all of the information. Much of this information probably makes no sense to you. After you have done that then you get to outline this information into eight categories; that sounds like fun. Are you still following all of this?

Then you get to write your outline for your rough draft. You must have all this stuff checked in on deadlines that are hard to make; you probably messed up along the way and now you get to fix it. So after all your note cards are corrected, you have to organize them into an outline and have it completed by another deadline. Now that you have your note cards outlined, you get to write a rough outline of the paper.

So your rough outline is done and you get that checked off but you probably screwed up somewhere and have to fix that too. After that is corrected, you get to start your final rough draft. That takes a couple of days, a lot of advice, and stressful thinking that my brain doesn't like to do. But you finally get it done and checked off and you make all your corrections. Only then do you get to write your final copy. This has to be immaculate. It has to be the best you have ever written. When you're writing this you have to remember to put in at least two quotes from each source. You survive. But when you think you're done, you still have more. Your bibliography is your final step in writing your expos paper. This is a pain because you have to know everything about each author, including where they grew up and went to school. Writing an expos paper has to be the biggest thing a student is put through in high school.

Writing papers that include no research is still a pain in the butt, but they are not as bad as college prep composition papers. I personally don't really mind these papers; however, I would rather not write any paper at all. I call it freestyle writing. This is when you express your feelings on a topic that you choose. This is nice. When I got to write about wrestling (see Chapter 3, The Student Reality: Activities and Sports), I hate to say it, but I actually enjoyed it. That just doesn't sound like me, but I did enjoy it. It gave me an opportunity that I have never before been given, to write about the sport that is most important in my life. All who read that paper I think now know what really happens in a wrestling match and what wrestlers go though in preparing themselves for the match. When you read something that has been written freestyle, it opens people's minds to think a little more and realize something new to them.

I maintain that writing research papers is a big waste of time. I still see no fun in it. But students all across the country write them and get them done. I am sure a lot of them will agree with me when I say "Writing papers is boring and a pain in the butt." When you get a research paper assigned to you, the first thing you think is: "This is going to suck. Why did I have to take this class? Why did I have to get this teacher? I really don't want to do this" and stuff like that. However, when you write a paper on a topic that you choose, you enjoy it and have a better attitude from the start.

[Editor's note: It is rumored that during the year prior to this writing, two students required emergency intervention for suicidal ideation citing problems in college prep composition as the specific precipitating factor. Usually it is one per year. The grading scale for the semester paper emphasizes form at the expense of function. Eighty-four percent of a student's grade is based on form. Only 16% is based on content, the function for which the paper was written.]

Ditching School
by Mingo Suarez

"Honestly, what can beat a day when you wake up at 11:00 a.m., take a shower, and finish today's and tomorrow's homework, all before your friends are even out of school?"

Mingo Suarez is an honor student for whom ditching may be more fantasy than fact. Mingo is on the varsity baseball team and plans to attend the local community college in the fall.

Many kids have busy schedules, particularly in high school. Students, for instance, work part-time jobs, compete in school sports, and have many hours of homework. How can one get around doing his or her homework with the many commitments students have after school? Well, it's called ditching!

A typical school day, for a junior or senior, consists of five to six classes with a free hour and a lunch hour. For example, a typical senior's schedule may be as follows: calculus, English, Spanish, lunch, introduction to social science, keyboarding, physics, and a free hour. Five of these classes pose a serious homework threat. However, because many students work in the evening from 4:30 until 10:00 p.m., there may not be time to do homework. Many students don't arrive home from school until 3:45 p.m. and before one knows it, it's time to leave for work. After a hard night's work, the student may arrive home at 10:30 in the evening. By the time the student arrives home, he or she is tired from work. The last thing on the kid's mind is homework. The first thing on one's mind is to hit the sack, especially if there's a nice waterbed waiting. Knowing one doesn't want to stay up all night to do the homework and lose 2 to 3 hours of sleep, the student decides to play hooky for the next day.

Now, sometimes one may have to suffer the consequences and lose those 2 to 3 hours of sleep to finish homework. Yes, it takes a lot of dedication to keep up grades along with a job, but ditching school should be used as an alternate way to keep a student on task. Honestly, what can beat a day when you wake up at 11:00 a.m., take a shower, and finish today's and tomorrow's homework, all before your friends are even out of school?

There are times when it is actually better to skip school than be there. For instance, when one wakes up in the morning, one should ask: "What will we be doing in class today? Is it really worth going to school?" Just remember, most classes are going to be those very long, boring, drawn-out lectures. Is it more worth it to wander off into space and have your teachers say something to you than to sleep in until noon or 1:00 p.m.? I don't think so.

The best time to ditch is when a big paper is due at the end of the week and there's no time to do it. There is much planning to take place before ditching. One should take home key books in order not to fall too far behind in classes. As long as one keeps up with work from all the classes and keeps on task, ditching school can provide valuable and necessary time to finish whatever.

There are many things to do if choosing to ditch. The most common is to get a good day's rest. Others take time off to catch up on some homework or do recreational things like going to Great America or a Cubs game. Ditching school should be used as relaxation. It's great doing homework while listening to the radio and having a nutritious TV dinner. Hey, have some fun! Live your high school years as much as possible! Just think, one way or another, for all your hard work throughout the years you probably deserve a couple of days off.

There are various ways to ditch. One way is "Mom, I feel sick today." This is the most common way. No trouble can result between the school and the student when Mom calls you in sick. Another way is to just plain ditch. Just pretend to go to school. Leave the house and return when all things are clear. Make sure if you're to go to far extremes to ditch school you make the most of the situation. There is also another sometimes risky but effective way. You can simply call in for yourself. Now when calling in for yourself, make sure you keep nice and calm, and talk like a man or a woman or else you'll be doomed from the beginning. The most effective way to ditch is to tell one of your parents straight on the previous night or even in the morning prior to school. This is the most effective way because most parents totally understand what is going on and will probably let you do it about three to four times per year. With luck, your parents will think back many years ago when they were under a lot of stress with homework. Make sure you don't overdo these excuses or you may lose their trust.

With ditching school, there may be some serious consequences you may not be willing to face. The consequences for ditching school without calling in is to serve two detentions and have a disciplinary letter mailed to the parents. The result of saying you're sick is simply being a little behind in a class or two. This can't be too bad. The consequence of confronting parents and asking them to stay home is practically nothing as long as you keep your promise and do what you said. Whatever the consequence may be, if you want to ditch, you should be able to take the consequences.

Ditching school is more than a game, it is an art. One who masters it can be more successful in life. Ditching is OK as long it is not an everyday thing. There are certain times to ditch and certain times to not. Be careful in what approaches you use. Good luck!

National Honor Society, *NOT!*
by Maria Gonnella

"The selection process is absurd. Those who have parents belonging to school organizations, or those students in certain activities, easily roll through the selection process."

Maria Rina Gonnella is a senior at Weberville High School, where she has volunteered at the local elementary school and has been in the band and Model United Nations Club. She is a member of the National Honor Society and a recipient of the Weberville Pride Award, a school award for achievement. Maria earned the social science department's year-end recognition as the social science student of the year. When not in class, Maria works as a secretary at her church. Maria enjoys spending time with her family, whom she loves with all her heart. She plans to attend Illinois Benedictine College in Lisle, Illinois.

The National Honor Society is the traditional social gathering of high school members across our nation who exemplify the highest possible achieved status as exemplary students. These students are considered to be elite. Students across the United States are introduced to this prestigious society as they enter high school in the hopes that they will aspire to work hard to become members during their third year. Many are selected to join the elite. Yet a greater number of hardworking students who constantly prove themselves to their superiors are turned away. I'd like to examine the National Honor Society, who is in and who is not, the application process, and other facets of this "prestigious" club. I will try to provide new insight on NHS.

Because I am within the top 5% of my graduating class and due to my experiences, I feel I have a basis for writing on National Honor Society. I was approached by the president of the branch at my school with an application to fill out and submit for entry and acceptance my junior year. This greatly pleased me, for I had always worked and studied hard in hopes of joining NHS. Having taken time to painstakingly fill out the application, I gave it back to be reviewed. After a month of anticipation, I received a letter. It informed me that I had not been accepted. Time has passed, yet a year later, I still feel my hard work, good grades, and especially my undying effort all have accomplished very little. I believe it is time to allow others a view within the system of the "elite."

The setting is typical: Anywhere High School, U.S.A. Though it may not be labeled "NHS," it seems all high schools across the country have an elite group of academic achievers within their social setting. The desire that grows within a student throughout his [or her] formative high school years is generated from a subtle, yet unmistakably present, influence. This subtle influence originates from two distinct sources: the school's administration and one's peers. The latter relates to the concepts of peer pressure, the structure of peer social groups, and peer conformity. Those within National Honor Society are considered by social as well as national standards to be at the top of their classes. Pressure of competition among peers (especially those of higher intellect) exists within schools to be the best and achieve all recognition possible, to gain admittance into groups of such caliber as NHS, conforming if necessary to fit an accepted profile. The former deals with the subtle influence felt by students from the administration. Though apparent only to those who care to look and admit it, students accepted within the circle of the National Honor Society are treated differently than the rest. It seems as if a new personal relationship becomes established with certain members of the administration (for example, the principal) once a student is admitted into NHS. Though superficially some students care not to agree, the majority just want to be recognized by the administration as true people and not mere serial numbers. Yet the only way, it seems, is to be within a group such as NHS, a group recognized by the administration as made up of hardworking people who happen to be students. Influences such as these within the typical school setting motivate students to achieve success.

My personal experience provides one illustration of NHS. During my first 2 years of high school, I observed an emphasis upon being a member of NHS. While looking at the model upper-class students of my high school, as all under-class students do, it struck me that everyone who was truly "anyone" belonged to the National Honor Society. The administration had a different relationship with these particular students, not one of just educator-pupil, but of one friendly party realizing the other's potential and intellect. This was all I wanted during my high school years, to finally be recognized for my potential and hard work and be looked upon as worthy of praise. The National Honor Society was my chance to prove myself to a seemingly skeptical administration. So, after having continued to work hard through the first 2 years, spending all weeknights and weekends studying, missing out on what was supposed to be a fun high school social life, and never neglecting even one facet of my academic schedule, I was finally asked to apply to the prestigious NHS. I opened the application and found it to be a request of all extracurricular activities I had accomplished. It was divided into two sections. The first and most lengthy part was a sort of checklist with every organized school club and sport. I was asked to go through this list and check off applicable items. Not being very active within school bounds, I was not able to check many items, but I did check several. The second section required a personal list of all activities done outside school. Simple enough, it seemed, yet the structure struck me as strange. It was as if the heads of NHS simply added another page to take up additional space, as if they had really no plan to review this part of the form. But I continued to fill out the application. I began to notice, though, that I was running out of space. I had more items listed in this section than in the other; I thought nothing of it. In fact, I thought the heads of NHS would be pleased that I had taken initiative and broken away from school bounds to work within the community.

I handed in the application and began an agonizing waiting period. Within 3 weeks, news had arrived in the form of a letter. I anxiously opened it, only to find my hopes and hard work repaid with a rejection form letter. No explanations were given for rejecting 3 years of total commitment, struggles, and what was a life's work. Never before in my life had I felt so worthless; all my toil and pain were swept aside by NHS as if they were nothing. After the depression lifted, anger rose within me and I scheduled an appointment with the principal for an explanation. The first part of what she described was just as I expected: Because of NHS being a national society, she claimed she could do nothing to help. Yet what sent a dagger through my heart was that she said the reason I was not accepted was because I did not "do enough for the school." I realized I was not in an extraordinary number of clubs or sports, but I had poured my life into the school to become an academic leader, and apparently being within the top 5% of my class was not enough of an example of "leadership" to suit their tastes. Therefore, my dream was taken away and there was no way to get it back, or even fight for it.

Looking back, I feel National Honor Society to be a bogus institution. But I do not feel this way because I was rejected; I would feel the same even if I were accepted or if I never had been asked to apply. My personal experience is just that. It has been included as an individual example. One must remember that many others may have more positive personal experiences to share.

I feel institutions like NHS instill the wrong values within the minds of students. The main reason applicants are turned away (after having been asked to apply) has nothing to do with grades, but everything to do with participation in school activities. Yet school participation is hardly ever associated with NHS as a deciding factor for acceptance. Participation is mainly proposed by the school with the idea of "getting involved" to feel comfortable within school society. What the heads of NHS seem to forget is that many students cannot possibly participate in school activities due to certain other obligations. For example, two different students are being reviewed by the NHS board. The first student is from a well-off family, perhaps an only child, an "okay" student with a 3.0 grade average, yet he is on the football team, in choir, in band, and perhaps is a peer counselor. The other student, one from a large middle-class family, is an excellent student with an extremely high grade point average, works hard academically, participates in a few school activities but not many because he needs to hold a job to earn money to put himself through college due to the family situation.

More often than not, it is the first student, the one who has enough time on his hands to participate in school activities, who makes National Honor Society. And, sadly enough, it is the second student, who has always worked hard in school but has not done anything "for the school" who is turned away. It is not fair to penalize a student who has other obligations. Why is a student who must work outside school to produce a future for himself [or herself], or might participate in numerous religious activities due to a closer affiliation with religion than with school, or needs to spend the majority of his after-school time studying, or is in other similar circumstances, not allowed to join the elite? To me, this is injustice at its worst.

The National Honor Society has always been a tradition. Those students considered superior provide the model for all others. Perhaps I have placed too much importance on NHS, but this is solely a response to social values. The selection process is absurd. Those who have parents belonging to school organizations, or those students in certain activities, easily roll through the selection process. It is a fact, one that many are not willing to realize, that belonging to certain groups gets one in more easily than others—especially highly respected sports and prestigious clubs (at my school this means football, band, choir, and peer counseling leaders). National Honor Society members are those who receive more than the majority of academic honors. Yet this society is a service organization that recognizes students *not for academics*, but for participation in extracurricular school activities. Those rejected from NHS are made to feel less important—as if their work all these years has meant nothing—especially at graduation, a ceremony in which much time is spent honoring NHS members.

I would just like to mention two final observations. The first comes from a friend who also applied to NHS, one greatly associated with the school as perhaps its major leader. She had a few disciplinary problems due to her acting upon her particular beliefs regarding the system. Despite being a very active member of the school, both academically and socially, she was not admitted. She pointed out that because the deciding board receives evaluations from teachers and staff with whom students may have had disagreements over the years, one teacher with whom one does not have a good relationship can blackball that student and ruin his or her chances of ever getting accepted. And finally, I would just like to add for readers who are part of the National Honor Society that I do not mean to offend you as a member. I am quite proud of those who are within NHS, those who truly *know* deep within themselves that they are there due to their own hard work and merits. But the National Honor Society is an organization in great need of reform.

[Editor's note: Maria was accepted into the National Honor Society during her senior year after the above essay was written.]

School: A Search for Meaning
by Amira Zaben

"School life for the most part is frustratingly empty. The school at-mosphere drains creativity and independent thinking. The foster-ing of introspection is practically nonexistent. School leaves me feeling confined and discontent."

Amira Zaben is a senior at Weberville High School and is involved in marching band, pep band, NHS, CAMP WHS (a readiness program linked with local feeder schools), the commencement committee, and PEER (a peer counseling program). Amira plans to attend the University of Illinois at Champaign—Ur-bana in the fall.

I entered high school with the crazy idea that school would teach me something related to real life. I know that everyone asks their math teacher, "When will I use this outside of this class?" but that is not what I mean. When I say that I am searching for meaning in school, I am looking for emotion-provoking classes, discussion periods where I can express my opinions and hear the thoughts of others, friends that I feel close to, teachers who interact with their students instead of just lectur-ing and giving notes, and relationships with members of the opposite sex that were not created as the result of any form of a note. Each morn-ing, as I enter the school building, I hope that maybe today will be sig-nificant to me; however, my hopes are crushed as I begin walking to my locker when on the way I am bombarded by little hoards of fresh-men girls huddled together, giggling and gossiping. Meaning is not a word that I associate with school. Ultimately, school is supposed to be preparing us for "life," which is exactly why I cannot understand why school revolves around memorization, research, and homework as-signments rather than emotions, world issues, and getting to know the people with whom you interact.

Each day I am reminded of my search for meaning. The most trou-blesome part of this never-ending pursuit is wondering if anyone can relate to what I am feeling. When I entered high school at the ripe old age of 14, I found myself in a totally different world. I felt surrounded by immaturity and a lack of concern for significance. Not to sound snobby, but I felt as if my level of maturity made it hard for me to relate to others. Males and females of all ages still acted as if they were just en-tering junior high. My dream of entering a world full of understanding was crushed by a reality of foolishness. I found myself struggling to find someone who could relate to the things that were of concern to me. My desperation led to deep frustration. Boredom set in. Forming friendships became a particularly difficult task. I sifted through many friends quickly. I seemed to know almost everyone, and yet I knew no one. More importantly, no one knew me.

Immediately after I walk through those sliding-glass doors, I become devoid of emotion. I feel nothing. I can only see, hear, smell, taste, touch, and think. My actions are hopelessly routine. School life is incredibly repetitive and dull. Like one of Pavlov's dogs, my actions are controlled by bells which sound every 50 minutes. My day is filled with thoughtless conversations about homework and boys. Robots teach almost all of my classes. My so-called teachers are for the most part unaware, unconcerned, and interested only in finishing all of the planned note-taking in the given 50-minute class period. This is the daily setting and routine I am in just about every weekday in the entire 8-month school year. School life for the most part is frustratingly empty. The school atmosphere drains creativity and independent thinking. The fostering of introspection is practically nonexistent. School leaves me feeling confined and discontented.

There are four main categories where meaning can be found. These four categories are: relationships, friends, teachers, and courses. All of these four categories are integral parts of a student day at Weberville High School.

Relationships between males and females are some of the saddest attempts to find the essence of life, that is, love. At Weberville High School the majority of relationships are started by a single note, passed by a third party, questioning the boy if he likes "so and so." These foolish pieces of literature capture the essence of immaturity. An important concept of life is exploited by these ever-so-intricately folded notes. Adolescent relationships revolve around physical pleasure and appearances rather than emotions and getting to know each other. Most teens keep their brains between their legs. Teenagers claim to be in love; however, the only things they can concretely say they have feelings for are sports, movies, pets, and if they are overly emotional children they might even love their parents. Pick up any note in the hallway and without a doubt it will be signed "love ya" by some airhead girl. In school we learn about sex education but not the education of love. We learn how to have sex but not why to have sex. The ideas of love and the ability to communicate and get along are either barely touched on or not stressed enough.

Meaningful friendships are extremely difficult to develop in the school setting. There is not enough time to have conversations with friends, let alone develop long-lasting friendships. Conversations with friends are so brief that not even a thorough discussion of the weather can be completed. If I have conversations at all, they are about homework or boys. Greeting someone in the hallway is even a problem for some teenagers. There is a hidden fear that lies deep within each student. This is the fear of saying hello to another student of the opposite sex (because if you acknowledge this member of the opposite sex he or she might think you "like" them). Friendships are also limited by the social structures that exist at every school level. Students are classified and grouped according to common tastes in either clothes, music, or school subjects. Once these classifications have been set, which is usually finished after the first week of school at the beginning of every school year, students rarely switch out of the groups they have chosen to be a part of. The social values ascribed to each group limit the students' behavior and interaction with students from other groups. Conformity plays a major role in most students' lives.

When I talk about meaning in courses, I am not just talking about classes that you can apply in "the real world." After all, consumers' education applied to real life, but frankly it was not too emotion-provoking. Due to tracking and graduation requirements, I have been enrolled in numerous classes that are unsatisfying. Class discussions or debates are a rarity, if they occur at all. My classes are taught by robots. Many teachers insist on being private and distant. A student rarely has much contact with a teacher. This lack of teacher-student interaction can be quite dulling; it can also make a student feel too intimidated to come and ask for help, whether it be course-related or personal.

Searching for meaning in school is an extremely frustrating task. It has left me feeling very unfulfilled. I do not know if searching for meaning in school is an activity carried out by all students at Weberville High School; however, I think it is safe to assume that each student searches for some form of meaning depending upon what is meaningful to that individual. Looking for meaning in school has had many effects on me. The first effect is built-in insecurity. At times I am quite scared of sharing myself with others. I fear being laughed at or just plain ignored. Expressing feelings in school is terribly taboo. I have also learned to search for meaning in places other than school. I, like other students, satisfy my need to be understood by turning to rock stars or TV celebrities. My search has had one positive effect on me. I have learned to give my own meaning to subjects and be somewhat satisfied with what little meaning I have found in a few of my classes. I find myself becoming quite enthusiastic when something is meaningful to me.

Although each student at Weberville High School may be searching for a different meaning, it is not impossible to integrate meaning into school life. I believe it is still possible to include meaning in each student's school experience. Because there are enough things in this world that are universally meaningful, there must be a way to integrate these common ideas. School should stimulate emotions and deal with universal issues such as relationships and communication. To me, school should be the place where introspection and expression are fostered and encouraged. After all, during the 8-month school year, school and school-related activities are where the student spends two thirds of his or her time.

A Failure in Suburban Education
by Garrick S. Greenblatt

"I'm not sure I started high school as cynical as when I left. High school was not what I expected. I left an angry young man. I guess the basic lesson I learned was cynicism . . ."

Garrick S. Greenblatt graduated in 1990. While at Weberville, Garrick was a starter on varsity Scholastic Bowl, the school's championship all-subject academic competition. Garrick was also active in Model United Nations Club. Garrick took accelerated and advanced placement–level courses. Unusually articulate and politically knowledgeable in high school, Garrick majored in political science at Northwestern University in Evanston, Illinois. He since attended and finished law school in Maryland.

I'm not sure I started high school as cynical as when I left. High school was not what I expected. I left an angry young man. I guess the basic lesson I learned was cynicism, cynicism about Weberville High School and suburban education as a whole.

Every sociologist knows that the primary purpose of education is to give individuals the knowledge, skills, and values needed to become a useful member of society. America's schools accomplish this task through formal education (a system of public schools and universities) and informal education (social organizations and the family). My high school was no exception. It combined formal classroom instruction with extracurricular activities and sports. However, I left Weberville feeling slighted. Weberville was a jock school and it was obvious. Many high schools today fall into this category. WHS officials can dispute much of what I say, but I do know their emphasis on athletics, student conformity and obedience, and statewide prestige over individualism, cultural diversity, and students' intellectual independence left me wondering if it were just for show, that intrinsic quality in the classroom was irrelevant. I'm not a jock; I guess it's obvious. Time after time I saw emphasis on athletics at the expense of academics and more intellectual programs. What is it about high school that causes it to shun anything intellectual?

These critical yet in my opinion true statements are based on my experiences as a Weberville High School student from 1986 to 1990. Although most of my classes were on the accelerated or AP track, some included students of all educational levels. My social interactions with WHS teachers were on two levels. First, I participated in several extracurricular activities at WHS, allowing me to see my teachers in an unstructured environment where students receive more one-on-one attention than in classes. The other level of interaction was conflictual. Unlike most of my classmates, I was quite vocal about teaching techniques or attitudes I didn't agree with, which led to a great deal of conflict between myself and various faculty. From an economic standpoint, I lived in a lower-middle-class neighborhood populated by a mix of white and Latino people, quite different from the all-white, upper-middle-class community known by most WHS students. My residence alone helped me see problems like gangs and racism in a different light.

Throughout my years at WHS, I learned that its administration prioritizes athletic ability, student conformity and obedience, and state-wide prestige in a number of ways. School sports are emphasized through the media and school awards. Half of each school newspaper is composed of reports on school athletics, far more than editorials, letters, or stories about academic achievement. WHS morning announcements and "pep rallies" honor athletes and athletics, while academic awards and honors are given little attention. WHS's administration emphasizes student obedience and conformity through its faculty and so-called "guidance" department. Several of my math teachers demanded total obedience from their students. When I openly criticized their teaching methods or lessons, my feelings were quickly classified as "insubordination," and like most critics, I was punished with detention. Weberville's guidance department encouraged conformity after high school as well. A lot of students were encouraged to attend the nearby community college or an Illinois state university, no matter what their abilities were. For instance, no guidance counselor ever mentioned Northwestern in my college search, despite the fact that I was a pretty good student and NU is known nationwide for academic excellence. Lastly, the WHS administration is very concerned with state-wide fame and prestige. Athletics are a high priority for Weberville's administration because of the media coverage it receives. Also, many productive classes have been scrapped at WHS in favor of an Advanced Placement track. Since AP scores are reported across Illinois and the U.S., WHS administrators have added students' AP success to the school's "brag sheet." Advanced placement classes can allow you to earn college credit. I took some APs, but let me tell you, they are nothing like college. For one thing, at Northwestern, my professors have Ph.D.s. The university gives them all the time they need to prepare for classes. In AP courses back in high school, I wondered if some of my teachers had anything more than the bare minimum education or preparation skills. Give me a break, I can read the book without them!

Because WHS administrators and faculty emphasize nonacademic factors, the consequence is the disappearance of students' interest in education, cultural diversity, and intellectual freedom. I think many WHS students pursued school awards on the basis of social status and their parents' achievements, rather than academic success. I also feel that there was a connection between having two parents belong to the parents club and being accepted into National Honor Society. I had only one parent, and she worked full-time while raising two kids. WHS policies also damaged cultural diversity and pride when I was there. Back then the administration seemed totally ignorant of Latino, Asian American, and Jewish students. I'm Jewish and I definitely felt alienated. The caroling in the halls at Christmas not only insulted non–Christian students, it distracted from academics. Distraction from classes leads to the alienation of dozens of students, some of whom consequently lose interest in academics.

WHS's loss of intellectual freedom is detrimental to the faculty as well as the student body. Before the administration became smitten with advanced placement, the teachers I knew well felt free to share curriculum ideas and teaching techniques with each other. In the past few years, however, some accelerated classes have been destroyed in favor of AP. One accelerated course I took had time for many debates. The papers we wrote were intelligent. In fact, this book is a compilation of the papers written for the anthropology course. The course introduced me to philosophy, anthropology, sociology, economics, and government. It was recently canceled and replaced with rigidly structured AP classes. Another accelerated course they got rid of in favor of AP was an independent study course in English. My friends who took it could work on one major project for the entire semester. Getting rid of it just didn't make sense. In short, the administration of Weberville High School considered school athletics, student conformity and obedience, and statewide prestige more important than students' individualism, cultural diversity, and intellectual independence.

Smart kids just don't have a chance at WHS. Maybe it's because they're outnumbered, but hasn't anyone ever wondered why they're outnumbered?

The Crooked School System
by Michael Lacey

"After a while in this classroom, I adjusted to my new surroundings. I turned from the quiet kid into a troublemaker just like the rest of the B.D. students."

Michael Lacey enjoys sports and hopes to attend the local community college in the fall.

I did very well in school up to the fifth grade. While I was in fifth grade, my parents were going through a bad divorce. The divorce was very hard for me. It hurt. It hurt a lot. It's very hard to see your parents happy all of your life and then one day watch their marriage just start falling apart. This really affected my life.

In school I was really distracted. I couldn't concentrate on anything. I sat in class and just stared at lot. When I looked at the teacher, I guess I just stared. I wasn't hearing anything she said. I think she even yelled at me to pay attention; however, I don't think I heard it. I'm not sure I even know if her lips were moving. I just sat in class and daydreamed. This teacher used to make me cry in class. I hated her.

I remember the people at school thought I was not capable of learning as well as the other kids. They wanted to give me an I.Q. test to measure my ability to learn. I knew myself. I knew I wasn't stupid. I knew that I was just having a rough time. So to prove to them that I really had the capability to learn, I took the damn I.Q. test. I scored a 128! But since my grades were so bad, they wanted to hold me back. This got me really down. It made me feel like a flunky.

Luckily they decided not to hold me back. I knew I was capable of learning. They decided my problems were emotional.

The school told me about a program called "B.D." It was a class for children with behavior disabilities. They told me that by being quiet, I was a "behavioral problem." Gee, I know of teachers who would give anything for a class full of kids who were quiet! The B.D. program, as the school described it, sounded very good. That was the biggest lie I ever heard! It was supposed to be a smaller class with more teachers so I could get more help. When it finally came around to the first day of school, it was terrible. I had to be bused to school in a smaller bus. So when we stepped off the bus, there was always a crowd of students making fun of us. They called us "retards" and other names. This caused me to get into a lot of fights. I got to know the principal very fast. When I got into class, all of the kids were very different from me. It wasn't what I was used to. I was very quiet. These kids were very hyper. When we went outside for lunch, the other students in the normal classes would pick fights with me. I ended up fighting someone verbally or physically every day.

After a while in this classroom, I adjusted to my new surroundings. I turned from the quiet kid into a troublemaker just like the rest of the B.D. students. I really hated being in this class. I figured, maybe if I tried real hard, I could get paroled. They told me if I got good grades, they would let me move into normal classes. By the end of the first semester, I was almost moved out. I always felt that for some reason they didn't want me out of the program. My father complained to the school explaining the program was hurting me and that students in the class were hurting me. He explained students in the class were being labeled. The school denied it. My father could not understand it. At home I wasn't B.D. At home I was a decent kid. At home I was smart.

In high school I remained B.D. But when I was out of school, at home or on the job, I wasn't B.D. My boss liked my work. If I was B.D., how come I was not B.D. on the job?

I believe these B.D. classes are in need of a lot of improvement because ever since I was in these classes, instead of helping me all they did was hurt me. I never got any better. All I did was get worse. I think the worst thing to do with children who have behavioral problems is to put them all together.

Well, to make a long story short, I'm finally out of B.D. classes. In fact, today is my first day out. I'm no longer B.D.! You see, yesterday was Sunday. Yesterday I graduated from high school.

Learning to Learn for Myself
by Anthony J. Lis

"I had a problem and I had to understand that it was up to me to find the answers to fix it."

Anthony J. Lis spent his years at Weberville High School on the stage. He plans to study acting at Illinois State University. Offstage, Tony is home playing guitar or weight lifting and dreaming of hitting Broadway.

It seemed like an endless road. Now it looks like one I started only yesterday. In a few minutes I'll leave for commencement. This high school diploma will symbolically signify the end of my childhood. I can't but think of all the turns in this road I have encountered since the start of the journey. The hills and underpasses have helped me to learn lessons about life I can pass on to my children.

I never thought I was slow at learning, but when I started first grade I was diagnosed with having a learning disability. My teachers decided for the next few years that I should have extra daily reading classes. Since the beginning of my schooling I was put straight into this program. Thus I hadn't realized I had a learning disability. I spent those years doing special exercises to help me read better. I never felt weird being there and I was able to enhance my reading to some extent. This was only the beginning of a road that widened. In order to get a head start on second grade I was enrolled into a summer school reading course.

As I try on my cap and gown, for some reason I'm reminded of when my parents and teachers felt it would be best if I was put on the medication Ritalin. Ritalin is a drug that is used to slow down a person's body to help enhance better attention and concentration. I was treated with this from second through fifth grade.

In second grade I continued my reading class and usage of Ritalin. I was put in the remedial reading group, which was the first time I felt different for being with the remedial students. What made this tougher to deal with was that my teacher was an old lady who yelled and scared all of us. She made our group read the same story together six times, making us all feel stupid. She got angry easily and was impatient with us. By the end of second grade I could read and was getting better at it. To help get my reading up to the level it should have been, I had a tutor for the summer. We reviewed the year's lessons.

In the third grade, along with my daily reading classes and Ritalin, a few more additions to my weekly schedule were made. My spelling tests were not as good as they should have been so my father wrote a program on our computer that would help. Every week I would put my spelling words in the computer and play different games to help learn them. I also started to see a counselor once a week for observation. Instead of asking about myself, she had me play games and put puzzles together. I guess she observed me to see how I thought, the depth of my learning disability, and how I would best be taught. This year I was lucky to have the best teacher I have ever had. She was the nicest lady and it was fun to learn from her. When summer came around she became my tutor. That summer I spent three mornings a week reading and taking tests. She gave me a special activity calendar with daily assignments. For added incentive, after I finished a month of activities, I got to choose a toy. I was tutored the following summer with this same teacher.

In fourth grade I started a different reading class where I learned how to read and do other activities. By this time I was starting to get fed up with all the extra classes; all I wanted was to be with the regular students. I started feeling stupid and did not want to be in the extra class.

Fifth grade came and I was still in extra reading classes. I was growing more impatient. After all that I had gone through, I think getting upset with all the extra work was a reasonable response. I did what I was asked, I worked hard, and made improvements, but I had been doing it for so long! I was growing tired.

After talking with my parents about not taking the extra classes and stopping the Ritalin, they decided to see how I would do in sixth grade without either. I managed to do okay. My only trouble spot was my spelling again. I was told that if I scored poorly on one more test, I was going to be put in the fifth grade spelling book again. When I told my parents that I was doing badly and that I had to score better or else, I got scared and worried I would not graduate to the seventh grade. From there on I started to bear down and really studied my spelling. This was the first time I had worked on my own. I started to bring my spelling book to family outings. I was writing the words out hundreds of times and I never scored less than a B on any test thereafter. That was when I learned how to learn.

As all this was going on, due to my usage of Ritalin, I slowly developed a weight problem. As I now look back, I realized the reason I learned to read so slowly was that I was not learning how to learn for myself. While I went to classes and counseling, took my medication, conducted my lessons, and did the summer programs, I still had not learned how to learn on my own.

I knew from there on that I could help myself, that I had to find it within me to go ahead and make the change. As I went to seventh grade I was placed in an average-level class. This is what I wanted. I was later placed in another reading class. I was angry. I was told my reading comprehension scores were too low, that I needed one semester to help raise my score. Again I was stuck in a remedial class. I again talked with my parents, asking why, why was I in all this again. After all I had been through, why did I still have this problem? I could not understand. I spent a lot of time thinking. What would make this time any different from all the others? Then it all made sense. All the previous times I had tried to improve my reading, it was because I needed to and that was not going to work this time. I had to want to improve my reading for me. I had to understand it was up to me to decide why I had to get better. After I realized this, I knew what I had to do. The rest was easy because I was doing it for myself.

I watched myself start off slow and then pick up. When I did an exercise wrong, I wanted to know why and how I could find the correct answer. So I spent a lot of time just fixing problems and looking for ways not to make those mistakes again. At the end of the program I learned how to learn for myself by myself.

The idea that I gained from this was that I had a problem and I had to understand that it was up to me to find the answers to fix it. All the efforts of anyone except myself would not solve what needed to be done. Once I understood what needed to be done my journey had begun and was moving along. Nothing is stronger than understanding myself and what I want to accomplish. I used this same principle when I was trying to lose weight. I had tried for years to lose weight but could not. I did not want it badly enough and did not understand what I had to put into doing it. Then one night I was thinking about it. It was up to me and only me, and the only way would be when I understood that it was only a matter of time. I came out of that knowing I had the ability to do anything I set my heart to. If I really want something, there is nothing that will get in my way.

When high school came around I was able to use what I had learned in many areas throughout school. I became involved in theater and choir. It was difficult for me to achieve what I wanted in choir. I was not born with a voice that could just be put in a choir. It was a voice that needed to be worked into something. When I started singing I could not hear the notes. I started getting discouraged. Then I decided if I wanted to improve my singing, just like my reading, I had to want to do it and then work at it. I started taking music home and worked at my voice and the songs we were learning. After a while I started to come around and made some definite improvement. This again proved to me that I was capable of doing anything to which I set my mind.

During high school I was put into average-level classes. I never again needed to take a remedial course.

The problems people think they face are not ones they cannot fix. What I did took a while and a lot of tries, but I did it. When I made up my mind that I had a problem and that I had no other choice but to fix it, then I did and it was easy. The work meant more to me. It was easier. When I wanted to get better I did. I used this to solve my weight problem, my choir singing, and many other problems in life.

I had done well. I went from a learning disability in elementary and junior high to high school without one. In high school I did remarkably well. I found myself in average-level classes, contrary to the odds. I performed well in the theater. I did reports in class. I enjoyed political debates in class. I developed a hypothesis and tested it using a survey in my social science class. I did reports on all types of topics. I started my own political movement to make college tuition tax-deductible. For this I collected more than 2,000 signatures on letters. I have remarkable memories. These last 12 years were a struggle, but they were the greatest. Oh my. It's time to leave for commencement. You'll have to excuse me. It's time to say goodbye to childhood.

The Effects of Long-Term Injury
by Erin Lindstrom

"A long-term injury such as mine can have devastating effects. It can result in loneliness, depression, low self-esteem, and jealousy."

Erin Lindstrom is a senior at Weberville High School, where she is captain of the speech team, a member of Orchesis (dance), and a member of National Honor Society. Erin plans to attend Indiana University and major in English.

Physical injury of any kind can present interruptions in one's normal lifestyle. However, when the injury, however temporary, takes months or even years to diagnose and treat, one's entire life is altered. When such a long-term ordeal occurs in an active high school setting, it results in months of physical, social, and emotional turmoil for the afflicted student. To understand these hardships and how they affect an injured student's behavior and academic performance, the situation faced by the student must be closely examined.

From the end of my junior year through the first half of my senior year, I suffered from severe pain in the lower left side of my back. During this time, I saw various doctors, physical therapists, and chiropractors in an attempt to find the cause of my mysterious pain. Later in senior year, I was hospitalized at Children's Memorial Hospital and underwent a bone scan that appeared to show the presence of fractures in the lumbar spine. I spent almost a year living in a rigid plastic back brace, best described as a removable body cast, that kept me highly immobile. I removed the brace only to sleep or shower. I was forced to quit dancing in Orchesis and could no longer participate in gym class and many other ordinary teenage activities. Throughout this extremely stressful ordeal, I was expected to maintain my high academic performance, heavy involvement in activities, busy social life, and general good nature.

Weberville High is fast-paced. Everywhere, students are busy with activities that require physical mobility. Injured students such as me have had to slow down everything and adjust to being dependent on others for simple things. For instance, if I dropped my pencil as I walked down the hall, I could not bend down to pick it up because of the restrictiveness of my back brace. I had to continually ask others for help. Students with long-term injuries must learn how to be spectators in a place where everyone and everything bustles with activity.

However, many students with temporary yet long-term disabilities seem to go unnoticed, as I was. Everyone expected me to keep my usual fast pace even though I physically could not handle it. Often I needed more time at my locker to get my books together or to simply walk to class.

The burden of wearing a brace affected my ability to concentrate, as I had to sit in small classrooms at desks for 8 hours each day, enduring terrible discomfort caused by the brace. The only relief I had was walking through the halls during the allotted 5-minute passing periods. Even then, I felt restricted by the hundreds of students swarming around me. In fact, everywhere I went in school I felt claustrophobic with so many people milling about, unable to escape the confinement of the school as well as my brace. I soon learned that school was simply not a place where I could be comfortable. I also knew that I could not avoid it. This is the case of many students who suffer from long-term injuries, unable to escape from the normal routine of life at school, and unable to adjust to it.

The year I spent in my brace typified the uncomfortableness felt by any student suffering from a long-term injury. Such students face limitations they are not used to—and experience emotions foreign to them. "Normalcy" is replaced by the word "adjustment." Rather than enjoy high school life, they must learn to endure.

The physical discomfort caused by the brace I wore was reflected in my performance at school. In the classroom, I was jittery and claustrophobic in the tight confinement of my brace. Unbeknownst to my teachers, I was unable to concentrate on lectures and tests as I suffered silently in my seat. It was uncomfortable for me to ask if I could stand up or walk around to relieve my claustrophobia—I did not believe that anyone could understand how I felt. In contrast to this immobility, during gym class I would tirelessly walk the shelf alone while my class-mates played badminton or volleyball. In this situation I would become claustrophobic from too much movement, causing me to be hot and in-creasing the uncomfortableness of the brace. The only option to this misery was to sit through study hall, which I considered to be the more unbearable of the two choices. Once I arrived home, I was so anxious to get out of my brace that I would take it off and go to bed early without even glancing at my homework. I adopted poor study habits for the sake of comfort.

Emotional instability also contributed to my worsening academic habits. Much of my time was spent in doctors' or physical therapists' offices, attempting to ease my pain. I worried about the seriousness of my condition, whether or not it would heal, and how long it would take. My motivation to do well in school seemed to have disappeared, as school had become my last priority. The most striking emotional blow came when I was forced to quit dancing in Orchesis, one of my fa-vorite involvements at school. This was the most difficult loss for me; I had to be content watching my friends perform the dances I had helped choreograph. I was extremely depressed throughout most of this, yet academically I was given no leeway because no one was aware of my emotional state.

Because of the seriousness of my injury and the restrictiveness of my brace, I was not allowed to participate in many normal social activities. My friends wanted to ride roller coasters at Great America and go bowling or dancing, and I could not do any of these things. Not want-ing to be a burden to my friends by keeping them from doing what they wanted, I often felt that I was limiting them and preventing them from having fun. Activities like watching movies and reading books became boring for me—it seemed as if there was simply no way for me to just relax and have fun. My friends supported me, but they could not know the envy I felt as I watched them, comfortable and pain-free in their own bodies. They possessed the one thing I wanted: freedom to live a normal life.

Students who are afflicted by an injury or limiting condition face the same problems I did. They give up normal lifestyles in order to get well. They attend school and social functions like other students, but they do not have the ability, physically or emotionally, to have fun. Their lives are dominated by and centered around one thing—their particular ail-ment.

A long-term injury such as mine can have devastating effects. It can result in loneliness, depression, low self-esteem, and jealousy. An af-flicted student may feel out of touch with the student body in general, his or her friends, and teachers. When an injury takes so much time to heal, one feels it is too late to ever resume normal activity. One year may seem short in comparison to one's whole life, but it is one quarter of a teenager's high school experience. Amidst trying to prepare for college, maintain good grades, and enjoy life as a teenager, the student has to deal with immense physical and emotional stresses, probably without the understanding of persons in similar situations. Thus, a student is likely to feel locked in by his or her injury, trapped in a situation without escape.

The injury is only a symbol of the problems faced by the student. He or she needs an environment compatible with the injury—a more relaxed place to learn where the student knows that although academics is important, his or her well-being is more important. Although students must be able to deal with crises such as injuries, they also need to know that there will be others there to help him or her along if such a situation should arise. Teenage life is full of unexpected occurrences, and an environment conducive to the healing of these occurrences is crucial to the general good health of the individual.

3

The Student Reality: Activities and Sports

Students often allocate much of their school day to school-sponsored activities. The club or athletic team to which a high school student belongs reveals much about the student. Although the majority of classes are scholastic requirements, and part-time jobs are often chosen by geography rather than personal interest, a student is free to join any extracurricular activity of his or her choice. As a result, students generally show more loyalty and commitment to their particular groups or teams than to their other responsibilities.

In the section on activities, Jackowski and Cutler relate the pride and accomplishment they feel from their association with student groups. They explain that organizations such as cheerleading and PEER (a student peer counseling program) build self-confidence, responsibility, interpersonal communication skills, and the ability to work well in groups. Randazzo relates a similar experience as a volunteer in a local nursing home. As the students detail, active involvement in activities leads students to easier acceptance and higher social status from their peers. Though the activities do take a considerable amount of time out of their schedules, the profits of such dedication are well worth the effort. Others are less certain.

Robins is not as confident that dedication to activities is worth the effort. After 4 years as an editor of his school newspaper, he is forced by an administrative decision to publish an article against his wishes. Disillusioned by this loss of control, Robins questions the weight of his accomplishments and concludes that the school paper can never be any more than a school's "brag sheet."

Minardo and Ulander share similar concerns about the school's drug-free and VOLUNTEER programs, respectively. For Minardo, the drug-free program greatly divides students. Athletes are encouraged to "tattle" on fellow students who may be using alcohol or other drugs and to ostracize them from social situations. In turn, those who are ostracized often have nowhere else to turn but to peers more heavily involved in alcohol and other drugs. Similarly, Ulander points out the hypocrisies of VOLUNTEER, a mandatory "volunteer" program begun by the school. Instead of teaching students the benefits of volunteering (as Randazzo eloquently illustrates), the school presented a nondemocratic policy that did just the opposite. To avoid oppression, many students simply refused to volunteer.

Robins, Minardo, and Ulander insightfully examine the negative effects of policy making without the student perspective. Decisions like these help only the school's cosmetic appearance and leave quality results behind. As a result, administrators and club sponsors should recognize the necessity that student-run organizations remain student-run. For example, the rash administrative decision against Robins implies that the student newspaper can remain student-run as long as it satisfies the needs of the administration. By imposing this rule, the school discourages creative input in an organization that could have thrived on its creative potential. Furthermore, it might discourage students from joining the paper or pursuing a career in journalism. Students are pulled to activities or sports that offer the greater status. For example, if football offers greater status, students with a talent for soccer might instead go out for football. Similarly, students talented in academics *and* sports rarely choose an activity such as newspaper or yearbook instead of sports. Generally, the most difficult newspaper or yearbook position to fill is that of a sports editor.

Similarly, the drug-free program and the VOLUNTEER program promote the exact opposite of that for which they were designed. Although their intentions might have been in the right place, the programs were designed in an institutional vacuum. Had students been consulted on how to approach the school's drug problem, there is no doubt that many students would have felt less anxiety and discomfort than they did. After all, these policies are important and can forever change the course of young lives. Student realities and emotions must always be seriously considered.

In the section on sports, Sinibaldo, Giutini, True, and Mann passionately explain the important lessons learned about teamwork and loyalty on the football and wrestling teams. These athletes stress that the skills developed create not only winning teams, but also winning individuals. The sports teams promote dedication, self-discipline, and healthy, drug-free lifestyles.

Kopeny and Sevak, on the other hand, intelligently criticize high school athletics for the promotion of what Noam Chomsky has called "jingoist fanaticism" (Rai, 1995, p. 46). This refers to the power of sports to marginalize the public by diverting its attention away from issues of greater importance. In our culture, the enthusiasm and analysis devoted to athletic competition is second to none. Naturally, high school is a place where this behavior is encouraged. In fact, Sinibaldo *proudly* relates a story in which he stayed in a football game after his knee twice popped out of its socket. Unfortunately, schools may actively support this behavior. Throughout the year, schoolwide assemblies (during regular school hours) celebrate the accomplishments of various athletic teams. Clubs or activities are not likely to receive similar treatment, scale of celebration, or support. Classes are shortened to fit pep rallies into the school day. Student attendance is mandatory and the library and computer centers are off limits. Students are corralled into the sports arena. Students who refuse, when prompted to stand, yell, and holler, are sanctioned by teachers assigned to monitor and positioned evenly throughout the stands by administrators.

Teachers in the school about which these students have written have contracted to receive salaries in 1998 as high as $86,500, besides generous fringe benefits. Coaches can receive, in addition, more than $7,000 per sport season. Assistant coaches can receive more than $5,400. There are three sport seasons during the academic school year. Many teachers of academic subjects coach and allocate time to coaching and their sport disproportionate to the hours their combination of teaching and coaching salaries would command. For teachers and also students, there are only 24 hours in a day. Imagine if teachers of academic subjects who coached instead spent a proportionate amount of time on their academic preparations.

Teachers are not likely to rock the boat. Given the salaries described above, if given a choice, teachers are more likely to follow an unwritten code of silence and obedience to the school administration than fight for what they believe would achieve academic excellence and critical thinking.

Sevak cites sister-school rivalries as a potentially dangerous example of this dedication to sports. He explains that although some good-natured rivalry can be great fun, the extremes to which it is carried are too much. He describes the burning of football fields and the physical assault on a principal as instances in which the importance of a game outweighed all moral and rational thought. Similarly, Kopeny attacks the teams themselves for the promotion of such behavior. According to him, high school athletes must conform their entire lives, including time, clothes, and friends, to the success of the team. The sport itself ceases to be fun and the team becomes more a way of life than an extra-curricular activity. The combination of rigorous preparation, undivided attention, single-focus devotion, and dedication demanded by coaches and backed with sanctions take sport out of sports and leave it devoid of any sense of recreation. Sports, especially senior year, become more like work and chores. Students who are not part of an athletic team may be viewed as less important. As Kopeny cites, the perpetuation of homophobia is a tool by which team members and others intimidate "outsiders."

With the apparent undivided support of the school, the message is clear. Students should either join or enthusiastically support athletic teams, and they must win. Despite the quality lessons that athletics can teach (as explained by True, Mann, et al.), they can also lead to a dangerous fanaticism that moves the emphasis of school away from the classroom and onto the playing field. Of course, a long list of state champions contributes to the cosmetic wealth of the school.

Think of the potential list of accomplishments from a school that instead promoted a "fanaticism" for academics.

Section 1: Activities

Activities: Preparation for Life
by Meghan M. Jackowski

"The life of a suburban teenager can tend to be insulated from the realities of the world. Involvement in extracurricular activities can begin to open a student's mind to the diverse conditions that exist outside the classroom."

Meghan M. Jackowski is a senior, a member of the National Honor Society and PEER (a peer counseling program), secretary of the Service Club, and involved with many of the school's bands. Meghan plans to attend the University of Illinois in the fall.

As incoming freshmen, my classmates and I were encouraged to "get involved." Some ignored this suggestion, whereas others discovered the essence of "Weberville Pride." Those who made the commitment to contribute to the school have gained a wealth of experience. At the same time, they have generally earned better grades.

Throughout my high school career I have been successful academically; however, no textbook lesson can rival the wisdom acquired through the involvement in extracurricular activities. I realize that analyzing four obscure lines from Dante for 50 minutes and knowing how to take the derivative of 2x are designed to make one's thinking process more acute. However, activities outside of the classroom give students practical experience as well as opportunities to expand their minds. Some of these lessons will be extremely valuable to me in the future. Success in a career demands much more than simply mechanically reciting memorized information. Educators who understand this and allow their students to experience more practical applications are better preparing these teenagers for the world outside of school.

The two most rewarding organizations that I have been a member of are PEER and Service Club. PEER is a peer counseling group of which I am a leader. Each week I meet with 10 to 12 teenagers who, like myself, are struggling with the many difficulties of being old enough to have many freedoms, yet young enough not to always know how to handle them. We share everything from crude jokes and gossip to discussions about drunk driving and pregnancy. In addition, the Service Club sponsors many activities each year. During the holiday season, we provide a Christmas party, Santa and all, for a low-income day care center. The club also hosts a pizza party for the physically handicapped attending our school. Furthermore, as new students enter Weberville High School, we give them a tour of the building and try to make them feel welcomed. Both Service Club and PEER allow teenagers to interact with and help people who are in need of support.

Although I have always been active in school functions, up until my junior year I was mainly focused on conscientiously memorizing every minute detail that I could possibly be asked to regurgitate on a machine-graded test. Social encounters always came second to academics. However, in my search for the "perfect college" I began to notice a pattern. Grades and test scores were important, of course, but a great emphasis was placed on extracurricular activities. Northwestern wanted to know how I would cope with a serious challenge. The University of Michigan was interested in which activities I considered to have had the greatest impact on my life. As I attempted to answer these questions, I realized just how much these activities had enhanced my high school experience.

Similarly, some administrators have become so engrossed with producing a certain level of academic excellence that they are unable to maintain an equitable balance between activities and schoolwork. For example, many conflicts arise upon an intrusion into class time. PEER groups only infringe on any particular class approximately one period a semester. This time can be made up by consulting with the teacher and other students about the day's notes and work. However, missing PEER is something that cannot be made up simply by receiving a quick recounting of the meeting. The leader, as well as every member, benefits from what each individual has to offer.

A 10-week PEER session begins with a circle composed of isolated links. Over time, these distinctive individuals blend into a united chain of confidants. A few weeks into our session, most members start feeling comfortable with the group, and many discussions arise. Teenage pregnancy, child abuse, and a suicide attempt were definitely the highlights of my last group. Volatile situations such as these require immediate attention and overshadow the value of one missed math assignment. Although I was overwhelmed at first, I began to gain a feeling of gratitude as I realized that the students had enough trust in me to share their innermost convictions. The confidences shared produce feelings of achievement and appreciation much greater than any good grade could accomplish.

Service Club meetings are held after school, thus reducing the time that a student can allow for homework. However, helping to feed a disabled child can prove much more rewarding than spending an extra half-hour studying for a history test. When I joined the club, I was uncomfortable dealing with the physically challenged. Now, I have learned to appreciate their determination and I realize that they have a lot to offer. Although I still strive to maintain a high grade-point average, I now ensure that I maintain a realistic balance between studying and interacting with others.

As a young child, I viewed the world from a very sheltered perspective. However, the world has much more diversity than any black-and-white textbook would like us to believe. In PEER groups, students can gain firsthand knowledge of the destruction that drugs and alcohol can create and the difficulties that accompany a teenage pregnancy, and they understand that no problem is so overwhelming that it lacks a solution. The ability to share problems and realize that others understand and have similar dilemmas enhances each student's personal life and thus contributes to their academic success. Similarly, Service Club allows students the extraordinary experience of getting to really know people who are different physically or socially. Lessons like those can be learned to some extent in a classroom, but have much more meaning when experienced in an informal setting with a chance to freely interact.

Leading a PEER group, I have learned that some problems are out of my control. It can be frustrating to realize that I do not have a ready solution for each problem; however, it is very rewarding to discover that one can make a significant difference in the life of a peer. Actively participating in peer counseling and Service Club has not only opened my eyes to many new aspects of life but also has provided me with a

clearer direction for my professional goals. It can be complicated dealing with the misfortunes of others; however, the rewards of helping
people overpower the difficulties.

The life of a suburban teenager can tend to be insulated from the realities of the world. Involvement in extracurricular activities can begin
to open a student's mind to the diverse conditions that exist outside the
classroom. Throughout my high school career I have acquired many
interpersonal skills that have allowed me to better understand myself,
as well as those around me. I hope that these talents will help me to
succeed as I leave Weberville High School, academically as well as socially and professionally.

Cheerleaders, Pom Pons, Flags:
Expectations of a Student Leader
by Barbara Cutler

*"My first 2 years were exciting and enjoyable; I liked performing
and learned how to budget my time. I expected the following 2 years
to be even better, but I have been too pressured to fully appreciate
my accomplishments."*

*Barbara Cutler is a senior at Weberville High School, where she is in acceler-
ated classes and captain of the varsity flag squad. She has also been active in vocal groups.*

Our high school has a unique organization of all the cheerleaders,
pom pons, and flag team members. This organization has been functioning for about 25 years with the help of both adult leaders (sponsors
or coaches) and student leaders (captains and other officers). Freshman year I was on the JV drill team, which performs both poms and
flags. My sophomore, junior, and senior years were spent on the varsity flag squad. I was a varsity advisor to JV drill my junior year, and as
a senior now, I am captain of the varsity flag squad. My experiences
have taught me much about the expectations of a leader.

Members of cheer groups are generally of low to average in academic ability and are frequently stereotyped as airheads. They are easily spotted on Fridays when dressed in uniforms and are derogatorily
referred to as "cheerleaders" or "rah-heads." Tryouts for these selective
groups are held in May, and the squads practice twice a week in the
summer and at least three times a week during the school year. Extra
evening or Saturday morning practices may be scheduled depending
on availability of floor time in the gymnasium. In addition to performing at all the home football and basketball games, the squads attend
several all-day competitions and State, the final competition, held in

March. The 11-month activity is time-consuming and unpredictable, so employment and participation in other extracurricular activities are strongly discouraged.

My first 2 years on cheer groups were spent observing the abilities of my many leaders. My friends and I often shared opinions of the different methods of leadership and complained about their faults. After evaluating our reactions to their various techniques, I formulated an opinion about the characteristics of a successful leader. I decided what I wanted and needed from my leaders, and that knowledge helped me earn my positions the following years.

The JV drill team is the largest squad on cheer groups and, as I learned my first day as varsity advisor, the most difficult to control. Many of the 24 immature, talkative freshmen only wanted to perform and try out for varsity poms. It is difficult to keep a squad with such diverse goals and skill levels focused on learning a basic flag routine. Remembering my year on JV drill with leaders who attempted to gain control by screaming insults and threats of demerits, I decided to try other, more positive, methods. I discovered the key to success was learning to balance the use of power with encouragement, praise, and constructive criticism. I also learned how to keep everyone involved and interested by choreographing what I hoped would be creative and exciting routines with challenging but appropriate skills. My methods did work much better than the insults, and instead of creating enemies, I made many friends, earning their respect, trust, and attention. I believe my leadership was successful because the squad received a first place at their last competition and much praise for their abilities from the judges.

The captain of a varsity squad should work with the squad to develop individual and group goals to accomplish during the year. She should then meet with the sponsor to schedule and plan so practice time is efficiently used. It is the responsibility of the captain to stay on task and accomplish as much as possible. I think the role of captain is more difficult than that of varsity advisor (a student), because not only does the captain choreograph and teach, but she also performs. The captain must be cautious with power because when the show begins, all are equal.

The leader of any group is a role model for team members and should be "perfect" in behavior and at skills required of the team. On flags, the captain is displayed as perfect and carefully watched for all fine points in every technique. Other squad members judge themselves in comparison to the captain and are disappointed and confused when their leader makes a mistake. The leader should be able to demonstrate and explain patiently all skills in whatever detail is required. After teaching the routine at a reasonable speed, the captain should critique and correct individuals and the group. The leader should ask for and listen to the suggestions and ideas of squad members. As captain, I cannot ask my squad to do anything that I am not able or willing to do.

The leaders, adult and student, must give both encouragement and constructive criticism in order for the squad to grow and succeed. Most leaders in cheer groups are quite capable of giving criticism, but it isn't always constructive. Occasionally I am forced to miss a practice, and I always dread returning because I usually hear that practice went poorly. My vice captain and sponsor realize there are major problems with the routine, but they are rarely able to help the squad improve. From members' complaints, I learn that my substitutes just wail and scream that "It looks like shit!" and "I can't believe that competition's in only 1 week!" The next day, after hearing from my vice captain and sponsor that they are ashamed to be connected with such a lousy squad, I try to piece back together my squad's confidence. I divide the routine into single tasks and help the squad concentrate on improving one technique or skill at a time. I constantly encourage and praise them for their accomplishments. Everyone likes to be congratulated for a job well done; praise is a reward for hard work and motivation to continue. I try to keep practice as fun and nonstressful as possible because everyone will be in a good mood and, therefore, more will be accomplished.

Cheer groups function only with proper communication between adult and student leaders and between leaders and squad members. Often the sponsor will have a short announcement at the start of practice to inform the team of the day's schedule. Squad talks are another important method of communication. The captain generally leads these meetings, so she must have good speaking and listening abilities. If a team member has a problem, she can approach a captain or sponsor in private or call a squad meeting. The captain must help in the problem-solving process, if possible, and suggest compromises. I frequently hear the complaints of squad members about the sponsor, the vice captain, or other squad members. I shouldn't take sides in any of these conflicts; I must remain neutral and help end the conflict. Squad talks are also used for discussing problems I'm having with the team's cooperation or concentration. Dealing with attention problems in this manner has been very successful for me. One very important reminder about speaking to a group of peers is, "Think before you speak." I have learned that a leader must know the team members well and what underlying meanings they might draw from the captain's comments. Some people are very sensitive and could be hurt if pointed out as an example. The captain is responsible for protecting the team's feelings.

Communication between the sponsor, the captain, and the vice captain this year, in my opinion, has been a problem. The sponsor made major changes in procedures without consulting or even informing the student officers. Because the sponsor does have the final decision in any matter, she may have become slightly power hungry and jealous of my success with the squad. I think she became jealous when I talked to a former flag sponsor and competition judge about our routine for the year. I believe she said that the vice captain and I were the squad's two worst enemies. She might realize that we have difficulties with communication but she seems unable to understand our problems or explain her ideas and feelings.

The many responsibilities heaped upon a student leader are stressful and incredibly time-consuming. Last year as varsity advisor I attended many extra JV practices and spent many hours choreographing. This year as captain I have been spending much more extra time selecting music, choreographing, and just thinking about the stresses and problems of my squad. I sometimes have difficulties establishing priorities between flags, a mostly accelerated and advanced placement class schedule, work, and sleep. Even if I'm having problems, personal or squad-related, I must always be confident and positive.

The cheer groups system of cheerleaders, pom pons, and flag team members provides a social atmosphere for meeting new friends and learning responsibility. My first 2 years were exciting and enjoyable; I liked performing and learned how to budget my time. I expected the following 2 years to be even better, but I have been too pressured to fully appreciate my accomplishments. The prestige and glory of a student leader attract many to the position, but only those with fresh new ideas and energy, who are truly prepared for the total time commitment, pressures, and responsibilities, will become successful leaders.

Freedom of the Press
by Mike Robins

"Quickly, I became disillusioned with the paper and my hours and hours of work each week no longer seemed worth it. A school newspaper without student control just appeared to be a waste of time."

Mike Robins graduated from Weberville High School in 1990. He served as editor-in-chief of the school newspaper during his senior year and as class president in his sophomore, junior, and senior years. Mike was chosen by his peers to give the commencement address at graduation. Mike earned a B.A. in cinema and photography from Southern Illinois University. He now works as a freelance writer and independent filmmaker.

When I entered Weberville High School as a freshman, I created two goals for myself to achieve before graduation: one, to become senior class president and deliver a speech at commencement, and two, to become editor-in-chief of the school newspaper. Although I achieved the first fairly easily (through, I think, a combination of general kindness toward others, several hundred silly campaign posters, and the fact that very few people ran against me), the second goal was much more difficult (it took a tremendous amount of dedication and work). Unfortunately, although I did become editor-in-chief my senior year, the fruits of my labor were not all that I had hoped for.

Writing for the school newspaper was something that I had thought about doing since I was a little kid. In fact, I think it had a good deal to do with the way "the reporter" has been romanticized out of proportion in movies and television. For example, I remembered seeing Peter Brady on *The Brady Bunch* making waves at his school by publishing a really hot scoop and changing the opinions of his fellow students. Although I certainly knew that television exaggerated everything, I longed for some of that excitement. In addition, I had always enjoyed writing and thought that the school newspaper would be a good creative outlet. Also, being strongly opinionated about many social and political issues, I thought I could use the school newspaper as a forum for discussing items important to the students.

Essentially, the school newspaper functioned quite similarly to any one of our school's athletic teams. Freshman joined on as reporters and learned the rules of newspaper grammar, style, and technique from the older students. Those who displayed great determination and enthusiasm usually worked their way up to an editor position (news, features, sports, editor-in-chief) by their junior or senior year. In addition, two faculty advisors made sure that deadlines were met and offered assistance to staff members. They also allowed the student editors great freedom in their decision making. However, this freedom quickly became superseded by powers outside of the newspaper office.

From the beginning, I noticed that students were not terribly enthusiastic about the school newspaper, and understandably so. Issues appeared once a month and stories focused primarily on applauding the successes of this team or that club, rather than presenting ideas that were of interest to the student body as a whole. In effect, the school newspaper was a newsletter or "brag sheet" for the school instead of a newspaper. As a result, I began to suggest story ideas such as film and record reviews or things for students to do on the weekends in order to gain student interest. In turn, I wrote two or more stories for each issue and during the second semester of my sophomore year, I was appointed features editor.

Immediately, my workload became much heavier and incredibly time-consuming. In addition to my regular class assignments and a 20-25 hours-per-week job at a local record store, I spent approximately 25-30 hours per week on the paper. Both my time and ability to relax diminished tremendously. Every other minute of the day seemed to be consumed with thoughts of late stories or future stories or deadlines. Fortunately, though, student interest appeared to be on the rise.

Slowly, people began to comment to me about a particular thing I had written and the newspaper began to receive more letters to the editor each month. Also, several teachers commended me and the staff on working so hard and noted that the paper was in better shape than it had been in several years. Although my workload was too much, I really did not mind it because the paper was functioning well and people felt it important enough to respond to. Unfortunately, I would soon find out that several members of the faculty and administration did not share my enthusiasm.

As my senior year began, I became the editor-in-chief and, at the same time, the United States Supreme Court decided freedom of the speech was for school administrations, not editors of student newspapers. Hence the administration had the right to censor the high school newspaper. As a result, I met with the school principal and he expressed that he felt no desire to interfere as long as things continued to go as well as they had been. In turn, along with the other editors and staff whom I had become very close to over the previous 3 years, I looked forward to a smooth-running year in which we might attempt to do some creative and thought-provoking stories. Often, we faced the choice of whether to do an entire story on the success of a particular team at a particular event (which might make a small group happy) or an important social issue such as the AIDS crisis (which might make a larger group happy). Generally, we chose the latter and on one particular occasion, our choice was met with great hostility.

One of the girls' cheerleading groups won a top award at a meet, and the school paper provided this information in the form of a small news brief on the front page. Very upset, the girls' coach entered the newspaper office the day the issue came out and requested that a full story be provided in the next issue. I tried to explain to her why the school paper had made the choice it did, but this did not satisfy her. Finally, I simply made it clear that there would be no story and that if she was unhappy with my decision, she should speak to the principal. She did.

Although the principal himself never mentioned this talk to me, I believe (though I'm not certain) that he did speak to my advisors. As a result, they urged the staff to write the story and did indeed (against my wishes) include it in the next issue. I felt betrayed by a school I had given so much time and heart to. I asked my advisors if all a coach needed to do was ask for a story to get one and they replied, with great hesitation, "It depends." Quickly, I became disillusioned with the paper, and my hours and hours of work each week no longer seemed worth it. A school newspaper without student control just appeared to be a waste of time. After working so hard to change the School newspaper from a "brag sheet" to a newspaper, my staff's work was completely undermined with one complaint.

I finished my year as editor only because I did not want to leave the advisors hanging, though I did so with much frustration. Throughout, I felt terrible pressure to simply spit out information rather than create. In addition, at the end of the year, our staff went to the annual NISPA (Northern Illinois Scholastic Press Association) conference and I received an award for an editorial dealing with student elections (incidentally, it was the only editorial all year directly related to our school). A professional journalist evaluated several of our issues and also commented that we were far too preoccupied with issues outside of school. Obviously, my staff and I were the only ones who felt the students themselves were intelligent and thoughtful enough to design their own newspaper. Robbed of our creative control, we realized that we were no more than pawns of a school administration very much in power.

I guess "freedom of the press" is a right beyond the reach of students and the editor is not "in-chief."

The Award-Winning Drug-Free Program
by Vinny Minardo

"Officials at our school try to brainwash everyone into thinking the program is a success. The community, the faculty, and parents all believe it is working. Take it from me. I'm on both sides of the fence. It is a failure!"

Vinny Minardo is a senior, captain of a varsity team, and member of the National Honor Society. He plans to attend Eastern Illinois University. He is well liked by his peers and much fun to be around on weekends.

I have been a part of Weberville High School's Drug-Free Program for nearly 4 years. This program is an attempt by the school to eradicate any utilization of drugs or alcohol by any members of athletic teams or school-sponsored clubs. Although many of its supporters feel the program is successful, repeatedly stating how beneficial it is for the school and community, from this student's point of view, they are only kidding themselves.

As a result of the Drug-Free Program, I have seen the spirit plummet and the sense of community damaged due to the increasing separation between those who are involved and those who are not. A sense of togetherness was once what this school had prided itself on. Now separation is the theme. No other person has felt the effects of this separation more than myself. There are countless numbers of reasons why this program is a failure and, to put it bluntly, wrong.

To begin with, I entered this school with feelings of both excitement and curiosity. What was high school really like? I had seen many different interpretations of teen life on television. Quickly after graduating from eighth grade, I went out for the football team. I attended all summer practices, and by the time school was about to begin, I was all geared up. A sense of pride and extreme content filled up inside of me. I was in high school, a football and baseball player, and basically on top of the world. It seemed as if high school was the way it was on television. Many times I heard about big parties with alcohol and drugs, loud music, and sex, but I never experienced it until late in my freshman year. Following the night of the first party I had attended, the taste of Weberville High School really hit me. It was not the little dream world that I had been living in for almost a whole year, but rather a complex maze in which for the rest of my high school life I would have to watch out for others snitching on me, coaches telling me with whom to and with whom not to hang around, and being told to tattle on my friends for drinking or use of drugs.

After a recent class graduated, the football coach devised a program that encouraged athletes to snitch on their friends and teammates for the use of drugs and alcohol. Soon after the football team established the movement, all the other sports followed. The previous rules of not drinking or doing drugs during season were destroyed and replaced with a drug-free contract. This document, given to each and every athlete, stated that he or she must remain drug-free for his or her entire time at Weberville High School. Also found in the text was that if any athlete found out about another athlete drinking or doing drugs, regardless if they saw it firsthand or not, he or she was required to snitch on them. I use the word "snitch" because it is childish, but "snitching, snitching, and snitching" is exactly what is going on at this school. One can only question what's next on the horizon. And today, this is what we have: a group of students who are athletes, do not drink, and tattle on their friends and a group who drinks, most of whom have already been kicked off a sport, have a twisted home life, and guidance that was needed earlier is no longer there for them.

For me, it creates a huge predicament. I have quit football but I am still a part of baseball. Baseball has always been my first love and I would never think of quitting it. However, many of my friends have been previously kicked off a team or have never been involved in a sport. The vast majority of these kids also drink or do drugs. As I have stated before, many of these children have had a lack of discipline in their lives. Broken families, parents who neglect them, and parents who themselves drink heavily and use drugs are part of what they have had to face in their lives. These kids are not bad. They just have fallen victim to their environment. On the other hand, I have had excellent guidance during my childhood. My parents have always looked out for my well-being and have kept me going forward in a positive direction. The problem is that coaches have said and even threatened that if I continue to hang around with some of my closest friends I will be asked not to come out for the team. This is ridiculous! I am the first to admit that I drink, but it is very seldom, and there is no harm ever done if I do. If I ever consume alcohol I always make sure that there is a designated driver. The fact that I drink every now and then does not make me an alcoholic. High school is a time for experimentation and growing up. All this program teaches is immaturity. For instance, if someone in the program catches me after I have consumed alcohol, they better have the balls to confront me about it rather than tattling on me to a coach. Tattling sounds like something that I would do in second grade! Besides, it is nobody's business but mine what I do with my life and how I live it. It does not concern them and I am not harming anyone. The coaches state over and over how much they care, but they really don't. They did not care too much about all the kids that they booted off of their teams! The bottom line is the students who need sports as a route to staying out of trouble get screwed and only become worse than they already are. In addition, it will be a cold day in hell before someone chooses my friends for me! Although I am not nearly as bad off as they are with drugs and alcohol, they are still some of the closest people I have ever had in my life and I will never leave them. Especially in a time of need such as right now. If nobody else cares about them, I do. As one can see, I am stuck between a rock and a hard place. Do not think I am naive to the situation that drinking is illegal for minors. But one must take into consideration that this is high school, and teenagers are curious and inquisitive about the world around them.

As Weberville High School gets more involved with the Drug-Free Program, the dilemma of drinking and use of drugs worsens. Officials at our school try to brainwash everyone into thinking the program is a success. The community, the faculty, and parents all believe it is working. Take it from me. I'm on both sides of the fence. It is a failure! As the number of kids who get kicked off sports for drinking increases, added is the number of kids who have nowhere else to turn but to alcohol and drugs. Think about it! This is not doing the school or the public any good. When I take a gander at the drug use among underclassmen compared to when my class was younger, I strongly believe the numbers, the potency of the drugs they are doing, and the number of times they do it have increased drastically. I wish that those who worked at our school saw what the hell is really going on here! This school is considered to be one of the best around, which it probably is for the time being. But it will only go downhill from here if we do not put an end to this program. It is only creating controversy within the school.

Because many of my friends drink or do drugs, they have been discriminated against by some teachers. Some of their ex-coaches have gone out of their way to make life as difficult as possible. For example, a football coach went out of his way to make the soccer team look like a bunch of losers by telling his team that they were a bunch of drunks just because one member of the team got arrested for the possession of alcohol. Now the soccer team has a nasty reputation at our school, when many of the most spirited and fun-loving students in the senior class belong to that team. In addition, a number of my friends who chose to participate in a multicultural assembly sponsored by the Cultural Awareness Club were stabbed in the back by many coaches and teachers. The teachers told the man who was organizing it not to involve them in the skit. Luckily the gentleman who happened to be running the show was one of the few teachers who gives students like this a chance to be involved and make something of themselves. All of this discrimination builds hatred against the school, hatred for the athletes and those involved with school, and dislike of many teachers. The school is destroying one's sense of belonging, encouraging separation resulting in alienation, and increasingly damaging the school spirit in the very same students in which it had intended to strengthen school spirit!

Weberville High School, like thousands of other schools in our society, is changing hour by hour, day by day, and year by year. In order to improve our situation, it is time for school officials to start listening to students about what is really going on and take actions that are much more feasible and sensible. I am a "people" person, I love to be with people and I always will. The Drug-Free Program discourages growth as a person. It discourages the acceptance of others who may be different. It encourages intolerance of friends who may be a little different. It discourages open-mindedness. I know that if there were no rules it would be havoc, but what is going on at this school is taking it way past the limit. When kids are told to try to get teammates and friends in trouble behind their backs, it destroys the almost-forgotten institution of friendship.

It is also unjust and un-American to require an athlete or anyone else to contract away his [or her] right to due process in order to play ball. Athletes "tattled on" do not get a chance to confront their accusers. They do not get a chance to defend themselves. The once-great school I attended has become a symbol of paranoia, frustration, and heartbreak. Deep down inside I know that many students who drink and do drugs are good, but the coaches never took the time to get to know them. It is sad to see people who have been close to me my whole life throw their lives away with nowhere else to turn. Sports would have been a way out, but there is no understanding and compassion. All the school cares about is its reputation and awards, not its content, not what really made the school so prominent. And that is everybody, the entire student body, together as one.

The Value of Volunteering Voluntarily
by Jeremy Ulander

"The VOLUNTEER program is one of the most anal-retentive programs I've ever encountered. I began before the program started. If I did not enjoy volunteering, I would have preferred to fail. The program should be designed for the students and not simply for the school and the number of awards it can compile. Overall, I would consider this program a complete and utter failure."

Jeremy Ulander is a senior at Weberville High School. During the school year he works 30 hours a week in order to save for college. He has volunteered in the emergency room of a major local hospital every free minute since the start of summer prior to senior year. This heavy schedule allowed no time for school-sponsored activities essential for acceptance by the National Honor Society. Jeremy enjoys volleyball, tennis, and golf. In the fall, Jeremy plans to attend Purdue University and study biology in a pre-med structure. His goal is to be an emergency room medical physician.

I have been volunteering since June of the end of my junior year in the emergency room of a major local hospital. The benefits of volunteering are boundless if and only if they are done for the right reasons. Nothing can be attained from this experience unless you are motivated by the desire to better yourself and most obviously to help others. As a volunteer, you get more out of volunteering than the agency that benefited from your services. There are sacrifices that must be made but they are all well rewarded. Experience can be invaluable. Through commitment you learn responsibility. This in itself is a lesson in life that cannot be taught in a classroom.

The hours I spent volunteering have had a most significant impact on me both mentally and emotionally. Through personal experiences, both positive and negative, I have become emotionally attached to the idea of helping others. It was a lesson in compassion and sympathy and, moreover, a truly sobering experience. When I first began the program, I thought I could prepare myself for anything. I had tremendous self-confidence. I thought I could not be caught off-guard in a critical situation. Although I did not perform life-threatening duties, I played an important role in what occurred around me. The first thing I learned was no matter how far you think you have gone, you can never be able to prepare yourself for the unexpected. I personally gained more from the program than I ever thought possible.

Since I started volunteering, I've been working anywhere from 4 to 8 hours every Monday, with a few exceptions. This is an obligation that I thoroughly enjoy. Boredom is never a problem. There is always something that can be done. You never get stuck in the same old routine. You learn something new every week. Whether information is from a doctor, a nurse, or an ER technician, information is graciously accepted. I have nothing but respect and admiration for all those I've come to know.

In today's society, leisure time for many is a rare commodity. How a person decides to devote that time helps shape their life. For a student, this is ever so true. Besides the rigors of the average school day, he or she has to find time to complete all assignments. This in itself is not very demanding even for an academically gifted student. If you add a part-time job or an after-school sport or activity, which requires a substantial commitment, you are left with no time to waste. To add volunteering to this already crowded schedule may be difficult for students who have already stretched themselves too thin in other areas. For this reason volunteers must truly enjoy what they are doing to make it all seem worthwhile. For some people it is painstakingly hard to grasp the concept of volunteering, which requires people to go out of their way to work for nothing. Others consider volunteering a responsibility owed to the community.

The definition of volunteer is one who enters into any service or undertaking of his [or her] own free will. Unfortunately, this concept is completely contradictory to the VOLUNTEER program established at my high school to get seniors involved in the community. The VOLUNTEER program is one of the most anal-retentive programs I've ever encountered. I began my volunteer work before the program started. If I did not enjoy volunteering, I would have preferred to fail. The program should be designed for the students and not simply for the school and the number of awards it can compile. Overall, I would consider this program a complete and utter failure. Many of those who disagree with this program do so because the idea of "forced volunteering" is a contradiction in terms. The concept is completely self-defeating: Those who object cannot possibly gain from the experience. This seems to be the opinion of many of the people involved in the program. For this reason, in my opinion, any attempt to impose strict regulation is, in the long run, completely futile.

Although the VOLUNTEER program has many faults, with luck they eventually will be ironed out. I see volunteering as a very beneficial learning tool for those who are actively involved and enjoying what they are doing.

Through volunteering one is able to explore possible career choices with firsthand experience. This was an incredible benefit for me. I had the unique opportunity of seeing the impact those whom I worked alongside had on the patients. The opportunity to save a life seems more of a privilege than an actual job. While you are there, you try to do whatever you can to help the rest of the staff. You must stay composed at all times, for it is the only way in which you can help others in critical moments. It can be emotional at times. Dealing with death on a regular basis makes you consider your own mortality. After enough exposure to death, you become accustomed to it and begin to expect it. After a length of time it no longer affects you. I've learned some valuable lessons while volunteering and I have been exposed to things most other high school seniors have not been exposed to. Volunteering is a rewarding experience and something I deeply enjoy. I look forward to every week.

Others, unfortunately, do not like the idea of volunteering as strongly as I do. They see it as more of an inconvenience. In the simple act of volunteering some of your time, you learn a lesson in life. The skills learned through volunteering can never be taught in the classroom.

The Benefits of Volunteering at a Nursing Home
by Julie A. Randazzo

"Volunteering made me realize that I want to work with people for the rest of my life. I have learned that my career has to be with people in career areas such as education or social services because I love working with people so much. I feel that I am making a difference in someone's life and I want to give something back to the people that have made a difference in my life."

Julie Randazzo is a senior at Weberville High School, where she is a member of Orchesis (dance) and choir, and performs in school productions. Julie volunteers in a nursing home. She plans to attend Illinois Wesleyan University and major in education or biology.

Volunteering is a very rewarding and beneficial experience for the volunteer and for those helped. By volunteering to help older people, I have become a better person and I have learned many things that school alone cannot teach me.

I have volunteered at two different places. I volunteered at an adult day center twice a week during the summer before my freshman year. The adult day center is a day care center for adults. In addition, presently I am volunteering at a local nursing home. I have had much experience dealing with older people through volunteering more than 150 hours to date.

As I walk into the nursing home, I see the familiar surroundings. Mr. Charming, Betty, and Millie are watching old reruns of *Gilligan's Island*.

Residents sleep in their wheelchairs. Others sit by the elevator greeting everyone who enters the home. I can hear someone in the background: "Nurse! Nurse! Somebody help me." The picture is often the same every week at the nursing home.

My duties at the adult day center and the nursing home are similar. At both I do activities with the residents; they are the people who live or stay at the places. At the adult day center I would do exercises, read news, and play games and music with them. At the nursing home I play Bingo every Sunday, and I visit the residents. I also attend to their wishes and calls for drinks of water and for the nurse. The responsibilities to the residents are not difficult, but they appreciate the help a lot.

The residents show appreciation for the volunteers' help through their actions. One week at the nursing home I helped a lady, Opal, play Bingo. Although she could place the chips on the card, she needed to be shown where the numbers were. She won three times that day, and when I left, she cried. Opal's actions are typical of the residents I have volunteered for. Many of the people do not have any family, or they do not get visits very often. As a result, simple gestures such as playing Bingo and balloon volleyball with them can be the highlight of their day.

The residents also enjoy when the volunteers visit because then they have someone to talk to. The people enjoy talking about their families: grandchildren, sons, and daughters. They also enjoy hearing about the volunteer's life and family. I was talking to a lady named Mary and telling her about the dance show I was in. Suddenly, her face lit up and she smiled: "My daughter took dance lessons when she was little, and she was very good." Something I said reminded her of her daughter, and that made her happy.

Sometimes the volunteer does not even have to do anything for the resident because just seeing the volunteer makes the person happy. Prudence, a resident of the nursing home, is very happy every week when I come in: "Beautiful girl, beautiful, nice, young girl. You are so nice to come in and help us older people." Another time a resident told me I reminded her of her granddaughter. Because many of the residents don't see their family or don't have one, a young face makes them happy. A volunteer can cheer up their day and make them happy because they enjoy what the volunteer does for them.

Volunteering can have a positive effect on the volunteer as well. A great reward for me is to see the joy on the faces of the people I help. I feel as though I am making a difference in their lives and giving something back to others.

By volunteering, I have also learned some interesting things about the past that I could not learn in my history class. One day I listened to a group of 80-year-old ladies reminisce about their social life when they were younger. I got to learn what the area I live in was like 60 years ago and what people did for fun. Surprisingly, things are still very similar today: fairs, roller skating, dances, and restaurants. By being with the residents, I have gotten an interesting perspective from people who have experienced a different era, and this is often not offered in school.

I have learned very useful people skills from volunteering. I have learned how to handle difficult situations. For example, at the adult day center, I saw Marge standing at the window waiting for her daughter to come pick her up. I knew the daughter was not due for another hour. Next, I heard the beeper go off, signaling that a resident was leaving. I ran to the door, only to find Marge heading for the stairs. "Marge, Marge!" I called, "Why don't you come back inside and sing with us," but Marge didn't want to. She needed comfort and reassurance that she would see her daughter soon. I had to learn to deal with similar situations. These situations happen often. I learned that many of the people think differently from most and I have learned how I must deal with them.

As a result of all of my volunteering experience, I have learned a very important aspect about myself that will affect my future. Volunteering made me realize that I want to work with people for the rest of my life. I have learned that my career has to be with people in career areas such as education or social services because I love working with people so much. I feel that I am making a difference in someone's life and I want to give something back to the people that have made a difference in my life. Perhaps this is the most important thing I have learned from volunteering. I learned this from an out-of-class experience and I enjoyed it very much.

Volunteering is a very rewarding, beneficial learning experience. Volunteering at a nursing home benefits the residents by bringing them joy, a companion, and activities to do. In addition, volunteering benefits the volunteer. Through volunteering I have grown as a person. It taught me about love and compassion toward others, and volunteering has helped me make a career decision. The benefits make the volunteering and hard work a worthwhile experience.

Section 2: Sports

Tearing One's Knee: The Homecoming Game
by Geoff Sinibaldo

"As I ran to get him, my knee popped. But I was a man possessed. Nothing was to get in my way and keep me from doing my job. I got to my man and hit him with every bit of energy left in my blood. I went to shuffle my feet to stay with him, but my leg just completely collapsed from underneath. I went down, but the play was over."

Geoff Sinibaldo is a senior at Weberville High School, where he is on varsity football and basketball and a member of the National Honor Society. He is also an altar boy at Immanuel Lutheran Church. Geoff plans to attend Carthage College in Kenosha, Wisconsin. Off season and when he is not writing papers, Geoff is outdoors enjoying a variety of sports including baseball, volleyball, basketball, street hockey, and football.

It is a great honor to be in the football program. I've been in football all 4 years. It is even a greater honor to survive the hard work and sacrifice it takes to stay in the program. My freshman team had well over 60 players. The varsity squad had 18 seniors my final season. Making the field in a varsity game is an even greater honor. However, the game is not without its risks. Football is a hard-hitting sport that takes its toll on a player's body. Due to the violent nature of this game, injuries are not that rare. A player's reaction to personal injury affects the prestige he is afforded.

All athletes risk serious injury. Football is a rough game, and an athlete who plays football is at greater risk. It is certain that all athletes do endure some kind of pain, whether it be sore muscles, cramps, whatever. Football players must be tough individuals because they must constantly play with a certain level of pain. Protective equipment is helpful if used correctly. Even with proper technique, however, injuries can still occur.

Senior year I sustained an injury that took me out for the rest of the season and post-season. I write not only to describe my personal experience but also to show different reactions to injury. The culture of Weberville football teaches the proper reaction to injury.

Football is fun and exciting. However, it is not always peaches and cream. Football has a proper mix of skill, strategy, and hitting. With violence come casualties. Coping with the trauma and pain of injury depends on a player's pride. One of the most important lessons is to learn that pride can overcome adversity. A loser will quit when things get tough. A champion who is proud not only of himself but of his team will rise to the occasion for his teammates. If that means sacrifice is involved, then so be it.

I'll never forget that bright clear day just perfect for a football game. It was after a rainy week of practice. I have always been the type of player that did not play much, but when I got my chance, I gave it everything I had. I had just recently started on kick off, and for our Homecoming game I was also on the kick-off return and extra-point teams. This game meant a lot to our team because we had lost the last two games by a total of two points after blowing out our first four opponents. The fans had their doubts, but by game time everyone on the team was pumped up and ready to go. When we walked to the stadium from the school as a team, we walked in a single-file line as the band marched next to us. The adrenaline rush a player gets from marching in next to a drum ensemble is so immense, it's to hard to describe. We got on the field, did our warm-ups, and were ready to play. We were going to kick off. We huddled up and ran on the field. I lined up on the left, and our kicker placed the ball on the right hash mark. (There are two hash marks on either side of the width of the field. They are used for marking the ball after a play, and they divide the field into thirds.) The other team missed the ball. We recovered! Our offense was on the move and we scored a touchdown. I blocked my man on the point after and it was good. This next play I'll remember until I die. The kick was right down the middle and I stayed in my lane as I sprinted down the field. The return man headed to the right and then cut back to the left. As I was changing directions, my right foot stayed planted in the ground. My right knee came in toward my body and I felt a big snap. I fell to the ground holding my leg. I got back up but our coverage stopped the ball carrier. I ran off the field with a limp, and started to look for the athletic trainer. I told him what had happened, and that I wanted to get back in the game. I had worked too long and hard just to quit on my team now. Pain or not, I was determined to play.

The kicking game coach took me off the kick off, but I was still in the game and that was all that mattered. The next extra point, I went in and blocked my man fine. It hurt, but I got the job done. When I was running off the field, my knee popped out again. This time I felt a quick sharp pain that shot up my leg. I knew this would probably be my last game, so I wanted to go out the right way. I attempted to walk the pain off on the sideline. After a couple minutes, I could tolerate the pain. This is when self-pride kicked in. My whole time in the program, what I really needed to learn was to become tougher. This was my test. The only way I was coming out of the game was for the coach to take me out. As long as it was up to me, I was in there, pain and all. I not only owed it to myself, but to many others. I owed my teammates because we have gone through so many things together. I could not quit on them. I had to show the coaches that I had not been simply going through the motions. When I promised to be alcohol- and drug-free for all 4 years, I meant it. My coaches trusted and had faith in me, and I was not going to let them down. I also felt like I owed something to the younger players in the program. We taught them over the summer and during the season what being a Weberville football player was about. I had freshman looking up to me. I had to be a good role model for them to show them they could accomplish things even when the odds were not in their favor. So I bit the bullet and went back in on kick-off return.

On the kick-off return, the team receiving the ball is required to keep five men on the line of scrimmage. I was on that front line on the far right. The way we block is the middle lineman blocks the kicker. The man to his right blocks the man to the left of the kicker. This means in order to block my man, I have to run from one hash mark to the other. Next the ball was kicked. I ran down and got one good hit on the man. Our ball carrier flew by. Then my knee popped. We got a decent return and I came off the field limping. I was still making an effort to run. That was near the end of the half. Shortly after, we went to our field house.

Inside, Coach asked me if I was all right to play. Even though the rational thing to do would have been to say no, I kept my "never-say-die" attitude and said I could play. We went back out and had to run across the field. My knee popped along the way, and I tried to stretch it out during warm-ups. The whistle blew and it was time to play. We were getting the ball for the second half, so it was kick-off return. I lined up and called out my man. As I ran to get him, my knee popped. But I was a man possessed. Nothing was to get in my way and keep me from doing my job. I got to my man and hit him with every bit of energy left in my blood. I went to shuffle my feet to stay with him, but my leg just completely collapsed from underneath. I went down, but the play was over. I felt like lying on the field forever, but I could not allow that to happen. I scraped myself up and hobbled over to the bench. This is something of which I am proud. I had always looked down on players who got hurt and just lay on the ground moaning until the trainer came to get them. I got up under my own power and walked off the field.

When I got to the sideline, Coach told me that I was done for the day. I found my back-ups and slouched over in complete exhaustion. Even though I was done, I was proud.

We went on to win the game. I went home and soaked in a hot, steamy tub. But it wasn't quite over yet. I taped my knee and went to the Homecoming dance. This wasn't too bright, but I had respect for myself and my date. I went to see the doctor the next week and learned I had ripped the ligament that runs in the middle of the knee, the ACL, completely in half. I had to have reconstructive knee surgery. Recovery took a few months. When I look back, I would not have changed a thing due to the pride I have in myself and my team.

This experience has made me a tougher person. I am more sure of myself. I am proud of my responses to adversity. I'm proud to live in a place where honor and pride far outweigh the cost of personal sacrifice. Sometimes a person will get down on himself when tragedy hits and say, "Why me?" A winner will look at the situation and say, "Why not me? I can handle this, keep it coming." The injury and my experience as an athlete through 4 years of high school turned me into a winner. I enjoy self-confidence. In the future, I know I will rise to the occasion when faced with a challenge.

Most people would probably view my injury as a tragedy. I view it differently. It made me a stronger person.

Football, From the Heart
by Jeremy C. Giutini

"The Weberville High School football program is not just concerned with winning (e.g., state championship) as much as it is dedicated to making winners."

Jeremy C. Giutini is a senior at Weberville High School, where he is a starter on the varsity football and varsity track teams. He plans to attend the University of Colorado in Boulder. Jeremy selected U.C. Boulder for its academic record, surrounding environment, and many outdoor activities. When not in school, he is lifting, enjoying athletics, and writing poetry.

In high school, the title "state championship" is just like any other title. In and of itself, it means absolutely nothing. What makes it so valuable is the hardship and effort put into obtaining the title. Football is a sport of punishment, contact, and all-out destruction, but there is more to the game. Football can become a learning experience where caring between friends and the ability to focus on a goal are among the most important aspects. The Weberville High School varsity football program attempts to combine all these facets in order to afford the team an opportunity not only to win a state championship, but also to be a winner in life.

My basis for writing this paper is that I have been part of the Weberville High School football program for 4 years. As a junior and senior I was a varsity starter, but this had little to do with superior athletic ability. The reason I was a starter was that I have an in-depth understanding of what the program really stands for and that its goal is to teach. Being with 35 guys after school for 4 years straight, you begin to eat, live, and sleep football, not because you have to but because you want to. Football had become more than a sport; it was all I thought, all I loved, and all I wanted to live for.

High school football is not something that takes place only on the football field for the weekday practices and at Saturday games during a 3-month period. It is everywhere, all the time. This is a program that consumes every minute of every hour for 365 days each year. If the team is not involved in actual practice, then the players either take part in an off-season lifting program, participate in activities set up by or for the team, or just do something with a teammate. Almost every Sunday of the season and the prior summer, players organize their own meetings to discuss an important topic, whether it is about staying drug-free, doing volunteer work, or setting an activity up with their huddle group. Huddle groups are groups of eight to ten players who work together for 3 or 4 months and engage in various focuses of the program. Everything is set up through the work of the players and the coaches. It is never one or the other. As a result, the spirit of the football team is not restricted to the playing fields, but instead the team is able to share what is learned with all the people of the community. The program does whatever it can to involve as many people as possible in any way that it can. Weberville football is a constant. It will never die out.

The Weberville High School football program is not just concerned with winning (e.g., state championship) as much as it is dedicated to making winners. There truly is no use in winning a pointless game, but there is importance in what is learned and how it pertains to life. Friendship, honor, and pride are the only three qualities that will get people anywhere in life. Without honor it is impossible to meet the right kinds of friends and it is impossible to gain honor. This is why it is a fight to become a better human being: No one is given respect; they have to earn it. A football program such as Weberville's provides teenagers with the opportunity to make themselves into the kind of people who can survive in the real world, not by making them superhuman, but by teaching them to fight for everything they want. These types of people are people who never give up. They are the kind of people with whom everyone else wants to associate.

A state championship is obviously a prestigious honor, but it is meaningless when compared to life. It is something hardly any of the world's population will learn of, much less remember. Forty years from now, no one will care. What people will care about is whether or not a person is an honest, respectable, and sincere friend, and nothing more. It is more important to learn and grow as a person and be a part of a team of winners than it is to be on a winning team. The team that won the Illinois High School Championship did just that. But that team, along with every other team in the state, was unable to accomplish the level of caring that was achieved by the Weberville High School football team.

There is no individual greater than another. It is a team effort. To accomplish any difficult goal, everything must be pushed into the background. As for football, one must focus only on football, academics, and building friendship and honor. The key word is sacrifice, not as an individual thinking only of oneself, but as a member of the team who cares for and loves his teammates. Excellence is attained through sacrifice, yet the amount of sacrifice has to be maximized. Teammates have to care more than what others think is wise, risk more than what others think is safe, dream more than what others think is practical, and expect more than what others think is possible. That is how they become winners.

The fundamental base of victory goes right back to being only as strong as the weakest link. If everyone does not understand what teamwork is, then there will be no winners. Coming together is a beginning, keeping together is progress, and working together is success. A team that is obsessed with becoming winners is obsessed with pride, respect, and honesty. Pride means doing everything to the best of one's ability. Every job is a self-portrait of the person for others to admire. Respect is something that people struggle endlessly to obtain. That is why jealous people try to take it away. Honesty is the important link. The weak try to fool themselves and others by saying they are not capable of understanding. The strong say what they mean and mean what they say. They are fanatically committed to excellence. That is a funny thing about life; those who refuse to accept anything but the best very often get it.

Commitment is what transforms a promise into reality. It is the words that speak boldly of your intentions and the actions that speak louder than words. It is making time when there is none. It is coming through time after time, year after year after year. Commitment is the stuff of which character is made; it is the power to change the face of things. It is the daily triumph of integrity over skepticism.

For anyone, whether it be students, athletes, teachers, or any person who has a mind, it is important to realize that it is easy to be ordinary, but it takes courage to excel. It takes courage to sacrifice, to work out when you are tired or sick, to seek out tough competition when you know you will probably be beaten; yet, this is what a winner strives to do. He strives to make himself better, no matter how hellish or terrible the torture, because in the end he has gained more than any lazy, drunken, wasted, self-pitying bum has a chance at. What makes a real man is the ability to stand by his morals when all those around him have no morals and to always keep fighting even when it seems he has lost. It takes courage to push yourself so hard and punish yourself so severely that it seems as though death is upon your shoulders. However, when you recover you always find yourself a better person. If you want to win at life, do not just set a pace for yourself. If you expect to win, always do everything to the fullest. Life is a pain, and pain makes the body stronger.

The football team had all the elements to win a championship in football at the 5A level except one: size. Unfortunately, in football the size of the players really makes a difference. Any team with large players that can pull together the type of program Weberville High School has is destined to win the State Championship. The best advice that can be given is to let the team develop its own will through a program that promotes honor, courage, and friendship. Then just let the winning happen.

Beyond the Goalpost: The Weberville Football Program
by Kevin True

"I have probably learned more about life since I've been part of the program than I would have ever learned if I had decided not to join freshman year. If you ask me, 'football' will be just as important to being successful later in life as all my years of schooling."

Kevin True is a senior at Weberville High School, where he is on the varsity football team. Kevin's intramural basketball team, the Bandits, took the championship. When he's not writing all these papers, he's earning money for college or playing basketball. Kevin plans to attend the University of Illinois in Champaign—Urbana.

I have been a part of the football program for 4 years. As a part of the team, I've participated in many things beyond football. None of this would have been possible without football. I am glad I got the chance.

For most football teams the setting is mainly at school—the gym, the weight room, and the football fields—but our program takes us away from school. We have volunteered our labor at St. Joseph's Home for the Elderly, Habitat for Humanity in Chicago, and even Sacred Heart Griffen, a school in Springfield, Illinois.

As an incoming freshman I began the football program in the summer. Freshman year was a learning year in which we learned a lot about how the game is played and the nature of the program. From the freshman team to the varsity, a lot of things happened. I found football really wasn't the most important thing to the coaches. What the coaches really cared about was helping us grow and learn about life.

One big part of Weberville football is being a part of the Drug-Free Athlete Program. This program began limited to football as a commitment to the team to remain drug- and alcohol-free, not only in season, but year-round until graduation. As word got around, other teams started to show interest and it was expanded to all sports and activities in school. Being a part of the Drug- and Alcohol-Free Program is a pretty big sacrifice for a high school student. It means not only staying away from drugs but also not drinking and not smoking or chewing tobacco. All of these things have been a problem for the team in past years. Obviously this is not an easy thing for most kids to do.

Huddle groups are also a big part of our team. Each year, the coach assigns one or two seniors to a group of people from lower levels of the program. The seniors, as mentors, help younger people with weight lifting, maintaining acceptable grades, and other problems that may develop.

The main aspect of the program is the activities we do off season with our huddle groups. Activities include things like rock climbing in

Wisconsin and going to a lake for the day with a team from Springfield's Sacred Heart Griffen High School. But not all the activities are just for our pleasure. In January of my junior and senior years, we went to Chicago and helped renovate an old apartment building for Habitat for Humanity. When the building is complete it will be used as low-income housing. Knowing that I helped provide some of the less fortunate with a better life is a good feeling. It is just one of the good feelings I get from being a part of a great thing like our football team. Something else we started is what we call the "Adopt a Grandparent" program. We went to a home for the elderly. Each huddle group took on a resident as a grandparent. We go and visit each month with our huddle groups and talk with them because they may not have any family left to take care of them. Just seeing the looks on their faces when we go to visit made me feel good. I feel like I really mean something to those people. I would never have had that opportunity if I hadn't joined the football team.

Although I might have joined the team simply to play football, the reason I stayed with it and like it so much is all the people we can affect with our program. Being on the Weberville football team has become much more than just football. It takes a lot of hard work and dedication. Some people may ask why anyone would want to put so much time and energy into a sport like football, but believe me, in the long run it will all pay off. I have probably learned more about life since I've been part of the program than I would have ever learned if I had decided not to join freshman year. If you ask me, "football" will be just as important to being successful later in life as all my years of schooling.

The Weberville football team has been known throughout the area as a top team every season and has made the state playoffs seven straight seasons. Most people see only what we do on the field and think it's great. Not many people know the kind of people we have in the program and the activities we take part in through the years. Our football program is more than just a team; it's a group of guys who really care about each other as well as the people around us, including our adopted grandparents and the people who will live in that apartment building we helped renovate, in addition to our fans in the bleachers. It takes a lot of dedication and sacrifice, but it's all worth it.

Wrestling to Win
by Dan Mann

"A fan sees about 10% of what is going on. If you are one of the wrestlers, you are constantly thinking 'What if he does this move or that move?' 'How will I score?' 'What will I have to do?' 'How will I do it?' and 'When will I do it?'"

Daniel J. Mann is a senior at Weberville High School, where he is captain of the varsity wrestling team. He participates on a wrestling team with the park district each spring. Dan plans to attend the local community college in the fall. When not writing papers, he is either wrestling, playing beach volleyball, or riding his motorcycle.

In the sport of wrestling there are many characteristics of a state champion and a state championship–caliber team. Because wrestling is mostly an individual sport, it takes a lot to be a state champion. You don't have the help of others while you are in your match. In this sport you need a lot of self-discipline, whether you are cutting 10 pounds or putting in extra time to perfect a certain move. But it is more than that. Most of all, it is having the proper mental attitude going into practice or into a match. You have to have it set in your mind that you are better than your opponent and that you will not be defeated. When a fan sits in the stands munching on popcorn and drinking Pepsi and watching two men grappling, he is not seeing what is really going on in that match. A fan sees about 10% of what is going on. If you are one of the wrestlers, you are constantly thinking "What if he does this move or that move?" "How will I score?" "What will I have to do?" "How will I do it?" and "When will I do it?" When two wrestlers are equal in strength and physical training, wrestling becomes a totally mental sport. It is probably the toughest, most grueling of sports there is. Your body is put to the test when you are in a match. For 6 minutes, you go all out.

I've been around wrestling all my life. My father is the head wrestling coach at a high school in a neighboring district. He has been the coach for about 20 years. I've been going to practices on Saturdays since I was 4 or 5. When I was in first grade I got into the local wrestling program. I was about 50 pounds then. I stayed in that for about 4 years. I had surgery that held me out for fifth grade, and this local wrestling program folded in sixth grade. I wrestled in seventh and eighth grades. I was conference runner-up both years. My junior high record was 50-5. For the last 4 years I have wrestled for Weberville High School in the fall and winter and the local wrestling club in the spring and summer. My freshman year I was 26-3. Then came sophomore year, and I got my first taste of state wrestling. I was the only sophomore on varsity. I ended up with a record of 8-14. During the summer of my sophomore year I went to state for freestyle and placed 8th out of 42. I missed a spot on the national team by one match. During my junior year I was ineligible because of grades until winter break. I closed out my junior year with a record of 10-6. During summer I competed at the Junior Regionals up in LaCrosse, Wisconsin. But in my second match I dislocated my right shoulder and was out for the summer. I spent that season rehabilitating my injury. Now I'm in my senior year and have a current record of 14-4, and I have placed third in one tournament and fourth in the Weberville Holiday Tournament.

During wrestling practice at Weberville, we usually warm up for about 20 minutes and wrestle technique for about an hour and a half. Then we wrestle "live" (as we would in a match). On Mondays and Wednesdays we have morning practices that start at 6:00 a.m. At these practices we run stairs in the pool area and do "live" in the afternoon. In practice I usually wear two shirts and a sweatshirt, not to mention my shorts and shoes. During practice I really try to concentrate on the technique of my moves. I usually have to cut anywhere from five to eight pounds a week. Toward the end of the week (Thursday and Friday), I usually cut the majority of my weight, and I am forced to work a little harder and wear more sweatshirts in practice. I try to make within a pound of 125 before the end of practice on Thursday. I will not eat or drink anything at all for the rest of the night or until weigh-in on Friday, which is around 5:30 p.m. That is one of the hardest things to do in this sport. But after weigh-in I eat and drink a little and after my match I drink some water. I can't drink too much because I have to make weight on Saturday also.

To be a state champion in this sport takes a lot of determination and sacrifice. When you prepare to wrestle you have to have an attitude. A lot of things run through your mind. "What if I lose?" You have to take that and say, "No! I'm going to kick his ass." I usually pray a little before each match. I think every wrestler with enough courage and balls prays. Before I wrestle I get so pumped up that no one can talk to me. I'm so concentrated I am like a bomb waiting to explode. I pace back and forth until the match prior is over, saying to myself, "Win. Kill 'em, destroy him." And right before I go on I get some last-minute tips from my coach. I then proudly carry with me my experience, my attitude, and my hatred for my opponent. We shake hands. The whistle blows. We are grappling and fighting for a takedown. When it is all over, win or lose, you listen to what your coach has to say and watch your tapes for hours, go back into practice, and make yourself better for the next time that you step onto the mat with your hated opponent.

Friends come and watch me wrestle whenever they get a chance. Sometimes one of them will take pictures. Wrestling seems to have a bigger effect on my parents than it does on friends. Mom sits in the stands and videotapes so my father can see me wrestle when he gets home from his own meets. We watch the tapes together. He tells me what I could have done and what to do. Watching tapes with my dad takes me one step further in achieving my highest goal, being a state champion.

Wrestling is very demanding and time-consuming. It takes a lot out of you, but it gives a lot back. If you work hard enough you will get what you deserve. It is one of the hardest sports a kid can put himself through in high school. You have to lose weight, and as a result you cannot go out and eat with your buddies. And it's a heartbreaker when you lose. But I have a love for this sport. To compete with the best you must have a love for the sport. You must have a lot of self-discipline. Perhaps that's what I've gained from wrestling.

High School Sports: An Indictment
by Sean Kopeny

"High school is a fragile time when personalities are being formed. We do not need a whole crop of insecure homophobes who believe manhood is demonstrated by who is dumb enough to cause the most serious injury to himself."

Sean Kopeny is a junior at Weberville High School, where he is captain of the Scholastic Bowl team, editor-in-chief of the school's social science magazine, and a member of the school newspaper and Model United Nations Club. He is also a Boy Scout who has achieved life rank. Sean is still pondering his options after high school, though college is a certainty. When not at school or sleeping, he's bagging groceries.

Here is my deep horrible confession: I have never been that good at sports.

I realize it is a horrible thing to have to admit as a student at Weberville High School, but sports have never been my forte. When I am out on the court or field, my effort is at its peak but my ability is at its usual low. My abilities have been average or excellent for street basketball or neighborhood baseball, but below average in organized sports.

When I entered high school I joined the soccer team. I was a week late in joining because they had been practicing for a week before school started and I had not known. Once school started there were 2 1/2-hour-long practices and a strong push by coaches for Saturday practices. I was not able to even think of joining any other activities until soccer ended.

Something horrible was happening to me that I did not realize until later. I was letting soccer define me. Soccer clothes were part of my daily attire and my friends were teammates on the soccer team. Few people with whom I hung around were not on the soccer team.

I will never forget how one day I overheard some of my teammates talking about the new soccer catalog. Deep contemplation about soccer started to set in. Wasn't I in this just for fun? Soccer is just a game, isn't it?

I cannot claim to be obsessive about much, and I am one of the most outwardly emotionless people I know. It may be that lack of obsessiveness, the lack of wanting to dedicate myself to any one activity, that led me to not participate in soccer sophomore year. Instead I joined and took leadership positions in other activities.

In my new activities—newspaper, Scholastic Bowl, Model United Nations, and a social science news magazine—I found release rather than pressure as motivation to become fully dedicated. The people I was with became my friends, not because we were on the same activity, but because we shared interests and got along well. Because I was in such a range of activities, no one activity could really define me. If I started leaning toward one activity, it was by choice and never for very long.

The boundaries of the clique I joined became less rigid, and my mind became more open. When on soccer it was "uncool" to associate with the so-called art freaks. I ignored them. Once I got to know the people in the art department I realized that there was little difference between "us" and "them." I have spoken little to those who were my friends because of soccer. It is not because they are bad people, but because I have little in common with them and it is unacceptable for them to go far outside the boundaries of their clique.

My argument with high school sports is not with the participants but rather with the way they are set up. Students are asked to dedicate themselves for several months or, in some cases, 4 years solely to one activity. Coaches hint that joining the summer program could get a student closer to that starting job. I fear for the football players at our school. They have been living football for 4 years and they learned little else of life than football. I have been called "fag" by several football players for the sole reason that I either did not indulge in high school sports or I simply annoyed the athletes. In spite of being completely straight and not even agreeing with the homosexual lifestyle, I found myself saying, "Do you really think you're insulting me by calling me homosexual?"

Activities have allowed me a chance at leadership that has taught me lasting lessons. As captain of Scholastic Bowl since junior year, I have learned to effectively balance the playing of as many people as possible while still winning. Junior year my team won its division, and I only violated the feelings of one member of the team who I felt was too tentative to be played in tight games. As an editor of the newspaper I learned how to delegate authority and got insights into journalism. As editor-in-chief of the school's award-winning student social science magazine, I learned the difficulties of trying to motivate a whole staff and putting together a publication from scratch. I enjoyed all these lessons because I am not in these activities to set up a career. I joined them to have fun.

Activities for me are a physical and emotional release because I get to hang out with my friends and goof off. In newspaper I stayed after school with the other editors, and we either played card games ranging from blackjack to "bullshit" or invented new classic games such as koosh volleyball (a koosh ball is volleyed with old yearbooks over a center line of chairs). The same central characters were in all the activities, so any time I went to activities I was hanging out with my friends.

For every problem there's a solution. For the affliction of making students overcommit to sports, I think high schools should make sports more an outlet for fun and less a money-making publicity grabber where the students are tools of a coach or a school. Conformity is not merely encouraged but forced by sports (and by some activities), and this is just wrong. High school is a fragile time when personalities are being formed. We do not need a whole crop of insecure homophobes who believe manhood is demonstrated by who is dumb enough to cause the most serious injury to himself. My advice to those entering high school is to join activities that you enjoy and that will not engross your entire life.

The Good, the Bad, and the Sister-School Rivalry
by Alex R. Sevak

"I was amazed at what some schools had gone through because of rivalry. Certain schools had their football fields burned, principal beaten up, and athletic teams locked in their locker rooms so that they would be disqualified from the game. It is obvious that rivalry between schools is often taken too far."

Alex R. Sevak is a junior at Weberville High School, where he is on student council, speech team, PEER (a peer counseling group), principal's advisory board, and the National Honor Society. He hopes to attend Eckerd College in St. Petersburg, Florida to pursue a career in pharmacy. When not sitting in class making fun of teachers, he enjoys going to movies, collecting shoes, and riding in golf carts.

Since we've been little, we have been in competition with many different people for many different things. For instance, many siblings are in competition with each other, whether it be over grades, sports, or affection from their parents. Rivalry is also present in the workplace. Almost all employees have an enemy or two in their department with whom they are in conflict. The rivalry that is most significant to me and affects me the most is the rivalry between sister schools.

I, along with many other students, feel qualified to write a paper on school rivalry. I attend Weberville High School, which has a sister school, Richland High School, just across town. The rivalry between the schools has been getting worse every year. Since I started attending Weberville, I have become aware of the increasing tension and competition between the two public schools within the same high school district.

As mentioned before, rivalry is present almost everywhere in our culture. Rivalry between schools can occur at many different places. At Weberville, as well as Richland, juniors and seniors have an option to choose an "off-campus" lunch whereby they get to leave school grounds during their designated lunch period. Some students go home, but most students opt to go to a restaurant with their friends. But with the restaurants situated in the center of town, students from both schools come into contact with one another and ultimately induce rivalry. Another place in which rivalry can take place is at local shopping centers or malls. Because malls are a major hangout for many teenagers nowadays, there is a great chance of interaction between students from different schools. But the most frequent instances of rivalry undoubtedly take place at school functions. Among the highest incidents of rivalry occur at football games. Whether it be at a store, restaurant, or school function, rivalry between sister schools will always be a problem.

Rivalry has both positive and negative effects. On the positive side of the spectrum, rivalry increases the fun and excitement at a game. Many people enjoy showing their school spirit and enthusiasm against rival schools. Rivalry can also cause the competitors and athletes to become more determined and win. As long as it is kept in a calm and reserved manner, rivalry can be a very satisfying part of high school life.

On the other hand, there are many more negative effects and consequences to the rivalry between sister schools. Excessive competition and animosity between students from rival schools can cause them to break out into a verbal argument. These verbal fights usually occur when groups of friends are at a restaurant or any other local hangout. Students argue in a vulgar manner, almost always for some irrelevant reason. Usually, it's because someone gave another person a dirty look, cut in front of them in line, or just in spite of arguing. This quarrel results in worse relations between the two people or groups of people and increased rivalry between the schools. I have experienced this fighting a great number of times. One incident that stands out was the day of the football game between Richland and Weberville. As usual, lunchtime rolled around and we decided to go to the neighboring Taco Bell. When we got there, students from Richland were there also. Commonly, we'd just get our food and ignore them completely. I wasn't aware of what induced the action, but a girl from Richland dumped a whole glass of orange pop on one of my friends. They began to yell and swear at the top of their lungs. Luckily, the restaurant manager saw what was going on and stopped the scene from going any further. Incidents like this one happen almost every day. Something definitely needs to be done to stop this foolish rivalry.

When the verbal abuse progresses, it commonly ends up in a physical confrontation. If the restaurant manager hadn't stopped the verbal fight, it probably would have ended up in a vicious brawl. By far the most occurrences of physical rivalry are apparent after a game. After football and basketball games, and even after wrestling matches, many people get so upset their team lost that they take out their anger on other people, usually from the rival school. I can remember one situation after a basketball game when my friends and I were driving away from the school parking lot. A carload of students from Richland forced us off the road. Luckily we were all right, but we were still scared at how it could have ended. Scenes like this one are not very uncommon and happen all over the country. I attended a student council camp this summer in Colorado. The objective of this camp was to share ideas and suggestions with the other delegates on how to improve our student councils. One of the issues that we talked about at camp was rivalry. I was amazed at what some schools had gone through because of rivalry. Certain schools had their football fields burned, principal beaten up, and athletic teams locked in their locker rooms so that they would be disqualified from the game. It is obvious that rivalry between schools is often taken too far.

Rivalry is often an amusing thing to be a part of. However, nowadays it has become an extremely negative concept. With so many occurrences of physical and verbal abuse between students from sister schools, it is hard to even imagine rivalry as a traditional event.

The effects of rivalry on students is phenomenal. The most obvious result of rivalry is the physical pain and anguish a person might go through. Due to many of the awful fights that occur, many individuals get severely injured. Rivalry also has many emotional effects. If a person were to get into a fight with someone, it would probably be in their minds for the rest of the day, if not longer. The effects of arguing with someone could affect an individual by lowering their grades, scapegoating their anger on other people, and making them feel guilty. Dating is another concept that rivalry can affect. Many couples nowadays are from sister or rival schools. For the most part this works out fine. But in some cases, the relationship does not work out because of differences of opinion or distance between the two is just too great. Rivalry has physical, emotional, and social effects. In most cases these effects are negative and have to be dealt with in an extreme manner.

Rivalry is apparent throughout society, but it particularly affects me and many other students. Rivalry can occur at many different places within the city or suburb. I have experienced rivalry firsthand. With a big rival school across town, I am constantly dealing with the competition. In some instances, rivalry can be pleasant, but in most cases it is not. The verbal and physical abuse involved in rivalry is getting out of hand and should be stopped from progressing.

4

The Student Reality: Working 3:25 to Closing

High school students frequently complain that teachers assign homework as if school were the only responsibility in their lives. For many students, however, part-time jobs take up as many hours of their week as academics. According to Geoffrey T. Holtz's *Welcome to the Jungle* (1995), between two thirds and three fourths of high school–age students worked during the 1980s. This chapter allows students to explain the benefits and detriments of that experience in their own words.

Bodzewski and Borkholder view their part-time jobs as extremely positive experiences, though from different perspectives. Bodzewski dismisses the "gloom and doom" outlook of certain analysts and explains that his job as a grocery store cashier has made him a better student. Besides reinforcing good communication and mathematics skills, his position brings him into contact with people of various social and economic backgrounds. By doing this work, he better understands the importance of the opportunities his parents and school provide. Bork-holder goes farther and concludes that the lessons learned at her job as a bank teller outweigh those learned in school. She attributes her greater self-confidence, responsibility, and assertiveness to her part-time job.

On the other hand, Clifford and Roberts warn of the dangers that teen employment can pose. Like Bodzewski, Clifford works at a gro-cery store but he experiences a very different reality. Despite the bene-fit of having extra spending money, his job steals too many hours away from his week and, in turn, away from his schoolwork, family, and ex-tracurricular activities. As he explains, the resulting stress and physical demands can often be too much.

From a desperate situation, Roberts describes similar negative ef-fects of working. To escape an abusive father and to help his mother pay the mortgage, he works three part-time jobs totaling 51 hours per week; yet he also attends school full-time. His resulting declines in mental and physical health serve as a wake-up call to administrators, teachers, and parents who do not yet realize the necessity of the stu-dent perspective.

Interestingly, both the positive and negative work experiences sug-gest that something is lacking in the school curriculum. For Bodzewski and Borkholder, work teaches valuable life lessons that they could not find within the classroom. As a result, creators of curriculum must again go back to the three basic curriculum questions:

1. What knowledge is most worthwhile?
2. Why is it worthwhile?
3. How is it acquired?

As Bodzewski points out, the assignments of his speech class be-come largely irrelevant if they find no practical application for the stu-dent. Teachers should investigate their students' experiences outside the classroom and then incorporate those experiences into course-work. For example, it would have been extremely beneficial for Bodzewski if his speech instructor had included work-type situations in a classroom exercise or had invited a local company's sales force per-sonnel trainer. With meaningful in-class exercises, students can begin to close the large gap between what they do within and outside the school.

Essentially, teachers and administrators should seek opportunities to introduce the "real world" to the high school classroom. Students in an economics class may calculate the value in dollars of staying in school compared to dropping out senior year. Foreign language teach-ers can develop lessons using the Yellow Pages of a telephone directory printed in a foreign language. A sociology teacher can invite a representative from the U.S. Census Bureau and review local census data for emerging trends. Health courses can teach students to read, compare, and decipher different types of health care policies. The community offers a wealth of free and appropriate resources. Educators who teach to the test risk depriving students of an education that is meaningful and relevant.

School must remain relevant for students like Borkholder who have decided that more hours at work resulting in lower-quality schoolwork is a worthwhile trade-off. It is troubling, though understandable, to note that students often treat work with more seriousness than school. Remember, for a moment, the scene in virtually every *Leave It to Beaver* episode where the boys come home from school and change into their *play* clothes. Today's teenagers do exactly the opposite. They come home from school and change into their *dress* clothes and go to work.

The issues Clifford and Roberts raise from negative work experiences remain more problematic. Constructing meaning between the worlds of work and school simply may not be enough. As Roberts passionately explains, the mental and physical exhaustion of working three jobs in addition to going to school full-time leaves him ineffective at school. Roberts' pride and strong ethos of self-reliance prevented him from approaching his teachers for understanding. For students like Roberts, teachers must first show concern. Next they must demonstrate flexibility. After all, students want to learn the lessons. Students want to complete the work. A simple and partial remedy may be to assign homework 1 week in advance. College courses often assign the entire course's responsibilities on the first day of class; high school courses could do the same thing on a smaller scale. For example, if students knew both their work schedule and their homework schedule 1 week in advance, they might be able to appropriately schedule work and homework and meet both responsibilities. Students who find out at 2:00 p.m. that they must read an entire chapter before class the next day, in addition to working to closing that night, will not be able to finish both tasks. Most often, it will be the schoolwork that will suffer. Advanced notice on assignments allows students the best opportunity for getting both tasks completed.

Moreover, teachers and administrators must demonstrate varying degrees of flexibility from student to student. Although a death in the family or a religious function immediately elicits a sympathetic response, so should overwhelming domestic situations like the one detailed by Roberts. Again, the more teachers understand student realities, the more teachers can address students' needs. Because statistics indicate that the rate of teen employment is not likely to decline, issues related to student employment should be a top priority for teachers and administrators.

The Effects of Work on Students
by Jeffrey M. Bodzewski

"The so-called 'gloom and doom' outlook taken by analysts has corrupted and biased people's thoughts against teens working."

Jeffrey Bodzewski is a senior at Weberville High School, where he competes on the varsity track team. He plans to attend Purdue University in West Lafayette, Indiana. When not writing sociology papers and drawing comics about his social science teacher, Jeff can be found working at the local Jewel Food Store.

Experts have rarely explored the effects of working upon school from the student's perspective. Many have claimed working is detrimental to a teen's development. They cite time constraints regarding studying and sleep. They fail, however, to explore all the positive effects a job and the responsibility that comes with it can have. Although at times work is a liability and does detract from school, a job's overall effects are beneficial and many times motivating.

I have been employed for nearly 2 years at Jewel Food Stores. While working there, I have done a variety of jobs. My tasks have included parceling, getting carts, stocking, and the present position of cashier. During this time I have averaged 18 hours a week. My performance on the job has been average to above average. This is determined through various on-the-job evaluations. In school, my classes range from average-level to advanced placement. While working these 2 years, I have achieved not a drop, but in fact a noticeable rise in my grades. This year, using college-level materials, I've gained an understanding of cultural anthropology, macro economics, sociology, and political science. I have developed proper writing skills in advanced English classes. Through my work and school experience, I feel competent to address the issues of school and work. More importantly, I'm a teen. I've experienced it.

My employer is Jewel Food Stores, a large grocery chain located in the Midwest. This specific store is located in a large metropolitan area. The town in which it is located is home to approximately 75,000 people. One of the Jewel chain's largest stores, it is also one of the newest and most modern, being only a year and a half old. This new store combines the newest techniques and technologies in the grocery industry. This Jewel is constantly being used as a testing center for new registers, forms, etc. As a cashier, I stand in the front of the store, waiting for customers. A total of 13 different registers can be employed and at times have been. As a cashier, I see between 100 and 700 people at each work session. This claim is verified through a customer count that the receipt contains. The people who work and shop here for the most part are from middle-income to middle-upper-income families.

The impact of working upon school performance and attitude is usually reported from a one-sided viewpoint. The so-called "gloom and doom" outlook taken by analysts has corrupted and biased people's thoughts against teens working. Moreover, the positive aspects of working have usually been ignored. I'd like to show you both sides from a student's perspective.

By working as a cashier, I've come in contact with all kinds of people. People of every economic class, age, and personality come through my line. Working as a cashier brings about a sense of appreciation for school and the opportunities given to me because of this contact with others. You cannot describe the fear of looking across the counter at another employee and seeing that his age is three times yours. These people have bounced from job to job for 20 years without achieving success monetarily. Without a good education and the opportunities needed to capitalize on that education, these people are now in a precarious situation. These people are making anywhere from one dollar less than I make to about two dollars more an hour. These people have no real job security. Each day could be their last with a "good-paying job."

The same is the case for people coming through my line. People may come through in short, tattered clothing about which an immediate judgment is made: that these people are poor, lazy slobs. Upon talking with them, I make a discovery. These are people who lacked the opportunities to capitalize on their talents. Without hard studying, I too could be presenting food stamps to a cashier in a couple of years. These two variables instill in me a sense of appreciation for the education offered at school.

I now appreciate more than ever before the quality education I'm getting. Although this may not show in my work every time, I am making a more consistent effort than ever before. Before working, I thought I would succeed no matter what. Living in this socioeconomic area, poverty and failure used to be just fantasy. Homework could be done later, if at all. School was just not important. After being exposed to the "real world," grades take on a much greater significance for me. Realizing that in 5 years I, too, could be one of them is motivation in and of itself.

Working can also have a negative effect upon schoolwork. If one works until late and there is homework to do, a student then has two choices. Choice one is to do the homework and be tired and inattentive the next day at school. Choice two is to go to sleep after a long 15-hour day. With this second choice, the homework's completion depends upon one's free time and a teacher's understanding. The advantage of this choice is that there will now be enough energy to take notes and understand the new material presented. With either choice, most teachers will be disappointed and label the student as lazy.

Nothing could be further from the truth in most cases. Choosing not to leech off Mom and Dad for spending money, this student has taken it upon himself [or herself] to get money the old-fashioned way, to earn it. School is going to suffer at times because of this. Long-term suffering should result in a reevaluation of the student's working, however. By no means is a high school job more important than earning a high school diploma and attending college. A simple balance must be maintained to get the most out of both school and work.

Work also adds a good complement to the lessons taught in school. I said "complement" because it is by no means a supplement. Although the lessons of life are a good teacher, you cannot approach them unprepared. A class entitled "speech" or one that emphasizes this topic does not give you actual hands-on experience. This experience is attained through practice. As a cashier I get better practice than just about anyone. During this time, a business demeanor must be maintained. The customer is always right. To convey a mistake on their part or mine is sometimes very delicate. By applying knowledge from this class, a good approach can be taken. If a mistake is made, then obviously that is not a good approach. The human relations aspect of being a cashier complements what is learned in school.

Work also adds a complement to mathematical skills learned in school. Coupons that offer a certain percentage off must be calculated by the cashier, not the machine. There is no mathematical pressure greater than having a customer looking at his watch while you're figuring out 39% of $3.16. Though these are basic math skills, they are enhanced beyond imagination as a cashier. Simple knowledge of these skills is essential, but so is lightning-fast use of them. Through a combination of work and school, students attain better mathematical skills.

Through a combination of work and school, a good balance of knowledge can best be attained. School will offer the background and knowledge to be able to do certain things. Work will give the experience to have confidence to really do something.

As a student and cashier, I can say that the effect has been a good one. One of these effects is the acceptance of responsibility. Just like real life, I am no longer able to go anywhere I want or do whatever I want at any given time. Even days that I'm not working are spent doing homework that will be due the day after a work day. This sounds good, but not many of the assignments are given in advance. Although most teachers realize the effects a job can have on time, few actually "accept" it. They prefer to think that 1 day's notice for a two-page writing assignment is good because their class is the only thing on the student's mind. Or so they seem to think.

Not all benefits, though, are economic or educational. At work you make a lot of new friends. Your personality can change too. I've become more serious because of the job. Life is no longer just fun and games. I now accept the responsibilities presented to me. My mom and dad are proud of me because instead of lying around the house, I'm contributing to my future. Scholarships can be attained through work. This would ease the financial burden on my parents to a degree. A negative social aspect, though, is time. Sometimes there just isn't enough of it. I don't see my grandmas as much as I did before. Sometimes I don't talk to my dad for a day or two because of work. However, we have all accepted this fact and it does not create much of a problem. Although there are some negative aspects, work has had a positive effect on me.

Work is beneficial to the student. At the same time the student is able to incorporate items used in the classroom, new situations are introduced by working. Working during the teen years enables a student to make adjustments early in life regarding a sense of responsibility and time adjustments. An appreciation of opportunities, both educational and financial, occurs as a result of working. This brings about a student more committed to the classroom. With an understanding teacher, work and school can be mutually beneficial to a student.

Pen and Teller
by Joy Borkholder

"It is nice to know that I can be successful at something besides academics and music. . . . School is no longer my main focus. . . . I feel much better prepared for college than if I had spent my senior year at my desk studying and filling out college applications."

Joy Borkholder excelled in school. She plans to attend Cedarville College in the fall.

This is about how working can affect a student in different ways. The reader should, however, consider that students have a variety of jobs. My job as a teller is one with a good salary and good hours for me. Working has had quite an impact on my present life as a senior in high school and on some of my plans for the future. The effects of a job on academics can be both good and bad, but some changes in a working student's school performance can also be attributed to the turmoil of senior year. For a student, working brings many new situations, people, responsibilities, and stresses. These changes are sure to influence school as well as other facets of the student's life.

My job as a teller at a bank is the first work experience I have had. I started in June after my junior year and worked full-time throughout the summer. Since school began in the fall, I have been working an average of 15 hours a week. Because of a bank's limited hours, I work three afternoons a week from 3:00 to 6:30 and Saturday mornings in the drive-up. It may not seem like much, but in addition to school and other activities it becomes a demanding schedule. Tomorrow, for example, I have to be at school early for a meeting, rush to work after school, rush to a National Honor Society meeting after work, and finally return home around 8:00 p.m., not having had dinner and having plenty of homework to do. I have seen firsthand this year how working can affect every aspect of someone's life.

The bank where I work is large for the suburbs. Located in downtown Weberville, it is the main building of about 10 branches throughout the north and west suburbs. The teller line is in the lobby, along with the customer service representatives. The loan department is upstairs and the trust department is downstairs. Also, two tellers work in the drive-up, which is where I am most of the time. The drive-up is attached to the building, but it is enclosed and private enough that the two tellers can eat, drink, talk freely, and listen to the radio. However, tellers in the lobby are always under the scrutiny of the customers. The teller line consists of about 10 tellers plus 4 college students who work when the regular tellers are home. The 10 regular tellers are all women ranging in age from 17 to 60, myself being the youngest. Four of those 10 work part-time only because they attend local colleges. Three of the ladies do not work in the summer or on breaks so they can be home with their children. This allows the college students to come back and work.

The most obvious aspect of working for a student is the money. I have a very good salary for a high school student. I have a checking account, a savings account, and a credit card. This responsibility requires budgeting, which I have done successfully without the help of my parents. I am getting good experience handling my own finances, which will help me in the future. Of course it is fun to spend the money I earn. After I put 60% of my paycheck into savings and give 10% to the church, I buy clothes, shoes, and craft supplies that my parents will not buy for me. The money I save will help pay for college and, I hope, will give me some spending money while I am there.

Working as a teller requires a lot of responsibility and knowledge. I still remember how frustrated I was during the first week that I worked because I did not know any of the procedures. It took me about a month to learn the bank "jargon" and the many different types of transactions. Now I do things automatically without much thought, but I still must remember many things. Possibly the biggest responsibility I have is being in charge of so much money. At first, counting out $100 seemed phenomenal. Now, I do not even think twice about counting $1,000. The most stressful part of the job is counting down my drawer at the end of the day. This is when I find out if I gave someone too much or not enough money. I have been off a few times, but not by too much.

Through my job I have also learned how to better relate to people. I have to get along with many different people, or at least pretend to, whether they are supervisors, coworkers, older people, college students, or customers. There will always be people that I do not particularly like or have anything in common with, but part of life is learning to get along with people in order to make things easier for everyone. I have been amazed at how rude or mean some customers are; however, I feel that the friendly customers make up for the terrible ones.

Working has affected me in some very personal ways as well. It is nice to know that I can be successful at something besides academics and music. During the first job review my supervisor complimented me for having initiative and for being responsible, prompt, personable, and trustworthy. My experience has made me more self-confident, friendly, straightforward, and assertive. At work I can be whomever I want to be, regardless of the fact that I might have changed a little within even 1 year.

The negative effects of my working have been that my schoolwork has suffered because of it; however, other factors have also caused this decline. Obviously, the time that I am working is time that I could be spending doing homework. In addition, work-related stress and fatigue decrease my ability and desire to study even after I return home. For example, I usually come home from work around 7:00 p.m., but by the time I have eaten dinner and feel refreshed enough to study it is around 8:00 or 8:30. In addition, this year I have had not only homework, but also private music lessons, school music rehearsals, and numerous college and scholarship applications to complete in my "spare time." I suppose I could quit my job, but I do like it, and it is a guaranteed job for me when I come back from college for the summer.

Overall, working has been a very positive experience for me. School is no longer my main focus, a fact that has caused some difficulties, but I am learning to keep things in perspective. To me, the personal growth that I have had outweighs the negative effects of having a job. In that respect, I feel much better prepared for college than if I had spent my senior year at my desk studying and filling out college applications.

Work and Teen Behavior
by Jim M. Clifford

"Eventually, on work days, I became so physically drained from the combination of work and school, I'd forget completely about homework."

Jim Clifford is an honor student and senior at Weberville High School. In the community, he is involved with the local park district. When not writing papers, Jim enjoys "messing with" electrical equipment. Jim plans to attend the University of Illinois at Chicago in the fall.

Working affects student performance and attitude. Most students have a part-time job for some of the year. For the most part, the students, as part-time workers, labor about 3 days a week. The added responsibilities of work can increase stress on students who already have very little time for recreation. Students of course are willing to cope with the additional burden of work because it provides auxiliary money for personal use, for college, or for whatever else they see fit. In my opinion, the problem originates when people are given more hours to work by their employer than they want. Even if a student is not granted many hours of work, it might provoke problems if he [or she] already spends many hours on sports or other activities. This is in addition to the stress parents can add concerning grades. In general, parents want their kids to earn extra money themselves for college and other expenses. However, when pressure for adequate grades is combined with pressure to work, problems can develop. These pressures can cause students to somewhat compromise grades for more money. When this occurs, jobs become more of a hindrance than a help. From the added constant pressures, a student's attitude and actions may be affected in certain ways. Students may become bossy and more easily irritated. In most cases, added work hours will likely affect the student's energy level. These students can be identified in a few ways. Late working hours may contribute to a student being late for school. These students may sometimes be found sleeping in class.

My first experience working was when I delivered papers. This job paid good money, but it had its drawbacks. I could not call in sick if I could not work. The job required that papers be delivered every day of the week. This meant I had to work every holiday. Because the papers need to be delivered extremely early in the morning, I needed to go to bed very early, often missing a favorite TV show or other night activity. Because the job became too demanding, I waited until I could find a regular part-time job. When my 16th birthday came around I applied to many places. I finally landed a part-time job at Jewel Food Stores. At first I was given about 16 hours a week. This is what I wanted. Because I stated I was available to close the store, I did just that. They scheduled me to close about 3 nights a week and, in addition, 2 nights each weekend. These hours made it harder for me to do homework. I got frustrated more easily. In general I was in a bad mood on days I had to work. This pattern of behavior continued until I was promoted to a different department. In this new department I was given 16 or fewer hours a week. My behavior returned to normal as my hours were re-duced.

The school I attend is considered excellent for academic achieve-ment. When it comes to academics, the competition is great. There is a lot of pressure to go to college. Because many parents do not have enough money to pay all costs of college for all kids in the family, many students get jobs to help pay for college and their personal needs.

The real question is how do jobs affect student performance. Al-though it does not happen overnight, some students fall behind in their studies. At first, students are able to handle the combined respon-sibilities of school and work. Eventually, it becomes more difficult to catch up on homework due to the decreased amount of time available for studies.

Working also affects a student's physical well-being. Jobs can drain one of energy. The added stress can age one faster. When students are overworked they tend to sleep in classes more often than nonworking students. Not too long ago, I saw a student actually sleeping on the floor. He told me that he works more than 30 hours a week and has al-most no time outside of school for homework. Since that day, on a few other occasions, he again has fallen asleep on the floor.

Less obvious is the subtle effect working has on a student's attitude. Some kids become bossier and more frustrated. Being overworked causes extra stress, which in turn causes gradual changes in attitude. In my case, especially on days I had to work, I became more demanding and bossy. Not only did it make me more easily frustrated and irritable, it caused me to get depressed. I would find myself working harder at work and less at schoolwork. Eventually, school became the place I rested from work. It became harder and harder to do homework late at night when I got home from work. After a while, I did just enough to get B's. This was not difficult considering that I had only a couple of ac-celerated classes.

Given a choice between working more hours and writing a quality paper, students will generally choose more hours and a poor job on the paper. Obviously this new desire for money can cause grades to suffer. At a certain point, the student, if he [or she] has any free time, may sac-rifice that for work, as well.

In my case, I got to the point where I made good money, but I started to hate work more and more. One reason was that I had only 1 hour be-tween work and school. When I would finally come home from work, it was about 11:00 p.m. At first, I did homework when I got home from work. Eventually, on work days, I became so physically drained from the combination of work and school, I'd forget completely about home-work. Under these circumstances, Jewel scheduled me to work 3 school days and loaded my weekends with working hours. Gradually, work became something I hated with a passion. Even though I had plenty of money, I had very little time to spend it. Actually, I did not care any more.

I am not the only one who has this problem. Many of the high school students who work at Jewel at first want more hours. Some of those students who work allow their grades to suffer. At work, I noticed something interesting. Most of the students say that they will not keep Jewel as their job. The smarter workers at Jewel usually tend to quit if they are scheduled too many hours or if their grades start to fall. The rest of the part-time workers, those who usually end up going to the local community college, keep their jobs at Jewel. Lucky enough for me, I got promoted. Promotion for me was being scheduled fewer hours.

Not all of the effects of working were bad. It provided me with extra money so I did not need to ask my parents for money anymore. The successes I had at my job gave me confidence that I could handle the responsibilities of a job. I have kept the job for more than 1 year. This accomplishment has proven to me that I can hold a job. Most of all, I learned to have pride in work I did well, whether or not I got compliments.

In summary, if a student is overworked, the effect on his or her attitude and performance tends to be negative. This leads to less student effort. The student may become depressed or easily irritated due to increased stress. On the other hand, if a balance between work and school is maintained, work can be a positive experience. The student can learn to have pride in his or her work. If the job is a good one, it can provide much needed money for college. If work is not too demanding or time-consuming, it might be a valuable learning experience for students.

Working Full-Time and Going to School Full-Time
by Bobby B. Roberts

"If working full-time seems hard, try working full-time and going to school full-time. There's nothing rewarding about it."

Bobby B. Roberts is a senior at Weberville High School, where he is a starter on the varsity Scholastic Bowl team, an all-subject academic competition. Bobby is involved in the Boy Scouts of America and is an Eagle Scout. When Bobby is not at school he works, works at a second job, and on weekends, works at a third job. Bobby plans to attend Northern Illinois University.

I have chosen the topic of students and work. It is important to me. This is not, like so many others, just some stupid writing assignment. This writing allows me to express my feelings and explain, in an intelligent and possibly satirical way, my life. I feel a need to explain how I have been living for the past 2 years. I have been going to high school full-time and working full-time, and it has taken its toll.

Although I have been working since the age of 10, I have been working full-time only since last year. In addition to school, occasionally I work more than 50 hours a week. On the average, I usually work about 40 hours a week.

My life these past 2 years seems scripted and acted out in four basic settings. The first is my school, an attractive school with seemingly caring teachers in a relatively affluent suburb northwest of Chicago. The second is the bowling alley at which I have the honor of being employed. On the average, I work there about 30 to 35 hours a week. There are two other places worth mentioning. One is a computer networking company where I work some weekends. This job gives new meaning to "weekends free." I usually work there from 8 hours to 20 hours a month. Then there is a farm at which I am employed other weekends. I work there most Saturdays or Sundays. In all fairness, I must say that these are fine places of employment and everyone treats me with respect.

If working full-time seems hard, try working full-time and going to school full-time. There's nothing rewarding about it except learning what could possibly happen to a person who doesn't get a proper education. I have seen many things that have saddened me and made me think about the future. In this respect I cannot say enough as to how work has actually given me incentive to aim high. My original reason for working was to save money for college. Before this could happen, however, I was dealt a lightning bolt from fate. You see, my father decided to get a little violent and was ejected from family matters. Strangely enough, we didn't receive any money from him until a jail cell persuaded him. During these 4 or 5 months, my mother had to deal with more than $1,000 each month in mortgage payments alone. My mom wasn't making enough as a waitress, and our house was going to be taken away. I did what anyone else would have done, and decided to help my family. I paid off the mortgage for about 5 months until we were able to sell the house. I am now in the process of saving for college and helping my mom pay bills.

Working full-time and going to school is hell on one's social life. I know because I lost my social life during sophomore year. I have no friends, except my team members on Scholastic Bowl, the school's interscholastic academic competition. All the rest are just acquaintances from the years when from I participated in extracurricular activities. So much for high school being the best years of one's life. I feel that I have been cheated out of the best years of my life. The physical strain is finally getting to me. Averaging 4 to 5 hours of sleep a day isn't exactly what health officials recommend. Sometimes I'm so tired, blowing off homework assignments doesn't really bother me. I've started to become a real professional at it, which is why I realize that I must take a break for a few months and start to become the student teachers once respected. Besides the presence of physical strain, there is also the mental strain that has come about due to my work habits. I have lost the ability to successfully fight off disease. Until the beginning of my junior year, I had a perfect attendance record. In the last 3 weeks, I've missed an entire week. Another example of my mental strain would be that I am unable to think in a clear manner.

All I can say is there is a tremendous effect on all students who make the decision to work full-time and attend high school full-time. There seems to be a strange feeling of disillusionment among us. We don't seem to receive very good grades and what we turn in is far from quality work. I hope this writing is an exception to the rule in that I have done my personal best.

However one looks at this issue, one can find advantages and disadvantages. No doubt benefits are received by holding down a full-time job; however, the effects on one's academic accomplishments are clearly detrimental. The proponents of work say lessons learned in the workplace teach vital skills such as responsibility and the ability to handle pressures of the real world. In the end, the balance of advantages and disadvantages must be weighed by each person. Are immediate financial gains more important than one's high school grades?

Well it's late, so much for my goal of 5 hours of sleep. If after I hand this in I doze off, at least you'll better understand. It's not your class; it's my life.

5

The Student Reality: The Family Hour

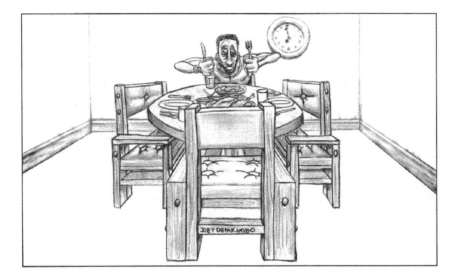

According to Geoffrey T. Holtz's *Welcome to the Jungle* (1995, p. 27), the incidence of divorce dramatically increased from 375,000 in 1961 to almost 1,200,000 in 1985. In addition, a 1988 survey by the National Center for Health Statistics found that students in single-parent families are two to three times as likely to have emotional and behavioral problems as those living with both parents. Despite these staggering statistics, schools have done little to accommodate students dealing with divorce.

Erics and Romanenghi passionately explain the effects of divorce on both their lives and their schoolwork. For Erics, overwhelming emotions prevented her from concentrating on assignments. Unable to find an emotional outlet, she became hypersensitive and looked at school as an inconvenience. Romanenghi explains that the emotional toll of her parents' divorce led elementary school teachers to believe she had a behavioral disorder. As a result, she was put in a class of children with emotional or behavioral problems and suffered from isolation. Educators must keep in mind that the decisions they make daily can have lifelong consequences for students.

Teachers and administrators must recognize signs of distress in students and make appropriate accommodations. For example, a concerned teacher might identify a decrease in the quality of a student's work, probe the source of the problem (as an instructor did in Erics' case), and lead the student to a social worker and the understanding that he or she is not alone.

Furthermore, teachers must recognize that all problems are not necessarily discipline problems. Romanenghi needed the help of a counselor or social worker, not removal from the class in which she belonged. Administrators and teachers need to better understand divorce and its effect on students.

Klein, Kurtz, Gribbon, and Ahmed discuss other vital issues confronting today's students. Parental alcoholism affects many young people. Klein and Gribbon explain that a problem of this severity cannot simply be left at home. The trauma of an alcoholic parent permeates every relationship, homework assignment, and group affiliation. As a result, the student becomes divided between a loyalty to that parent and the desire to break away from the problem. Similarly, Kurtz examines the pervasive influence of strict authoritarian parenting on a student's social life at school. The inflexibility of his parents dominates his thoughts and concentration on schoolwork becomes impossible. Finally, Ahmed discusses the interdependence between religion, family, and the student. For her, the strength of Islam and her family have provided a strong foundation for a quality education.

Teachers and administrators must be willing to incorporate many voices into the curriculum and daily classwork. For example, a serious discussion of alcoholism in a health course can lead to understanding for both the alcoholic's child and his or her peers. A sociology course may examine the various styles of parenting and the pros and cons of each. Religious discussions should include not only Christianity but also Judaism, Islam, Buddhism, atheism, and other theological approaches. Simply put, school must be made relevant to the reality of today's student. Schools must decide if they want to confront today's issues or shrug them aside. It is a convenient cop-out to long nostalgically for the family values of yesteryear on a Sunday morning news show. This may score political points, but unfortunately accomplishes little else. A serious debate about family values will occur only when teachers, administrators, parents, and politicians decide to view and listen to reality from their students rather than from their television set.

When Parents Divorce
by Elisabeth Erics

"My way of dealing with the divorce was to worry constantly about everything. I became very easily upset and developed every sign of depression. I started to give up all hope of ever being happy again. School became boring and more of an annoyance than anything else. I hardly ever completed assignments."

Elizabeth Erics is a senior at Weberville High School, where she has been involved in business technology, dance, speech team, and varsity softball all 4 years. Elizabeth received the honors of State Scholar, National Merit Commendation, and mention in Who's Who in High School. *Elizabeth plans to attend Northern Illinois University and study psychology. When not doing something else, Elizabeth is definitely reading.*

A divorce is difficult for all sides involved. Not only is the couple divorcing affected, but their children are also hurt. Divorce has a profound effect on the children regardless of their age. In high school, there are a lot of pressures put on the student: schoolwork, extracurricular activities, and a job. Students need all of their energy just to get through the day. When faced with the additional pressures of a divorce, lives are turned upside-down. No one can really realize how depressed one may feel. Teachers, especially, have a hard time realizing why students can't get work done. The intention of my paper is to help others realize exactly what a person goes through when his or her parents divorce. Also, I want to help people whose parents are divorced.

The basis I have for writing this paper is simple. My parents are in the middle of a divorce. This is not an easy divorce, because both sides are fighting for every inch they can get. A lot of time has passed since I first found out about my parents' divorce. After I learned about this, I did not want to do homework, I did not care about my grades, and I especially was not looking toward the future. Most teachers did not know what was to become of me or how to deal with my change in attitude. My friends didn't even know what to say to me. Now, however, I have learned how to deal a little better with my parents' divorce. I have learned how to tell my friends what is wrong and how I am feeling. Unfortunately, teachers still have a hard time realizing what happens to a student who is going through what I've gone through. I'm writing this paper to show adults and teachers what happens to students when their parents divorce.

It is said that one out of every three marriages ends in divorce. Divorce does not discriminate by color, race, income, or intelligence. This means that no matter how rich or intelligent a person is, they can still feel the effects of a break-up between parents. My family is a typical white, middle-class, and fairly intelligent household living in the suburbs of Chicago. It consists of my mother, my father, my younger sister, and me. Both my sister and I are involved in many activities in school. My parents both have decent, well-paying jobs. In all ways, we appear to be a typical family. Unfortunately, looks can be deceiving. Divorce has affected all our lives in many ways. Being "not poor" did not guarantee us "a perfect life." Instead, we learned the hard way. Divorce is an awful and cruel thing.

Most students favor one parent over the other. They might see one parent as the bad guy, and the other as their "best friend." It is hard enough to lose the parent who was unfavored. When the parent who was supposed to be your "best friend" betrays them, the hurt is sharply more substantial. My father and I were best friends since I was a little girl. When I learned that it was my father who caused the divorce, I was hurt. It was as if my whole world had fallen apart. A parental figure who meant so much to me had done the very worst he could have. Some students believe that divorce is their fault. This could not be farther from the truth. These students are only trying to protect their parents. It is important to remember that divorce is never the child's fault. It is a result of a problem that cannot be resolved by parents. Regardless of which parent demands the divorce, the children are still alienated by their parents' choice.

When someone first learns of the divorce, the initial reaction is one of disbelief. What could have gone so wrong that a divorce is necessary? For children of divorce, their first question is simply, Why? Their disbelief evolves into anger. How could this happen to me? They want answers. What happened? Can't it be worked out? What will happen to me? All these questions run through their minds. Parents are not ready to answer these questions. Tempers can run short and people get hurt even more. After a long period of great misunderstanding, life settles down; this is where depression begins.

Different people have different ways of dealing with emotions. Some might throw themselves into activities, others may choose to be by themselves. They may read, play an instrument, or even go running. The most important thing on their mind is to feel better about themselves. Some people, however, do not participate in one or more of the activities listed above. These people are very likely to become extremely upset or even depressed. My sister became involved in school and in band. I was not as lucky.

My way of dealing with the divorce was to worry constantly about everything. I became very easily upset and developed every sign of depression. I started to give up all hope of ever being happy again. School became boring and more of an annoyance than anything else. I hardly ever completed assignments. It got to a point where I was really jeopardizing my grades. Then one teacher reached out to help me. Slowly, I became more confident of myself. Still, it took a very long time until I was able to do well in school again.

The biggest problem, however, was not my schoolwork. It was the fact that I couldn't keep my emotions together. I cried often and easily, for no reason at all. Other students and teachers tend to feel uncomfortable and often don't know what to say to someone who is crying. I really couldn't tell them what was wrong because I didn't really know myself. The people who really cared stood by me and helped me. It was very scary not being able to know why I was feeling so sad.

I have had other friends whose parents are divorced. I tried to be there and help them deal with it. When it happened to me, I didn't know what to do. Friends, family, and teachers reached out to me, but I couldn't reach back to them. It was a long and hard process to get where I am today.

If you ever are faced with a student or a friend who is suffering from a parent's divorce, try to be patient with them. Students undergoing a divorce are very confused and scared. I hope that by sharing my experiences, I can help at least one person become aware of this situation.

Mislabeled for a Year
by Taryn Romanenghi

"In the second grade I was put in a class of all boys who had emotional or behavioral problems. I found myself even more alone because there were no other girls in the class with whom I could be friends."

Taryn Romanenghi is a senior at Weberville High School, where she is involved in tennis. College plans include the local community college and a major in elementary education. When she is not in class, Taryn is serving pizzas and entertaining kids at Chuck E. Cheese.

Divorce isn't easy for anyone to go through. It doesn't matter if you are 6 years old or 20 when your parents divorce. The feelings are the same: sadness, hurt, fear, and confusion.

Not only do the parents suffer through a divorce but the kids do also. A first reaction of the parents might be, "Oh my gosh, who is going to get the house or the car," or whatever their financial concerns are, with no thought to the child's feelings.

The child has to learn to accept the fact that there may be some form of separation from one of the parents. It's a good thing to talk to the child about what's happening before it really happens. This way the child can get a better understanding of the changes that are going to take place.

The reason for choosing this topic is that my parents got a divorce. It affected my education. I was 6 years old and in the first grade. It was very difficult for me to understand at first because of my age, but my parents sat down with me and talked about it before they actually separated. Being an only child, I felt really alone because I didn't have anyone to share my feelings or concerns.

It seems that nowadays kids' families include more stepmothers and stepfathers than natural parents. In a survey done in my family living class last year, out of 14 students only 7 lived with their natural parents. One of the students from that class was adopted. Some of the students said that their mom or dad started to date right after the divorce and they didn't like that. Maybe the parents feel that they really need someone during this difficult time, but what the kids need is attention from their parents, not a relationship shared by an outsider.

After my parents got a divorce we became a one-income family and my mom had to work. During the summer I went over to a friend's house and spent most of the day over there playing. At times it was hard because they had this big family and a father that would come home and eat dinner with them. That may sound kind of weird, but to me it meant a lot.

It was difficult for me to spend a certain amount of time with one parent and all the other time with the other one. In some cases a family may feel that it is better to live in the same school district so the child can live with one parent for 6 months and the other parent for 6 months. I personally don't agree with this because then the child doesn't have a steady home. When my parents first got a divorce I spent every Saturday afternoon with my dad. When I became older I stayed the night every other weekend. Once I got into high school I didn't stay overnight because of my busy schedule, but I would frequently go out to dinner with him and his girlfriend.

I remember a show on TV I saw about a 9-year-old girl whose parents got a divorce and remarried. The little girl lived with her mom and stepfather. She would see her father and stepmother on the weekends. Her natural mother and father really didn't get along with each other. They would never talk, and if they had something to say they would have the daughter talk for them. The parents had no idea what they were doing to the child. What they should have known was how they were hurting her because they wanted to hurt each other.

The difficulties of divorce can be very hard for the child. When the child finds out her parents are getting a divorce she may think it is her fault. Although this doesn't happen with all kids, it is very traumatic when it does. The child may feel that she was bad, that she should have made it easier on the parents and should have done everything they asked.

Sometimes divorce can affect the child's learning. When my parents got a divorce I was having trouble in school. First-grade tests did not show I might have a learning disability. The principal of the school and my first-grade teacher learned my parents were getting a divorce. They assumed that the divorce was causing the learning difficulties. It was recommended to my parents that I be placed in a behavioral class for the second grade. In the second grade I was put in a class of all boys who had emotional or behavioral problems. I found myself even more alone because there were no other girls in the class with whom I could be friends. In the middle of the second grade, my teacher told my mother he did not understand why I was put in his behavioral class. By the end of the second grade it was decided that I should be placed in a learning disability class. This is an example of how false judgments can be made during a divorce and how it affects the child.

My mom and I saw a psychologist every week during the summer my dad left. Sometimes we talked to the counselor together but mostly individually. I also attended a church-sponsored program called "Rainbows Children." This group was for children of divorced parents, and we were able to share our feelings with each other.

There are many things that family members can do to help each other in a divorce. One of the best is to keep communication open where the child is concerned. Another way is to not put your child in the middle by having him or her be the spokesperson for both parents. If necessary, seek outside counseling.

The first few years of my parents' divorce were the most difficult because of the hurt and anger they both felt toward each other. It has become easier for me because my parents are now able to talk to each other where I'm concerned. Birthdays and special family occasions are celebrated together.

Parental Alcoholism: A Teen's Perspective
by Katherine Klein

"At school, however, I was able to disguise my hurting behind many extracurricular diversions, such as sports, romantic relations, and most importantly my peer counseling group."

Katherine Klein graduated from Weberville High School in 1990 after an amazing high school career. She was a peer counselor in the PEER program helping fellow teens, played 4 years of varsity soccer, and excelled in the classroom. Katherine attended the University of Notre Dame as a psychology major and member of the women's soccer team. She is now completing a Master's in social work at the University of Chicago.

The trauma of living with an alcoholic parent does not begin when the first sip is taken and end when the last bottle is drained. In fact, the real tragedy is the pain of everyday life, watching a parent disregard pleas from the family to stop abusing himself and continually doing so despite knowledge of the sadness and frustration he creates. It is always the same at my house—a glass of wine after work to "calm the nerves," then a little with dinner, and soon after that the popping of cork after cork, together with the increasing number of bumps and bangs that thunder throughout the house awaken me regularly to the nightmare of my father's addiction. It took me about 5 years to realize his obvious dependence on the drug and just now, 5 years later, am I able to understand the effects of the confusion, anger, and deep-seated pain he inflicted upon me and other family members. However, these unsorted feelings throughout high school, during a time when I felt inferiority under the fury of my father's bad temper, coupled with my feeling of being trapped in a very conflictual household, often made me doubt myself. Moreover, it had a profound influence on our father-daughter relationship, not only during his drunken bouts, but more detrimentally during his state of sobriety.

The basis for this writing rests on the transition in thought that I experienced during my high school years that made way for my understanding of the emotional distance created between my father and the family. In my first 2 years in high school, I breathed easy coming home late at night and seeing my father in an incoherent state because I knew he would not be in a mood to argue, let alone remember the events of the latter half of the evening the following morning. But in the final years of high school, I came to associate nights of late and heavy drinking with early-morning shouting matches between my parents, inconsiderate and unfounded remarks toward my sister and me, and an incurable nervous feeling inside me for fear of his unpredictable mood. The tranquility of the prior evening inevitably created irritableness within my father, who then directed hurtful words toward my mother, sister, and me and made it unbearable for us to be close to him, both physically and emotionally. And although he could later come home from work, having recovered from a hangover throughout the day, and carry no grudges from that morning's dispute with the family, it was impossible for us to simply forget his biting words.

The relatively small three-bedroom house has further contributed to conflictual familial relationships resulting from my father's alcohol dependence because we were forced to witness the progress of the destructive disease. When the upstairs living room light was still on at the time when my sister and I came home at night, it became the unmistakable indicator that the glass of wine with dinner had become a bottle, which had become many bottles. The ashtray and surrounding table space was full of butts, drops of wine lay scattered across the table with an occasional spill stain on the tablecloth, and his notebook would confess his gradual alcohol-induced loss of control throughout the night as was evident in the illegibility of the latter sentences or paragraphs. Our bedrooms were just down the hallway from this room, and the clanging about from his clumsiness always awakened me. The limited space in our house made it impossible to hide from the hated scenario when he stayed up late to drink, and therefore I, too, would feel the physical effects of his drinking by being awakened late at night, only to face a nervous feeling created out of worry for and anger toward my father.

The father-daughter relationship during high school was plagued with hidden resentment and emotional withdrawal from disclosing to him aspects of my high school life. Our relationship revolved around a vicious circle; it would begin with his staying up late to drink, which chased the family away from him in the evenings because we did not want to watch the physical and mental dissipation, followed by morning hangovers and the subsequent use of the family as a scapegoat for his irritableness. This led to my blaming myself for upsetting him, in addition to despising him for so angrily pointing out his disgust in something I had done, followed by my not being able to count on his genuine interest in my life at the time because of his unpredictable mood swings. The fact that my sister and I did not come to him with personal problems upset him further, which resulted in familial isolation and encouraged his drinking.

The resentment came about because I often felt that my father chose alcohol over interest in my life. During the first half of high school, as previously mentioned, I was comforted coming home late to see him drinking because he often inquired about my personal affairs and expressed concern. It seemed that the only time it was safe to avoid arguments over the personal aspects I could dare share with him was when he swayed in his seat and looked at me with bloodshot eyes. But after a while I realized that although he expressed genuine concern for my well-being at the time, the following day held for me nothing but disappointment. Whereas just earlier he listened intently to me and praised my successes, the next morning he verbally attacked me for not doing well enough academically or not being socially mature enough to participate in activities that on the previous night he agreed to let me do. His memory loss suggested to me at the time that his late-night fixation encouraged a false interest in my life that was lost the next morning to the side of him that had undergone a personality change and had become infected with a need to make us hurt like he was hurting.

The double-sided personality he displayed during those years weighed heavily on my mind and made me feel torn between feeling sorry for and excusing him because his "uninfected " side had good intentions, and blaming and resenting him for allowing alcohol to foster this monstrous dark side. My conscience was torn between feeling bad for excluding him from my personal affairs and reasserting and justifying having distanced myself from him. I justified my withdrawal from him not only on the grounds of self-defense from his temper and violent words but also because I sensed the same distancing from my mother and sister, which reassured me that he, and not I, was to be held responsible for his own misery. In fact, whereas I used to feel guilty for being happy those nights when he was out of town on business, I discovered the painful yet relieving truth that my sister and mother felt the same way. But prior to this knowledge, I remember thinking of myself as disrespectful and ungrateful, probably two false images of myself that I picked up from an early morning verbal rampage.

At school, however, I was able to disguise my hurting behind many extracurricular diversions, such as sports, romantic relations, and most importantly my peer counseling group. I became dependent upon my boyfriend at the time, often walking into his house with tears dripping from my eyes, and used him as an excuse to my parents to be constantly out of the house and away from the fighting. However, my participation as a peer counselor, both running group sessions for younger students and speaking out in sessions for the group leaders themselves, allowed me to put my problems in perspective and helped me to get control of my emotions so that I could absorb myself within other activities and people instead of my own misery.

Through group interaction and encouraging other members to emotionally purge themselves, I learned to channel my frustration and anxiety away from self-despair and invest it, instead, in helping other students cope with their problems. Hearing my peers' overwhelming problems made me realize several things about myself. First, despite having an alcoholic parent, I had a lot of positive factors in my life that some students were not fortunate enough to have. In addition, it forced me to consider that when a student with so many problems can cope with them well enough to leave the group sessions smiling, I could also harden myself to the effects of an uncontrollable and painful issue. Most importantly, though, I realized that my genuine concern for each group member, along with the comfort found in sharing very powerful emotions disclosed in meetings, seemed to ease the suffering of that individual as well as myself. Moreover, I found that making them feel the slightest relief from the weight of their dilemma and knowing that they could breathe a little easier after meetings had that exact same effect on me; the purging of their emotions and my encouraging of further release, in a sense, became my own emotional release, and suddenly counseling was just as cathartic for me as it was for those I counseled.

Since high school, I have discussed with my father the detrimental effects of his addiction on family dynamics, unfortunately usually in the form of shouting battles between the two of us. Being at college helps me deal with the disease; I am not forced to witness it at nights when I come home late, I do not wake up to the drunken clumsiness, and I do not have to hear his furious uproars the following mornings. But I still have to deal with the reality when I come home, with the excuses and denial of anything serious (he can "always stop when he wants to"), with the late-night scene that occurs and recurs despite emotional breakdowns in front of my father, begging him to cut back and seek help. His emotional wall is built, cemented together with years of excuses and resistance to familial concern, and is sealed with anger over the "harassment" he receives for having what he insists is a responsible and controllable amount to drink. But he does not see what I see: the impact of the disease and the truth of addiction. He does not see the loss of control or the threat of physical harm. He does not witness the dozens of times my sister and I have struggled with him at 3:00 a.m. over a set of car keys just before he attempts to drive off or our convincing him to go inside and warm up rather than take a bike ride down the middle of our block or our helping him stagger to his bedroom as he is unable to mutter anything coherent. He does not understand the unfilled gap we feel as a result of not being able to depend on our own father's support or the hatred built up from witnessing the repeated disrespect he displays through verbal abuse toward my mother. He does not realize that my feelings of obligation and devotion toward a man whom I love very much get repeatedly and painfully chipped away every time he subjects himself and us to a drunken stupor. He does not see the detachment from his family in order to "unwind" from a hectic day. He refuses to acknowledge our hurt and the resulting withdrawal from him over an addiction that can be overcome. This, unfortunately, is the reality of living with an alcoholic parent.

Religion, the Family, and the Student
by Sobia N. Ahmed

"From my religion, I have learned that teachers are as much a part of my life as are my parents. Thus they should be treated with the utmost respect at all times. This, to me, makes perfect sense simply because I spend as much time in school as I do at home, if not more."

Sobia Ahmed is a senior at Weberville High School, where she is a member of Amnesty International, Foreign Exchange, and Ecology Club. She is an active member of the local Islamic religious community. Sobia plans to attend Aga Khan University. When not writing papers, she enjoys reading and traveling.

I am a student who strongly believes that my religion, Islam, together with the particular way in which I have been brought up, has had a tremendous role in forming my attitude toward school and education.

My family is not large. It consists of only four people—my parents, a younger sister, and myself. My parents come from a long line of devout Muslims and are themselves deeply religious, highly educated, hardworking. Communication, openness, honesty, sincerity, and respectfulness are key points that have always been stressed in my family and that I have come to value. As a whole, I would describe my family as one that is close-knit.

There are many things that go into forming the personality of an individual. Religion and family are two things that have played a tremendous role in my development as an individual and therefore as a student. It is, in fact, my belief that without the influence of my family and religion, I would be incomplete as a person.

Religion and family, in my opinion, are interdependent. Personality, character, and the development of principles and morals are the essential elements of a person as a whole. Islam has taught me the importance of such things as family, health, and education, while instilling the values of honesty, sincerity, hard work, patience, and diligence. My family has nurtured me, and in so doing, provided me with a sense of belonging and meaning. Religion and family, together, have given me my sense of faith and pride. It is my belief that when we have faith and pride in ourselves, we work harder to achieve our goals in life while exercising our rights honestly in all walks of life.

The learning experience, I believe, begins in the home. For instance, I have always been told by my parents never to give up under frustration. "Those who ultimately succeed are the ones who accept the challenge and work with a vengeance to achieve their life's ambitions" is a motto that I have grown up with. I can vividly remember the countless times that I have gone to my parents, literally in tears, when more than anything, all I wanted was to give up something that I was finding difficult and instead take up something easier. Advanced placement physics for some reason stands out in my memory. This saying, taught to me by my parents, has always helped me get back my determination when I felt frustrated and ready to give up. This saying, as I learned some time ago, was taken almost directly from the Quran, the Islamic Holy Book. It is evident, therefore, that my parents have used Islam as their main source of guidance. They have always applied the teachings of Islam in our everyday life.

Though my parents believe that exercising independence is a necessary part of growing up, they have not brought me up to be completely and totally self-reliant or liberated. I can remember just last year when I argued with my mother when she refused to let me take public transportation and go to the city. My reasoning was that I was old enough and that I should know such things as learning how to use the subway.

I later saw the right in my parents' reasoning. They believed that such things would be taught to me when need and time came and also that I should not rely totally on myself because, according to Islam, it is the duty of parents to provide their children with an adequate living and education and to inculcate in their children proper manners and discipline. I no longer envy those friends of mine who were allowed to travel to the city by themselves.

I have also been taught that shortcuts do not always provide the best of solutions and that I must try all possibilities and, in so doing, open up for myself more options. In addition, my parents have always stressed the acceptance of responsibility—in the sense that I should not look to them for sympathy, though they will always be there when I need them. Instead, I must face facts that may be realities of life, fears, or my own responsibilities. Also, it has been ingrained in me to do the best that I can at whatever I have to do, and only after I have done my best should I be satisfied with myself.

My religion has also taught me the importance of health. Health, above all, is the greatest blessing of God to humankind. Though my parents are not very keen on exercise, they do believe in exercising moderation in our eating habits, and almost everything else. I, on the other hand, love exercise. I find that it helps me to clear my head. It is my opinion that one must be in good physical health if one is to achieve his or her goals in life. Good health rewards a person with endurance. Take the college entrance exams, for instance: Without proper nourishment, a student lessens his or her chances of doing well. A person who is healthy will probably do better simply because, physically and mentally, his or her span of endurance has been augmented by proper nourishment.

My upbringing has also influenced me in the way that I look toward my teachers. From my religion, I have learned that teachers are as much a part of my life as are my parents. Thus they should be treated with the utmost respect at all times. This, to me, makes perfect sense simply because I spend as much time in school as I do at home, if not more, and so why should my teachers not exercise as many rights over me as do my parents?

My parents have also stressed such things as soft-spokenness and gentleness. My religion teaches me that these two qualities will always help me to achieve better results than if I were to resort to raising my voice and yelling. I believe that these two qualities, in particular, are things that my friends, classmates, and teachers alike appreciate most in me. In addition, I have been taught that I should never keep myself secluded, but instead, to explore everything, and in so doing, lead myself away from narrow-mindedness, discrimination, and prejudice. It is because of these things that I have always been able to make friends easily with people of various ages, races, and backgrounds. The ability to make friends easily is essential in the learning experience.

As stated in the beginning, the personality of an individual plays a key role in a person's attitude toward school and therefore education. My personality is a direct result of the way in which my religion and family have influenced me. I have developed for myself three main principles. These principles will probably grow in number as I grow older. My principles are:

1. To always keep my word of honor, I should never make promises that I cannot or do not intend to implement.
2. To value honesty and truthfulness in myself as well as in other people. Though I cannot say that I have never lied, I can honestly say that whenever I have, my conscience has never let me rest until I have gone back and told the truth.
3. Wealth is a clean conscience, good health, and happiness, not just of myself but of everyone around me and for all those for whom I care.

Someone once said, "O wealth you are not God yet but, by God, you provide every human convenience and protection to personality against all evil deeds." In so saying, this person has summed up my views of wealth.

These values that I have learned have a great effect on my attitude toward school. I am not a model Muslim, as I'd be the first to tell; nonetheless, I treasure my values. Such values, and not intelligence alone, have kept me on the honors track. It can be said, in conclusion, that my personality is a by-product of my upbringing. Who I am has been defined by religion and family. As I stated earlier, the learning experience begins in the home, and what we learn in our homes we use throughout our life. It is my belief also that it is because of the absence of sound values inculcated in childhood that so many families now face the problems of drug abuse and teenage pregnancies.

Values are essential in life. My own motivation to do well in school and to succeed comes from what I have learned and continue to learn from my religion, family, and from my teachers.

The Effects of Authoritarian Parenting
by Dan Kurtz

"Even though my parents now will let me go out, it's too late to join a clique."

Dan Kurtz is a senior at Weberville High School. He plans to attend college, double major in computer science and business, and have his own consulting firm after he graduates.

I am writing this paper based on personal experiences only. I have 17 years of experience. I feel like I've been locked up for every one of those years.

My parents rule my house, and I have nothing to do with any decisions made concerning my life. If I try to argue a rule, I am told, "Shut up! This is none of your business!" A few years ago, I wanted to grow my hair long in the back. This seemed like no big deal to me. My parents wouldn't hear of it. That was when I was in eighth grade. That same year, I wanted to pierce my ear. Again, no big deal. Wrong. It didn't matter to my parents how much I wanted either of these things, I could not have them.

When I started high school, my friends were going out on weekends to parties and the like. I asked my parents if I could go, too. Of course they said no. They said there was no reason in hell why I had to go to some stupid party. They never let me do anything. I may sound like just another teenage brat complaining about his parents, but believe me, this is quite a different matter. My parents would not let me go to Great America with my friends for some stupid reason. You'd think they'd run out of "stupid reasons." No such luck.

For every action, there is a reaction. Where there is a will, there is a way. Well, I found a way to have fun without my parents knowing. I started to use marijuana. That way, I wouldn't have to go out to have fun. When I got home from school, I rolled a joint and smoked it before my parents got home. I had fun just sitting in my room.

Finally, during my junior year, my parents let me go out to a mall to see a movie or go to an arcade, but I had to be home before 10 o'clock. I was 16 years old. I had to be home by 10 o'clock! Ten o'clock! Ten o'clock was ridiculous.

Well, lately, things are a little better. For the past 2 weeks, my parents seem to have changed from an authoritarian style to one that is a little more democratic. They finally decided I needed to get out once in a while. Perhaps they finally realized that all other people my age go out on weekends.

Authoritarian parenting can have many negative effects on teenagers. For example, people in certain cliques may go out together. If your parents are authoritarian, chances are you can't go out. It's hard to have friends and be part of a clique if you can never go out with them. The result is very few friends.

This authoritarian parenting style can also cause teenagers to feel inferior to others. The reason for this is that on a Friday, the teenager might hear his peers talking about what they are going to do over the weekend. The teenager would feel like the others are better than he is because they go out on weekends and he doesn't. I know it bothers me very much to hear people talk about what they're doing on the weekend.

Even though my parents now will let me go out, it's too late to join a clique.

Authoritarian parenting can affect a teenager's performance in school. I know, when I ask my parents if I can do something and they say no, it makes me mad. Then, when I go to school the next day, all I think about is my jerk parents trying to control my every move. I don't hear a word the teacher says.

Among other negative effects authoritarian parenting has on teenagers is the dangerous behavior it can lead to. For example, sometimes when I'm driving, I think because my parents can't see me now, I might as well have some fun. One example of fun is flooring the gas pedal and flying down the road at 110 miles per hour, going all the way from one large mall to another in under three minutes, never stopping to think about the danger. When I did this, I remember thinking, "That's one thing I can do to have fun without my parents telling me not to." I remember thinking, "Hah hah, my parents can't stop me from doing this!"

Well, I hope you can see, authoritarian parenting has many disadvantages. It can really screw a person up. Just imagine what a person brought up in such an authoritarian family could do once the kid moves out of the house. It will be like letting an animal out of a cage after 18 long years.

Why Teenagers Don't Give a Damn
by J.T. Gribbon

"Believe me, when only three people go looking for a person who is on a suicide run, it gets very scary."

J.T. Gribbon is a senior at Weberville High School. Formerly diagnosed as learning-disabled as a slow processor, J.T. demonstrates that such a disability has not affected his talent for conveying a strong message with powerful stopping power from which all can learn. Out of school he plays in several types of bands, mostly "death metal." He is active in church and the church group LIFT (Living in Faith Together). In the fall he will attend Northland College in Ashland, Wisconsin and study wildlife management. When not writing for the school's social science magazine, J.T. is writing poems or songs for his bands. He enjoys "listening to groups from classical music all the way up to death metal." One of his many jobs has included hanging billboards by the highway.

I want to tell you why teenagers don't give a damn.

People, or should I say kids in school, have enough stress built up inside of them that they sometimes think they are going to explode. It might be because of their teachers or their friends that they hang around with. It could also be what is going on at home. A lot of kids get into trouble (just like me) because our grades aren't good enough or they aren't up to our parents' standards. In school, we not only have to worry about the way we act in class, but also the way that other people perceive us. Do you get my drift? So now you have to worry about your reputation, the other bullies or gang-bangers, and your grades. And sometimes (or should I say a lot of times) this just causes too much stress and we plain and simple give up. Some people just don't understand why we give up, but for others it is easy to see. Some kids, including myself, just cannot take this and we get to the point where we don't care if we pass or fail.

But even outside of school there is so much stress on us. We have to make some kind of money either to allow us to get a higher education or to blow off and just have some fun with. For some it might be drugs while for others it might be that new car stereo that they have wanted.

We also have a lot of other problems. I have a lot of problems at home, but I can imagine so does every other teenager. I can't always do what my parents are telling me to do, like what is wrong to do and what is right to do, or like having to spend so many hours with them a week. I mean, you can't possibly tell your parents everything that is going on because they can't help you with a lot of these problems. I am not saying that I keep things away from my parents, but all these little things cause more and more stress, to the point where you are ready to explode.

Little things like these sometimes leave us with more stress than what an adult can handle, and we're only kids. Think about it for a second: teen suicide, drugs, sex, abortion, depression, giving up on something (religion, because something went wrong), divorced parents, and the list goes on and on. How many teenagers do you know who have been through at least one of these things?

Example 1: I have a friend who is in my church group. The group is called LIFT, which stands for Living in Faith Together. Well, this friend, his name is Tom, was getting ready to go to college. His parents did not get along at all. His older brother sold pot and acid. Tom got so heavily addicted to these drugs that he started not hanging around his friends anymore. He started to completely isolate himself in this fake world. This is what messed up the band we were in together. He got so much into this stuff that at the time we thought he was on a suicide run. Believe me, when only three people go looking for a person who is on a suicide run, it gets very scary. Those three people were Mike, Chris, and me. The only reason he had gone on a suicide run was that he wasn't remembering all the good memories we've had. Now, does that cause stress!

Example 2: I have a friend. His name is Chris. His parents got divorced when he was a little kid. His dad used to beat him. His mom was an alcoholic. Just recently she was put in the hospital for the third time for cancer. Right now as I type, she is in a hospice dying. Chris and his sister live with a father who does not care about either one of them. Chris is 17. Laura is 12. Their dad does not care if they fall off the end of the world and die. He does not pay for anything. Their grandfather pays for things. I am his best and only brother, if you get my drift. I pay a lot of times for Chris and his sister just so they can get food. Their dad won't even feed them. So you can just imagine the kind of stress he goes through day after day. And I am with both him and his sister every day.

Example 3: I have a friend. Her name is Jenny. She has been pregnant three times and has had an abortion every time. She never believed in God. Her boyfriend walked out on her. And her parents don't even talk to her. She gave up on her faith a long time ago. I have known her for 5 years, and she is probably the best person I have ever met, next to my brother Chris. We just helped her through a major crisis. We finally got her to believe in God. Just recently we got her parents to talk to her. Now everything is just a little better.

Example 4: I just broke up with my girlfriend, Joanne. I went out with her for close to 2 years. Everything seemed to go wrong when I broke up with her. Maybe it was for a good reason. I could not really tell you, but I felt like hell and went through 2 weeks of just the worst feelings. I think everybody knows what I mean.

All of these things increase stress in our life. A teenager's life is not as much fun anymore. It becomes harder and harder as the years go on. It's not like we don't have pressure at all. The only thing that was a problem in the past for kids was the draft. In today's world, we have more stress than they ever had. Sure, a lot of the stuff is the same, but a lot of it is completely different. There are more suicides, mass killings, drugs, and the worst thing about it is that we teenagers are looked down upon as druggies, burn-outs, gang-bangers, and irresponsible. Not many people can see a good side of us. This really hurts us. Give us a chance and you will see a big change in today's youth. So you can see that all this stress is what changes us.

6

The Student Reality: Facing Society

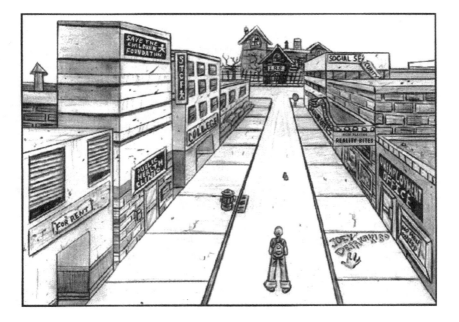

This book has tried to demonstrate that the real lives of today's students are complex and varied. The current generation often struggles with issues such as gay and lesbian pride and awareness, racial equality, and the AIDS epidemic without adequate guidance from school, and they often do so alone. At the same time, traditional adolescent questions of identity and self-actualization become even more confusing. This chapter allows students to illustrate the importance of a wide range of societal issues that demand attention both within and beyond school walls.

Levy and Whitehead expose their searches for individual identity. For Levy, the key to success involves seeking individuality from within through personal excellence in music. Whitehead explores racial issues and their importance in developing a consciousness of race. Whitehead's greatest lesson was "learning" that he was black, an identity he questions as being imposed. Whitehead's difficulty parallels that of many minorities.

Knight and Van Cleave investigate the roles of peer pressure and friendships in their lives. Knight explains that friends can make or break a student's success in high school. Van Cleave questions the sincerity and the meaning of several of his friendships while expressing the disappointment experienced when let down by friends in crucial situations. His disappointment is compounded by teachers who see only what they wish to see.

Panagakis describes his experience as an openly gay student. Despite the support of several close friends, he relates the difficulty in dealing with a constant barrage of vicious, hateful insults from other students. This behavior was especially distressing as it continued in class with the apparent acceptance of his teacher. Teachers need to know that hate leads to self-hate and low self-esteem. Gay- and lesbian-bashing is not only ugly, it is dangerous. Existing school policies must be actively applied to protect gay and lesbian students. The student who taunted Panagakis disrupted class, used profanity, and committed assault.

Lenart, Dean, Curda, and Owen discuss what, until the current generation, may have been described as "adult problems." In an extremely emotional and frank piece, Lenart describes the details surrounding the loss of a close friend to AIDS. She explains that most "unpleasantries" are hidden in Weberville, and her story suggests the need to confront fears, not hide from them. Dean passionately describes what it feels like to almost become a teen parent. His family and friends' reactions create an emotional turmoil greater than the impact of the pregnancy itself. At the same time, Curda's horrible experience as the victim of a stalker suggests that no words may accurately describe the reality of today's teens. Her brave account forces adults to recognize the weight of the issues discussed here. Similarly, Owen expresses the tremendous stress that high school seniors feel. The combination of advanced placement classes, college applications, extracurricular activities, and part-time jobs simply adds up to too much. Although many students appreciate pressure to perform, teachers must know their students well enough to recognize when flexibility and support would be more appropriate.

Bonds emotionally details the difficulty of arriving at a new school during the most celebrated year of schooling. During senior year, students are more likely to end friendships than cultivate new ones. It is a difficult time to join the "in crowd." Students were friendly in class, but no one called her after school, during evenings, on weekends, or during

Christmas vacation. School policy compounded the pain. Bonds, a varsity cheerleader at her former school, was told that because tryouts were peer-judged the prior spring, it was too late for an outsider to join.

Blume discusses the effects of racial tension within high school. Although he expresses genuine concern about the ways minorities have been treated throughout U.S. history and on television, he also questions to what extent minorities have contributed negatively to their social progress. His comments admirably strive to break through racial biases, but he finds this process extremely difficult.

Navarro reminds us of what many take for granted: U.S. citizenship. For as long as Navarro could remember, he thought his parents were overly protective. Only at age 15 did he learn the reason: He was "illegal." Educators need to understand the human dramas (and in some cases war stories) experienced by the many foreign-born students in today's classrooms. Educators should choose to view these students as multicultural resources from which all can learn.

Finally, Watson, Carrubba, and Arshad compare the experience of Weberville High School with other high schools. Watson explains the differences between a predominantly African American grammar school in the inner city of Chicago and a predominantly white school in Weberville. Despite starting off behind his suburban peers in classwork, Watson's difficult though positive transition leads him to believe that a peaceful future between the races can exist. Carrubba identifies the differences between a small school in upstate New York and the larger one in Weberville. Lastly, Arshad explains the economic and technological disparity between Weberville and her former school in Pakistan. The lesson for teachers is clear. Students notice a lot more than we give them credit for.

Due to the wide-reaching nature of the topics in this chapter, it is more difficult here to draw large conclusions than in other sections of this book. However, this alone is a most telling point. Teachers and administrators must recognize the great racial, economic, and social diversity of each new class of high school students. The classroom, while retaining basic curriculum goals, must strive to be as diverse as its students. Each student brings a different reality to the classroom, and teachers should encourage students to share their experiences with fellow classmates. Schools are a human institution that must promote diversity, individuality, and self-respect. An inclusive curriculum will not wallow in relativism as some have feared, but instead will teach young people to respect the realities of the people with whom they will share the larger society. To get there, schools must begin to sincerely consider the student perspective.

Achieving Popular Status: The Realization of the Self
by Eric Levy

*" . . . the key to true fulfillment in high school is finding your own
individuality and displaying excellence in whatever you pursue."*

*Eric Levy graduated from Weberville High School in 1992 and attended North-
ern Illinois University, where he studies music. At Weberville, despite numerous respected varsity teams winning state championships, Eric, a musician
and honor student, was the "big man on campus." He was widely respected by
peers and teachers for his musical talents at percussion and piano and his mod-
est and thought-provoking demeanor. While still in high school, Eric frequently did gigs at jazz clubs in downtown Chicago.*

The structure of high school society is not overly conducive to discovering who you are. Certainly, instructors attempt to ease the process by initiating extracurricular clubs involving such subjects as science, math, and foreign language, which allow students the
opportunity to interact with others who share similar interests and
make career-oriented decisions. The use of these groups, as well as
other educational techniques, does indeed aid the student in nurturing
his or her abilities, but there are immense obstacles that stand in the
way. There is constantly an onrush of pressure coming from parents
and teachers to find the right college, to have one's major decided by
one's junior year, to score well on the ACT, and to keep up one's GPA.

Throughout the midst of the confusion, when most high-schoolers do
not share a strong relationship with their parents, the obvious place to
turn is to their friends. Students feel the best way to determine how to
live their lives is by the example of their peers. For this reason, the social
structure of the common high school has an innate disposition and is
doomed from the start because it places far too much emphasis on following others. It's like the blind leading the blind, and the results destroy
lives daily. Attributes such as being athletic, having good looks, and having charisma are embraced, while strong academic skills and responsibility are overlooked. Why should one believe his or her parents and
instructors, who teach that the student should concentrate on grades,
when doing so will only lead to rejection by classmates? Of course, one
will gladly drink at parties instead of studying if that will lead to acceptance; hence the state of perpetual rebellion in which the student lives,
and his or her constant reasoning, "They just don't understand." True, it is
possible for a rare few to toe the line and find acceptance while achieving academic success, but it's a difficult life to live. After all, how many
valedictorians will you find inebriated with the football team on a Saturday night? Fortunately, I feel that there is a very tangible solution to
this unending circle of tragedy, and it lies in finding one's self. Basi-

cally, this simply means discovering who you are and what strengths you have, then achieving excellence in those areas. I feel that I am living proof of how this process can and does work, and by using my life as an example, I can personally relate the nature of finding one's self.

I feel very lucky always to have been good at whatever I applied myself to, but my main area of focus turned out to be music. My father, who was once a full-time musician, began teaching me piano when I was 5. I loved to play but hated the discipline of reading music and practicing, and always preferred to screw around and try to play melodies that I had heard. My mother worked out a system whereby I would practice for half an hour a day, playing music for my lesson for 25 minutes, and getting 5 minutes of "free time," during which I could play whatever I wanted to. Needless to say, it compelled me to play for much longer than half an hour.

Although I had a great love for music, it was never at the forefront of my life, only something I did with spare time. Throughout junior high, I was avidly involved in computer programming, and I was sure that I would spend the rest of my life doing it. I severely lacked social skills at the time and was perceived by my classmates as being a dork. Like most junior high dorks, I desperately wanted to go to a party, to drink my first beer, and, most importantly, to be accepted. Finally, I got my chance. On a warm summer night during my first few weeks of school, freshman year, I was sitting in my living room practicing when some of my classmates came to the window. I talked with them for a few minutes, then they walked away. My mom told me to let them in, so I went outside to find them. They were walking down to the reservoir, located down my street, and invited me to join them. We got there, and I realized that this was it: a party. All of the most popular freshman were there, along with cases of beer. I didn't really know anyone very well, and as I was completely consumed by the situation, I basically kept to myself.

After everyone had been drinking for a while, a girl who had liked me for years approached and asked me if I wanted to f— her. I was young and scared, and said no, but she was persistent. Meanwhile, others sensed my fear, and started to offer me beer. It was like a movie: I can still vividly remember the crowd of people enveloping me, hearing "Drink this" in one ear, and "Come on, let's f—" in the other. I don't remember how long this lasted, and I don't know why I continually politely said no to everyone, except out of fear. After all, wasn't this what I had been waiting for? Here I thought that good beer and sex with a pretty girl were the answers to life, but when they were handed to me, all I could say was no. Suddenly, an overpowering spotlight hit the concrete, and everyone scattered. It's hard to define the emotions that seared through my mind as I raced through the tall grasses away from the reservoir. Through the confusion, I somehow found the realization that I didn't refuse because I was scared or because I had been told my whole life that drinking and sex are wrong. I refused because I would not allow myself to be pressured into anything, even something I wanted to do, and I then discovered that it was my stubbornness to not conform that had prevented me from being a member of the popular crowd. This was my first big step in the right direction.

Soon after, music seemed to become more and more an active part of my life. I began performing in high school shows, meeting new people through them. My new group of friends was very supportive and encouraged me consistently by feeding my ego and telling me how great I was. It felt good to have a talent that people respected, and the more recognition I received, the more I practiced, and the better I got. Slowly but surely, I became steadily more respected and known by my classmates for my musical achievements. Then, during January of my junior year, I played and sang a song I had written for a few friends. They made me perform it for the school choir director, who asked if he could arrange it for the choir to sing. I said yes, and the repercussions were staggering. The choir performed the piece at their concert in March and after I was done accompanying them, I received a standing ovation from the audience. I had suddenly grown into the status of being a walking, living legend, setting me up for a phenomenal senior year. By the beginning of my 4th year, I had completely evolved into my own individual self. I entered the year wearing a beard and kept it well after I graduated. I was a member of the National Honor Society and I had gained a tremendous amount of respect from all of my classmates. I submitted three of my compositions to a state competition hosted by the Illinois Music Educators Association and placed first in all three categories I entered. This was a major accomplishment in my life, and I gained unimaginable amounts of recognition for it. I was named student of the month by both the National Honor Society and the local newspaper and was awarded a plaque at a district meeting. By this time, I was clearing $100 to $200 a week playing nightclubs on the weekends and my musical career was really taking off. My graduation had a storybook ending, as I composed another piece for the choir to sing at the commencement ceremony. At commencement, I received a standing ovation from my class. I was also voted "most likely to succeed." My hard work in the field of music and my commitment to excellence had obviously paid off. After graduation, I was invited to numerous parties all summer, those same bashes with the same people I had encountered freshman year. Now, instead of trying to test me or pressure me, they would celebrate my presence, shouting "Levy's at my party!" These same jocks and cheerleaders whom I had once longed to be like would crowd around me and beg me to play or to give them tapes of my work. Although I genuinely enjoyed the parties, I still sensed that I was not like these people, nor did I want to be. By being myself I had eventually found the most extreme form of acceptance: respect.

So, the key to true fulfillment in high school is finding your own individuality and displaying excellence in whatever you pursue. I'm now studying music at Northern Illinois University, and the philosophy continues to work. If you really do something well, people will eventually recognize it and respect you for it. You see, in the confusing world of high school, where students can only rely on each other to find answers, it truly is like the blind leading the blind. Only when someone who can really see, one who has found himself, steps into the circle, can the vicious circle have a constructive effect on the life of the high school student.

The Meaning of Black
by Evan Whitehead

"As I approach graduation, I've still not answered these questions: What do white students know after 13 years of school? They don't learn they're white first and a student second, do they? Why is it that we as minorities learn we're black first and student second? Why is this the major lesson we've been taught? Will we ever be measured on an equal scale?"

Evan Whitehead is a senior at Weberville High School. A member of the football team, Evan won a scholarship to attend and play football at Wyoming State University.

I'm going to tell you about the life and times of an African American in a predominantly white affluent school. This is my story.

I'm a young African American male; more specifically, I'm what is considered an "endangered species." There are not many of us who are "about something." This refers to having a higher level of education, having a job, and not being some kind of addict. And one good reason I'm *not* an endangered species is because of my parents. Another reason I'm not "endangered" is because I've seen examples and I am determined not to become one.

The school I attend is in an affluent suburb. But not everyone perceives themselves as affluent. If you talk to minorities, they'll tell you that this is a very affluent community. Most blacks and Hispanics live in apartments, so they sure as hell are not affluent. And the school is relatively a mirror image of the community; its minority population has grown, and they still have a lot of growing to do, but it has come a very long way.

I was not born in the inner-city ghetto. I was born in a predominantly white college town. I was born there because that is where my father attended and graduated from college. And shortly after my birth, my parents moved us back to their hometown, which is 15 miles outside of our state's second largest city. And, remarkably, that's where I first about learned black inner-city life. The city is approximately 30,000 in population and about 25% to 30% black. This is where I witnessed welfare, unemployment, violence, gangs, drugs, and poverty. This was my community until age 5. I didn't realize white people had existed in town. Once, out of innocence, I asked my grandmother where all the white people were. Soon after my 5th birthday, we moved back to the college town.

When we moved back, I experienced my first racial tension. This may have been partly due to previously having been too young to realize racial differences and because there weren't any whites. My first friend was Chris. Chris and I became good friends. It didn't matter that he was white and I was black. The first "different" feelings I had toward white people was when I had to attend a speech class for a lisp. My father was outraged and wanted it cured immediately. As I got older, I realized it just would have given white society an excuse to say blacks are slow or stupid.

My next really big racial issue occurred in the second grade. I was in the "fastest" of the three second-grade classes. As the only black student in the class, I felt the teacher believed I didn't belong. For that reason, my father and my teacher had many conferences regarding my "attitude." "Attitude" is what she termed my challenges to her academic tasks. She tried to disprove my intelligence. Regardless of this I still pulled all A's.

Moving to Weberville where I now live, man, it was a drastic change. I moved from a "liberal" college town to a very conservative community. The first question that was asked of me by a white student was, "You must feel really bad." I asked, "Why is that?" He replied, "Well, because there aren't any black girls for you to date." And that's when I realized how conservative this community was. But up until the eighth grade, I wasn't even attracted to girls that much. Eighth grade was the first time a black girl had been interested in me.

When I decided to try sports in junior high, I was expected to be the great basketball player and great track athlete because I was black. And this was the first sign I had that society and one's school environment instructed me on what it means to be black. Because if a white athlete didn't do something, he wasn't expected to be a super-jock hero before he ever unleashed his skills. And eighth grade was also the year I became interested in the Nation of Islam and the Honorable Elijah Mohammed and Minister Louis Farrakhan. The reason I practice and study Islam is that my father gave me "The Book." By this I mean *The Autobiography of Malcolm X*. This book has opened my eyes ever since.

Once I entered high school, my whole environment changed. There were enough blacks to give me the opportunity to become close to people of my race and enjoy a black social atmosphere. My best friends were now black, and yes, now even my girlfriends were black. And the only time conversations with whites came up were in class, or in a sports atmosphere, but not as weekend enjoyment and social life.

I now heard ignorant comments that were made by white students because they didn't understand "a black thing." But it really didn't bother me as much because now I understood that the reason for most racism and prejudice is ignorance. Now, my new awareness has changed my view of athletics. What is a minority's role in athletics, especially in high school? Are we pawns in a game? Is it because we're heroes to nonminorities in the stands, but as soon as we exit the playing arena, we're just another "nigger" or "spic"? I have learned that I'm a student-athlete to white society, so I must look out for myself first. Our role to society is black first, person second. We do not say, "Oh look, there's a white police officer"—it's just a police officer. Or if there's a doctor available, it's not "oh, a white doctor"—it's just a doctor. But if it's a doctor who happens to be black, they are "black doctors." And do we contribute to the plan by society by acting out what they want to see? Why is it when a student in a black community gets good grades, his peers consider him to be acting white? Why is not getting in trouble considered acting white? And what are we supposed to do as minorities in an affluent white school? As I approach graduation, I've still not answered these questions: What do white students know after 13 years of school? They don't learn they're white first and a student second, do they? Why is it that we as minorities learn we're black first and student second? Why is this the major lesson we've been taught? Will we ever be measured on an equal scale? And finally, when are we blacks going to stop getting sucked into the trap of trying to be black and instead, simply be people, people who can function in society?

Friends Are Vital
by Jessica E. Knight

"In the large social structure that exists within my school, I have discovered the hard way that friends are exceptionally vital to have and difficult to exist without."

Jessica E. Knight is a senior at Weberville High School and involved in choir and Foreign Exchange Club, a club that hosts students from other countries and later visits their new friends overseas. Jessica volunteers at a local hospital and the local library. Jessica plans to attend Southern Illinois University. When not writing papers, Jessica enjoys reading, singing, and modern dance.

In the hectic and demanding life of a high school student, having good, dependable friends is exceptionally important. In addition, friends allow a person to become more sure of themselves and more comfortable around others, a skill necessary in order to succeed in a future career. However, sometimes making friends can be a difficult task if that person lacks the required essentials. In order to make friends, one must be congenial and sociable so that others can get to know them. The problem arises when that person is also timid and frightened of rejection. Overcoming this fear requires a lot of effort, but the end result is assuredly worth it.

All of my life I have been extremely shy, even around people I have known for a long period of time. I never talked all that much unless I was at home with my family, and even there I could often be found sitting in a room by myself reading or playing in silence. In addition to my quiet nature, I have lived my entire life in the same location, and thus have not really ever had to make many new friends. The ones I already had I had grown up with, so when I went to high school and was confronted with so many people I did not know, I was terrified. Nevertheless, I slowly gained companions and they assisted me in acquiring the faith in myself that I needed to make other friends.

Friendships develop and exist everywhere. Students talk to each other as they walk together on their way to classes. Whispered and the not-so-quiet conversations held during classes as the teacher talks on and on promote the development of friendships. Elaborately folded notes initiating friendships may be passed from student to student. Sitting in the cafeteria at lunchtime, friends may hold lengthy discussions on various topics. Sometimes friendship can be communicated with only a smile across a crowded hallway. Friendship is something so universal it is impossible to place physical limitations upon it in any way.

I used to be extremely shy, especially freshman year. In the mornings I would ride the bus to school, go to my locker, and sit silently, all alone, working on homework. When the bell rang, I stood up and traveled somewhat automatically to my first-period class. Panic set in if the door to the room was locked, the teacher not having yet arrived, and I was forced to stare unseeingly into one of the books in my arms so that I did not have to talk to anyone else waiting around me. Once inside, I went directly to my desk and sat down, eyes front. I opened my books without a sound, eagerly awaiting the commencement of class, not for love of the subject, but out of fear of being forced to look at someone I did not know and unknowingly offending them.

What I did not completely realize then and that I am trying to act upon now is that it is impossible for a person to like or dislike someone they do not know, and that it is necessary to be somewhat bold, or at least amiable and open, when attempting to begin a friendship. The catch to that, however, is that it is extremely difficult to be outgoing and open when you are shy and scared to death of being hurt by others. Human intuition teaches us to protect ourselves from pain, and it takes a certain amount of effort to overcome that teaching and to not be afraid of a little emotional pain if there is also the possibility of great joy to be gained by it.

So as the months went by I slowly began to learn. If I accidentally, or after a while intentionally, made eye contact with someone, I smiled pleasantly at them. I sometimes even began talking to them myself, though I often could not think of much to say. When I was among the people with whom I had become friends, I was decidedly more relaxed and honest and not afraid to speak when I had something to say. However, I have discovered that most often I enjoy just listening to people, and as a result I became friends with those of my peers who liked talking about topics that interested me. These friends helped me expand my interests and decide for myself what I was truly interested in. They gave me confidence in myself I had not formerly possessed and made my years in high school remarkably easier.

During my years in high school my interests have varied to some extent, thus slightly changing with whom I was friends. However, their role in my life is still very important. We can have fun together in an attempt to get away from the normality of everyday life. My friends are extremely interesting to talk to and often make me see another side of an issue that I had never thought about before, thus forcing me to think harder the next time. My friends provide me with the support and self-confidence I need when I am feeling unsure or even scared about a problem I am facing. But most significantly, they have equipped me with the social skills that are imperative to survive in the demanding high school atmosphere and eventually in a future career.

My personal experience has shown me what it is like to live both with and almost completely without friends. Thus I have learned exactly how indispensable they are and have striven to keep those I have and gain those that I do not. In the large social structure that exists within my school, I have discovered the hard way that friends are exceptionally vital to have and that it is difficult to exist without them.

The Side of Teens Teachers Never See:
Delinquent Behavior in Exemplary Students
by Ryan Van Cleave

"I feel strongly that my high school experience was a negative one, not only because my closest friends reneged on our friendship, but also in that the teachers chose to award others with honors merely for being talented in athletics or a certain subject, not for being a well-rounded individual."

Ryan Van Cleave attended Northern Illinois University, where he was a member of marching band and Sigma Tau Delta and in the University Honors Program. He has since earned an M.A. in English from Florida State University, written three books, and published poetry. He graduated from Weberville High School in 1990.

This paper will examine the growing gap between the student and his two best friends, Brian and Steve. All three were moderately to fairly successful students at this time (high B average), and were active members of the marching band. All three had been best friends since seventh grade, and they were considered by most who knew them as having a "three musketeers" type of loyalty and devotion.

During my sophomore year, it became increasingly obvious to me that my two best friends were deviating from socially acceptable behavior and beginning to experiment with drugs, alcohol, and vandalism. They sought to include me in these activities, despite a close run-in with the police and two serious talks from their parents. The pivotal incident occurred in the first half of our sophomore year, in the house of Brian's affluent parents.

The incident happened on a Thursday in late October at Brian's house, when he held his first unchaperoned party. I went with my junior girlfriend—neither of us drank alcohol—even though we knew that Brian's older brother had bought a large supply of beer for the evening. We arrived early and went downstairs to watch a movie with some other party-goers. An hour later, I went into the kitchen and was surprised to find that Brian was drinking and smoking with a group of more popular kids whom Brian had been making fun of a week earlier. I grabbed a bag of chips and began to head back downstairs when Brian jumped up from the table and offered me some beer. I declined, but Brian said, "Come on—don't be such a fucking pussy!"

I blanched noticeably at Brian's words. People stopped talking and were staring at us, laughing quietly at me. Brian laughed and took a long drag of his cigarette, apparently intoxicated as much by the popular kids' approval as from the alcohol. I fortunately thought quickly and managed to say, "I've already got a six-pack downstairs. When it's polished off I'll come back for some more." This empty boast seemed to have the desired effect because people turned back to their drinking and talking, largely ignoring Brian and me.

Brian sneered, muttering, "Yeah, right!" under his breath. I weeded my way through the crowd and down to the basement, collected my girlfriend, and left immediately. As we were walking back to her house I recalled seeing my friend Steve sitting in the corner throughout the incident, watching with an amused grin on his face as he sucked up a layer of foam from a pitcher of beer. Steve is epileptic. His mom is a nurse, and I remembered her telling Steve that drinking was especially dangerous for him because of his epilepsy.

The next day at school, I barely saw Brian or Steve, who chose to hang out together while ignoring me. That evening, I received a call from a friend in Wisconsin, where I had lived for my first 14 years. My friend called to talk about Jason, a mutual friend who had a difficult early childhood. Jason had some genetic disease in his liver that killed his older sister when she was 12, and that forced Jason to take some 30 or so pills a day just to stay moderately healthy. He had always been sick, but seemed to be getting better when I moved to Illinois. We were both 12 at the time. He got increasingly better after I left but we did not talk often. My friend called to say Jason had died; he was only 15.

I called Steve immediately after getting off the phone with my friend from Wisconsin. I briefly informed him of what happened and then said, "Look, I know you may be unhappy with me about the party and everything, but I really need to talk about this. My parents just won't understand. Is it all right if I come over?"

Steve paused for a moment before saying, "Well, let me get back to you in a bit. I've got to ask my parents first."

I acquiesced and hung up. I waited until 11:34 and then gave up on him and went to bed.

The next day I found out that Steve and Brian had gone to another party the night before and had gotten intoxicated with their new friends. It seems that they also went around the neighborhood, egging houses and smashing mailboxes. Someone egged my house that night, also, but I never found out who.

During band on Monday—the class we all shared—I was admittedly telling dirty jokes in a loud manner that was disrupting class. The teacher glared menacingly at me and held me after class for a quick word. She gripped my shoulders tightly as she peered into my eyes, as if trying to determine what would possess a student to be so awful as to disrupt her class. She chastised me severely, saying that I should be better behaved. I agreed, but she felt I was merely trying to placate her. She grew infuriated and started shaking me, asking why I was so mean to her. Then she abruptly let me go, shaking her head sadly as she said out loud, "Why can't you be more like Brian?" to no one in particular.

I grew red-faced and said, "Blow it out your ass, lady! You don't have a clue!" Then I stormed away from the flabbergasted teacher, who felt it necessary to give me a C for the class when every other semester I had received a B+ or an A–, though I had no further run-ins with her and did not act up again in her class.

These types of incidents have led me to develop and foster a negative attitude about having friends. To this day, I have a hard time putting trust into a relationship with either sex. A similar distrust for teachers has developed, causing me to mouth off at the rude teaching assistant

(TA) in my introduction to logic class freshman year, which resulted in an F for the semester. I later took the class again with a different teacher and TA, while only attending class one quarter of the time, and still managed to get an A for the class.

I feel strongly that my high school experience was a negative one, not only because my closest friends reneged on our friendship, but also in that the teachers chose to award others with honors merely for being talented in athletics or a certain subject, not for being a well-rounded individual.

Brian went to Illinois State University, where he quickly got involved in the sale and usage of drugs, yet he did so poorly that he never returned. Steve has had a few encounters with the police, yet he still drinks regularly despite his epilepsy. Steve's parents have always maintained that I was a bad influence on their "precious Steve." Both Brian and Steve were National Honor Society members, but this type of behavior is unacceptable, during high school and after. Steve and three of his friends (not Brian), however, were kicked out of NHS during their senior year for going to a drinking party at a partially built house that the police were watching. After Steve's parents complained to the principal on their innocent little Steve's behalf, Steve was miraculously restored to full standing.

In conclusion, it seems that Weberville High School was an environment in which students were encouraged to behave appropriately in school, whereas out-of-school behavior was largely ignored or irrelevant to in-school success and standing. This is a deficiency that needs correction; after-school behavior is as important as in-school behavior. It is an unfortunate tendency for those with high levels of scholastic, social, and athletic achievements in high school to deviate from this path in college and later work experiences. I have noticed that the people who were considered the elite of my class are now content with mediocrity while others are striving to succeed in life despite relatively unexceptional high school achievements in academics, social settings, or athletics. Though this is not true in every case, I have watched three of the five students from my class who were voted most likely to succeed fade into the woodwork.

There seems to be a disturbing trend at Weberville High School to honor the letter of the law rather than the spirit of it; moreover, when awards or recognition for all-around achievement are given, those in high-profile positions (athletes, valedictorians, etc.) are disproportionately represented, whereas people who do after-school volunteer work or community service are more likely to go unnoticed. People who are outgoing and fairly popular, such as Steve and Brian, are encouraged by their peers to act irresponsibly out of school. This inappropriate after-school behavior, even when brought to the attention of school officials, is quickly brushed aside because teachers do not want to believe that model students can act in this manner—even when caught red-handed, as Steve was.

Out in Class
by Chris Panagakis

"What I experienced in my last 2 years of high school was hate, pure and simple."

Chris graduated from Weberville High School in 1995, where he was a member of the National Honor Society, speech team, Foreign Exchange Club, and Photo Club. He performed in the fall play, dance show, variety show, and spring musical and served the yearbook as photo editor. Chris won the Silver Key and the Scholastic National Portfolio Award for Photography.

This essay has no perfect beginning. I have tried and tried to open with something prosaic or witty or funny. I can't. There will be no recollections of a moment when I felt like I fit in and came to love Weberville High School. No such moment ever came. I do recall hatred, discrimination, and disgust. I remember name-calling, taunting, and not being able to use the bathroom at my senior prom because most of the football team was waiting inside to beat me senseless. Just who was I? What did I do? I wasn't the only black student in an all-white class. I wasn't disfigured or disabled. I didn't have a third eye on my forehead. I was gay and made no effort to hide the fact. That was enough. I must now ask you to put aside your personal feelings about homosexuality and just listen to what it is I have to say. It's nearly certain that you will have a gay or lesbian student in your class; the only question is whether or not they will ever feel comfortable enough with themselves and you to let that be known.

I always knew that I was gay. There was never a question in my mind that I preferred boys over girls. I was terrified of this knowledge for the first 16 years of my life and worked my hardest to pretend that I was just like everyone else. For some reason, I decided that, on my 16th birthday, I would tell my two closest friends. I had braced myself for rejection and ostracism. Instead, I got complete support from them and the other 10 or so I told by the end of my sophomore year. The violent and hateful reactions wouldn't come until later. By junior year, I had grown fearful of slipping up and letting people know what I really was and feared one of those I had confided in might slip up also. Rather than having to deal with random and malicious rumors floating around the school, I decided that it would just be easier to be completely honest. I began to write about being gay in my English class, talk about gay issues openly with my friends at lunch, and answer "yes" when people said, "What are you, some kind of queer?" Looking back, this may not have been the best decision. I knew of the intense homophobia in my high school. The support of my friends, however, inspired a bravado that got me to follow through with it. It was only after graduation that I learned that of my closest circle of friends who were my loudest supporters, all but two were gay or lesbian. They tell me now that they wanted someone to have the courage to do what they couldn't. I must say it would have been easier if one of them had joined me! Oddly enough, during my entire junior year, life was pretty calm. It seemed as if those in the school who had a problem with me kept it to themselves, and the rest accepted it. The relative calm that was my junior year ended with graduation that spring. Nearly all of my friends who had been supporting me were a year ahead of me. I was left without my defenses. I still had a close group of friends, but they went from 20 in number to 3.

When my senior year began, so did the harassment. At first it was just a couple of muffled comments in the hallways. The number of big jocks knocking me into lockers seemed to have increased dramatically. Times were changing. Where I used to pass between classes with large groups of friends, now I was only with one or two. More often than not, though, I was alone. Those who had kept their opinions to themselves now saw that there wouldn't be so many dissenting voices to counter them. High school had almost been a haven for me to this point. I had come out to my parents some time before. Mom was completely supportive of me and made it clear that she would support me no matter what. My father was a different story. If he could have kicked me out of the house, he would have. Home was not the most pleasant place for me to be. Luckily, I was very active in the speech, drama, and art programs and spent a good deal of time at school with my friends. I was still spending as much time, and often more, at school my senior year, but I soon ceased to feel safe there.

The first truly memorable and scary incident came in one of my classes. One of the louder and large guys in the class decided that he was going to do his best to make my life difficult. He began by screaming "fag," "fairy," "queer," or my personal favorite, "ass bandit" whenever I walked into class. What was I going to do, scream back at him? It would have been useless, so I just kept my silence. When he saw this wasn't getting him anywhere, he would scream these same things randomly during class. Somehow my teacher never seemed to notice. After a point, neither did I. Seeing that this too was not getting to me, the guy decided he would take a seat behind mine one day. What followed was one of the most brazen displays of hatred and discrimination I have ever seen outside of some movie about the civil rights movement. This guy, and I refuse to dignify him with even a "changed-for-publication" name, began by leaning forward and whispering every possible obscenity in my ear. I will pause here to say that I seriously contemplated whether or not I should include what he said. Part of me thinks it so disgusting that it doesn't deserve publication. The winning part, however, knows that it must be retold to be believed. It began with him whispering "fag" and "queen" at me. From there he got more creative. "I'll bet you want me to bend you over and fuck you up the ass right now, don't you?" "Why don't you suck my dick, you faggots are supposed to be real good at that." "Goddamn faggot, why don't you just get AIDS and die already?" When I turned around to tell him to shut up, he said, "Look at me again, faggot, and I'll make sure you're dead." These phrases, and some others, went on for the full period. Toward the end, he began to kick the back of my seat and try to knock things off of my desk. Somehow, all of this went unnoticed by the teacher. At the end of the period, I stayed behind. This was partly because I saw that this guy had met up with some of his friends, and I wasn't in the mood to have my ass kicked, and partly because I was too furious to move. I wasn't so much furious with the guy for doing it as I was with the teacher for not stopping him. Not wanting to waste a good rage, I went up to the teacher and asked what the hell this teacher's problem was. Didn't the teacher see what was going on? Was the teacher deaf? Blind? Plain old stupid? I wanted some answers. Weren't teachers supposed to stop this kind of crap?! This particular teacher also happened to be the teacher of a class that included teaching understanding and acceptance of other cultures. I expected something intelligent, if not politically correct. Instead the teacher told me that there was nothing that could be done. The teacher would talk with the guy, but questioned what did I expect? I was free to transfer to another class if I wanted, though. Perfect, I thought, I was being forced to change my schedule because of some backwards bigot. Not wanting to stay in the class, I transferred.

Similar incidents occurred in other classes. When I approached the teachers to tell them they could either do something about it or forget about my attendance, few were willing to do something more than offer a different section of the class. They always asked me what I was expecting. After all, I was openly gay. What they were referring to is that I didn't hide the fact. I wasn't walking through the hall in a ball gown with a tiara and scepter waving a big ACT UP! sign. I rarely brought it up in discussions. In fact, the times that it did come up in class, the issue was pushed by a teacher. I didn't go through the halls making passes at other men. Except for not hiding the knowledge from others, I was pretty much like everyone else. Knowing the attitude of the school, I did everything possible to be as inconspicuous in class as possible. What always astounded me was that if a black student was called "nigger" in class, the whole school would be called in for an assembly on multiracial awareness. Somehow the word "faggot" wasn't so powerful for the teachers and administrators. This from a school that had recently gotten on the bandwagon of political correctness and cultural awareness. We knew all about the plight of some obscure tribe in another continent that numbered about 100. Not a word was ever said about the millions of gays and lesbians who have gone through our schools. The most frustrating were the encounters I had with teachers who told me how much they admired and respected me for what I had done and then turned around and insulted me by asking me not to talk about gay issues around them. Apparently I was asking too much by expecting them to care. The most extreme case of this was when I was passed over for the most important position in a major senior year activity. I later found out that the sponsor told the group at their first meeting that he knew I was the best but that he didn't agree with my "politics." Of course, there were the precious few exceptions to the rule. Some teachers made a real effort to make sure that I was safe and not threatened in their classes and they honestly cared about what I was going through. These teachers and my friends are what made my life bearable.

And so senior year passed with all of its harassment, name-calling, and hatred. When it was over, I wanted nothing more than to escape. I was thankful to my friends and sympathetic teachers, but too broken and disillusioned to want to remember any of it. I think seeing the words "Die AIDS fuckers" scrawled on the comment scroll when the National AIDS quilt came to our school finally did it. How could people behave in such a way? How could teachers and administrators act as though it was acceptable? What I experienced in my last 2 years of high school was hate, pure and simple. It is similar to what happened when the schools in the South were integrated. There was a national outcry then. The only outcry over my passage through Weberville High School was a group of jocks screaming "faggot" when I received my diploma.

When AIDS Becomes Real
by Sara C. Lenart

"I began to see life in a new perspective as Jon deteriorated before my eyes. My schoolwork was more and more of a nuisance."

Sara C. Lenart is a senior at Weberville High School, where she has been actively involved in music and theater. A member of the National Honor Society, Sara plans to attend Bradley University in the fall and major in secondary education with an emphasis in English and a minor in the performing arts. When she's not "playing dumb," she's writing poetry about life and singing.

At the beginning of my senior year, Jon P. Alan (name changed for privacy) died of AIDS. Jon had known me since I was nearly 4. When I lost such a friend to AIDS, I suddenly lost much more. I lost the veil that had covered my eyes for my whole life. To me, AIDS was something out there, but it wasn't in my world. Suddenly an invisible killer was on the loose in my life, and suddenly AIDS was real. I was brought into the game of Real Life, and, everywhere I looked, people were dying of AIDS.

Very few things of importance happen in Weberville. No one ever hears of someone dying of anything like AIDS. In middle-class suburbia, sex is a dirty word. Adults don't want to hear about it, much less talk about it. It is for this reason that teenagers in the suburbs are protected somewhat from the everyday horrors of a more urban area. It is unlikely that you would see a homeless person walking the streets of downtown Weberville. Yes, there are homeless people in Weberville, but it is unusual to see them. In a sense, most unpleasantries are hidden in Weberville. Teenagers are also having sex in Weberville. The adults know that teenagers have sex, but it's not their children. The same veil many times covers the same eyes of those that try to cover ours. That same veil covers the eyes of Weberville to tragedies like AIDS.

When I was told that Jon was HIV-positive, my breath caught in my throat. I knew he would die. We all knew. Of all the facts that we knew, we knew that AIDS meant death. So there was no doubt about it; Jon was dying. What we didn't know was how he would die. I thought that someday it would just be over, and that Jon's life would cease. I was wrong. The way he died was beyond all imagination. Nothing could have possibly prepared his loved ones for the way that AIDS stole Jon's life bit by bit.

When Jon was diagnosed he had already been infected with the HIV virus for at least 3 years. He had had AIDS symptoms for 1 year at the time of his diagnosis. These symptoms were unlike anything those around Jon had ever seen before. Some days he would come in with big spots all over his body. Some of the treatments made his face swell, and some made him look emaciated. It was difficult to predict just what each treatment would do to Jon. As the disease progressed, we saw less and less of Jon. He tired easily, and he was sick nearly all of the time. Soon he began to lose weight. One day Jon was six-foot-three and 180 lbs., and the next day he was 120 lbs. As his murderer kept stealing Jon's life, I began to see AIDS as real.

I began to see life in a new perspective as Jon deteriorated before my eyes. My schoolwork was more and more of a nuisance. I became a strong advocate of safe sex among my friends. My poetry was the only thing that reflected my true feelings. During the second semester of senior year, I began writing a poem for Jon's funeral. It took up most of my time for nearly a week. That poem replaced any words that I might have said. It also replaced a void that was left when Jon died.

By June, we all knew that our good friend Jon would not live to see November. He would not live to see another snowfall, or another changing of the leaves. This realization killed a small place in all of our hearts. When he was placed in the hospital for a lung tumor, we each wept inside. The tumor was removed, and, miraculously, Jon survived. However, a few weeks later, Jon passed away.

Jon's death affected everyone in their own personal way. I never read that poem at the funeral, but I did give it to his lover. In my heart, I know that my poem was written solely for that purpose. It was written to remind Jon's lover of the special bond that they shared. When we put together Jon's piece of the AIDS quilt, that poem will be on it as a symbol of the special memories we have.

The effect of Jon's horrific death was nearly undetected. His death affected our hearts, minds, and souls. I started changing my attitude toward life little by little. No longer did I think how horrible my life was. Instead I was grateful that I still had a life. I began to appreciate the little things. In a year's time, I had matured greatly. In fact, the only truly detected change resulting from Jon's death was my sudden maturity to realize that I didn't want to watch life pass me by.

These days I still advocate safe sex among my friends, and many of my papers for school are about AIDS. I have been wearing a red ribbon since Jon's death to promote AIDS awareness. For every person who asks me why I wear a red ribbon, I pray that they at least have one thought about the dangers of unsafe sex. As a teenage girl, I now feel as if the veil is at least lowered a little, if nothing else. It is a tragedy that the only way that the tragedies in life become real is through experience, but I believe we learn more through experience. I have learned that unsafe sex cannot mean only pregnancy anymore, but now unsafe sex is playing the odds with Death himself. AIDS is a death sentence right now. Perhaps someday there will be a vaccine or treatment, but, for now, AIDS is a killer that strips your life away day by day. AIDS is real.

[Editor's note: Many adults could take a lesson in maturity from Sara. Despite the overwhelming emotions that can incapacitate one in the midst of a tragedy, Sara persevered and became an advocate of safe sex to her peers. Educators need to meet the challenge of AIDS with the same level of maturity. As Randy Dean similarly illustrates, sex education must become one of school's top priorities. Besides important safe-sex information, students need to understand the social, economic, and psychological effects of AIDS upon their future. With luck, then, they will be able to humanely deal with the numerous victims AIDS will certainly claim before a cure is found.]

A 17-Year-Old Daddy—Almost
by Randy Dean

" . . . and the fact that I was going to be a 17-year-old father, my thoughts were turning to suicide. What other choice did I have? My life was fucked. I had ruined my reputation. I really didn't think anyone would miss me. I honestly believed that. I had it all planned out. How I was going to do it, where I was going to do it, and when I was going to do it."

Randy Dean is a senior at Weberville High School. He plans to major in psychology. Randy remains with his girlfriend of 2 years and hopes to remain with her forever. At 18, Randy moved out of the family home. He hopes the situation between himself and his parents will someday improve.

"I think I might be pregnant." These are not the words that every junior in high school longs to hear. Unfortunately for me, though, I heard them. And I heard them loud and clear. A million thoughts go racing through your head when you hear this. Is it really mine? Are we going to keep it? Maybe we should get an abortion. What are my friends going to think? And, Oh God, what are my parents going to do to me when I tell them?

My name is Randy. I was at the ripe old age of 16 when my 17-year-old girlfriend, Andrea, rang out that horrifying word—pregnant. I'll tell you up front that Andrea was on the pill. It's not like we weren't using any protection. I don't want you to think that getting her pregnant wasn't on my mind, or that I'm some asshole who didn't care if she got pregnant and if she did, that I'd leave her in the dust and not take care of her. She never missed a day of the pill. The doctor said that the prescription just wasn't strong enough.

After a long discussion, we decided that we were going to keep the baby. Neither of us wanted to get an abortion, and neither of us could handle adoption—not knowing where it was, not knowing if it was getting as much love and attention that we could've given it, etc.

It really changed my life around. I blew off more school than imaginable to me before. I turned to more drugs to get away from this and my other problems. I was so incredibly depressed that I was hours away from suicide. I just didn't know how to handle it.

Blowing off school seemed to be one of the answers at the time. Do you know what it feels like to be walking down the hall, or sitting in class, and hear your name in every conversation of every clique you pass? What are they saying? What are they thinking? Is getting your girlfriend pregnant really going to have that much effect on your friends and friendships? You bet.

You find out who your real friends are when something like this happens. They are the ones who stick by your side—no matter what. They're also the ones that stick up for you when other people are talking shit about you. How many of these people were by my side when I'd take time off from school? None. Not one.

I would drive myself nuts thinking about my situation from every possible viewpoint. When I finally decided to return to school, I was so far behind, I had no idea what was going on. Needless to say, I did very poorly that quarter.

Because I was driving myself crazy, I needed to get away from all of this bullshit. I called up one of my "friends" and asked him to roll me up a big fat joint. He said, "No problem." He was over in a matter of minutes. Shortly after that, we were stoned out of our minds. Every day we would go out and smoke a joint. After a while, we were getting high four to five times a day. Then we were smoking "primos." These are joints with cocaine laced into the marijuana. I finally gave it all up, at least for a while, when I realized that I was stoned more than I was straight.

My life was really falling apart. My parents lost all faith, trust, and confidence in me. I was not brought up the way I had been behaving. My parents are strict Mormons who follow their religion 24 hours a day, 7 days a week. When I finally got up the courage to tell them, they about had heart attacks. Telling them wasn't exactly easy, but it wasn't the worst part about it, either; seeing their reaction to the news was. Watching them cry their eyes out made me burst out into tears, which I told myself I wouldn't do. So much for that. I had really crushed my parents, and it about killed me to know that I had done something to hurt them in any way, even though it wasn't intentional.

I couldn't stand to be around my parents because I thought they couldn't stand to be around me due to what I had done to them. I didn't want to be around my "friends," either, because I never knew what they were saying about me behind my back. For these reasons, and the fact that I was going to be a 17-year-old father, my thoughts were turning to suicide. What other choice did I have? My life was fucked. I had ruined my reputation. I really didn't think anyone would miss me. I honestly believed that. I had it all planned out. How I was going to do it, where I was going to do it, and when I was going to do it.

I was within minutes of going through with it, but then something made me turn around and get hold of myself. What was I doing? Life goes on. People make mistakes. It's a good thing I picked myself up when I did, because later on that week, Andrea told me that she had had a miscarriage. Oh my God! Talk about mixed feelings!

I was thrilled and disappointed with what had happened. I had finally accepted the fact that I was going to be a daddy. Everybody and their mother knew about it—literally. I would go to a friend's house and end up talking more with their parents about my situation than I would with them about whatever. I had made plans to graduate early from high school and to get a job. Andrea had already been buying things for the baby. We were even going to a prenatal class on Monday nights. So now what? The baby isn't coming any more. I had to tell everyone again about our situation but this time tell them about the miscarriage. Did they believe me? Or were they thinking that we had gotten an abortion, and we were using a miscarriage as an excuse? Once again, I was driving myself nuts thinking about what other people were thinking and of what they thought about me.

As time went by, things cooled down, and nobody has really said anything since. As you probably know, in high school there is, and always will be, something new and more interesting to gossip about than the old stuff that is going around. As for school, I got back on the honor roll. I'm not a nerdy brain, I just inherited a good mind, I guess. As far as the drugs go . . . well, let's just say it's not as bad as it used to be. Now I do them more to have a good time than as an escape or a way out of all my problems. Suicidal thoughts haven't crossed my mind since that day, and I pray to God that they never will again.

Life had thrown me an interesting curve that I didn't know how to handle. What else can you expect, though? You can't go through life without meeting up with challenges, or else you'll die from boredom. I just hope that if you (or anyone else you know) come face to face with any kind of a problem, no matter what the caliber, you'll be able to keep a cool head and a clear mind. Don't worry about what other people say or think, because sooner or later, the problem will blow over. I promise. Also, don't go about things the way I did. I realize now that the way I handled things was not the way it should've been done. School is important. Without it, you're not going to get very far in life. Drugs are bad news. Once you get started, it's only downhill from there. Why anyone would want to kill himself boggles my mind. Things do get better. Just roll with the changes and everything will work out.

Andrea and I are still going strong, every day adding to our wonderful, yet interesting, year and-a-half relationship.

Stalked Senior Year
by Valerie Curda

"Being stalked has also affected my concentration on school work. I often find myself thinking about Glen and me before all these problems started. I find myself daydreaming about what would have happened at work or the night Glen should have been arrested."

Valerie Curda is a senior at Weberville High School, where she is the only girl in building construction, a course in which each year the class builds a house. In the fall, if the streets are safe from Glen, Valerie will attend the local community college. If they are not safe, Valerie will go straight into construction.

I am a victim of stalking. My ex-boyfriend has been stalking me ever since we broke up. This has become an incredible problem for me. It has affected my life and my schooling. I do not feel safe knowing that he could be somewhere watching every move I make or that his friends could be watching me. It has affected my schoolwork because it has prevented my movement around the community. For example, I couldn't complete the mandatory volunteer work my school requires. We are required to volunteer 10 times for 2 hours each time. I had signed up to volunteer at a social service agency in the community. In addition, I had trouble looking up stuff for a major paper because I had to avoid the public library. In both cases, my ex-boyfriend or his friends made these places he could find me.

I know that this is not only happening to me. It is happening to adults all over. I am hoping to make it known that this is also happening to teenagers. When it happens, teachers need to be understanding. Although I always want to get my schoolwork done, there are things that get in the way.

My ex-boyfriend lives in a suburban town 20 minutes away from Weberville. Knowing he lives so close to me and my friends is a problem. When people hear about a teenager being stalked, many think it is just an exaggeration. They may realize it is real after it is too late. Many people did not believe me when I said my ex-boyfriend was stalking me until he came to my work with a pair of handcuffs and a sawed-off B.B. gun. Then things started to click in to my friends and family that I was not lying. It was almost too late for me. Luckily I was not scheduled to work that night.

Glen and I grew up together as family because our parents were best friends since high school. Our parents never dreamed of us ever going as boyfriend and girlfriend. But when the day came that he asked me out and I accepted, our parents could not have been happier. Now they regret it. Glen and I went out for almost 2 years. After we hit the 1-year mark, his attitude toward me changed. He started to be more protective, wanting to know where I was going and when I was going to be home. When I went out, he wanted me to call him as soon as I got home. He really did not want me to go out with anyone else unless he was going to be there. At first I really did not mind. I was a teenager. I thought he was only doing it out of love for me. Boy, was I wrong!

After a couple of months, I decided I could not handle it any more. So I told him either his attitude had to change or I was going to leave him. Well, it changed for a few months and then he was back to old protective Glen again. A couple of days before I broke it off with him, I met someone new. His name is Rick. I am still seeing Rick today. He has been a big factor for me during this whole situation. I really got to like him, so I told Glen that it was over. I was through with him and his attitude. Well, that was the day that set him off.

A couple of days later I realized that he was following Jessica, a friend and coworker, and me home from work. One night he followed us for almost half an hour. In the morning she woke up to find that her car was vandalized. The first person we thought of was Glen. But we could not pin it on him. Weeks went by and I did not hear from him. I thought things ended. October 30 was the day I will never forget. I was with Alan. Jessica came to Alan's apartment and said I had to go with her because something had happened at work. Once we got to my house she told me that Glen was at my workplace with a sawed-off B.B. gun and a pair of handcuffs. When she told me, I felt like I had a death wish put on my life and Glen was the one who was going to fulfill it. But I guess I had an angel looking over my shoulder.

I filed four police reports on Glen. We had a court date for November 30 and the judge put Glen on supervision for 6 months.

This has also affected my school work. For my social science course it is mandatory that we do a volunteer program called VOLUNTEER. Due to Glen, I was not able to complete the volunteer requirement. It turned out Glen's girlfriend attended the school next to the place where I started to volunteer. As a result, Glen often hung around and there was no way to avoid him. I tried a different volunteer project but ran into him again. Regardless of the grade penalty for not volunteering, I wanted to do the program. Volunteering is a good idea, but nothing worked out. I'm glad my teacher asked what was going on. I had not said anything. I expected the penalty because no one was supposed to be excused from the program. It seems the school couldn't think of any reason someone would ever need to be excused from the requirement. My teacher refused to penalize me. I hope he doesn't get in trouble.

Also for my social science course, I was supposed to use the local community college library to find background readings for a paper. I couldn't because that's where Glen takes some courses. Thankfully my teacher showed me other ways of finding the materials I needed.

Being stalked has also affected my concentration on schoolwork. I often find myself thinking about Glen and me before all these problems started. I find myself daydreaming about what would have happened at work or the night Glen should have been arrested.

High school is said to be the best 4 years of one's life. Well, only 2 of the past 4 were the best. The past 2 years have been hell! I just hope I can live the rest of my life in peace and not have to worry about anyone following me, bothering me, calling, or sending me unwanted letters.

Transplanted: Surviving Senior Year as a New Student
by Darya Bonds

*"The introduction of a new life during this self-exploration period,
senior year, is the most devastating encounter I have ever faced."*

*Darya plans to attend Wayne Sate University. Some flowers are so precious
they should never be transplanted.*

The formal dances, the immense parties lasting till dawn, the responsibility of vacationing alone, spring break, and the final ceremonies that fulfill the freedom of adulthood, these are all aspects within the hype of senior year. This is the time everyone looks forward to as a child. There are no worries, no stresses, no faults, just pure perfection. Where do you turn when the dream goes sour? The conscience of a transfer student is never at rest.

I had this ideal world painted in my mind for many years, as most of America's youth does. I had it all, a caring boyfriend, a friend on every corner, plans for my senior trip, and hopes for a beautiful graduation ceremony filled with family and friends, people who really care about me. As I clutched onto the truth in this imagery, my parents pulled me away. Within the first weeks of my move to Weberville it was easy to deny that I had left my life behind. It merely seemed like a vacation in the beginning; at times I would even smile with the thought that I would be home soon. After months passed, I made myself realize that there was no chance for a return. This was it—Weberville was my new, temporary residence, never to be called my home. Since my move, I have experienced different attitudes in people, style I was never accustomed to, and an educational program that is very foreign to my previous background. One could believe that the changes would be minor shifting from a suburb of Detroit to a suburb of Chicago. That assumption is unmistakably false. The introduction of a new life during this self-exploration period, senior year, is the most devastating encounter I have ever faced.

In one aspect, I feel much anger in the form of blame toward my parents. Blaming the people you are closest to is often the easiest way to release anger. Although our change of location is the fault of no one person, seeing a face behind your tragedy makes accepting it a whole lot easier. The continuous screaming competitions, the nerve-shattering guilt trips, and the refusal of any affection between my parents and me isn't purposely acted out to bring them to heartache. It's just that the anger and frustration I drown in day by day leaves me no other escape as relieving as projecting cruelty.

I believe that if I could only bring my parents down to the trenches of pain in which I suffer, they then could reason with my displacement.

If we once leveled our understanding to a state of communication we might even conclude with a compromise. Maybe we could accept an approximate median between our opposing views. But in a home where the walls are thick and the lights are dim, very little communication, much less compromising, is accomplished.

Many teenagers know that their parents love them but they become trapped in a slump that forbids the acceptance of this undying love. The saying goes, "Parents know what is best for you," but when you feel tremendous amounts of pain and discomfort, it's hard to believe there is anyone on your side at all. I've heard the speeches on why we had to leave, and I've listened to the lectures on preserving family unity. I just wonder where my satisfaction comes into play. I feel that if at 17 years of age I am considered an adult by law, I should be trusted to make intelligent decisions. Among those decisions, my first would be whether to continue my life in the path it was headed or keep the bonds within my family strong.

Unfortunately, my parents do not feel that I am mature enough to take on the responsibility of important decision making; therefore, I must still focus through their eyes until I leave for college. Trusting my ability would not have been a mistake. I would have done my best not to let them down. In addition to the complications in the relationship between my parents and me, my entire social life has been damaged.

Although family should always claim first priority in your life, friends and acquaintances are a very important part of senior year. That special feeling of acceptance enhances your interest in attending school and school functions. When you know that it matters whether you come to school or make an appearance at the activities after school, you are provided with the strength to involve yourself in these activities.

Attempting to start from the bottom in the last year of high school is not easy to pull off. Presenting yourself as a senior with the self-esteem of a freshman will force you to prove yourself all over again to different people in order to gain a sense of respect. Until you have accomplished respect from others, you will never receive acceptance.

I have experienced a change in my own personality while trying to earn a feeling of belonging in a brand-new world. There are days when I feel so down that I believe God himself couldn't raise my hopes, yet I'll pretend to be joyful in case there is a friend waiting to be made that day. This is nothing like the person I once was. I am the type of person who loves to express her true feelings, whether good or bad. The problem may be that for the first time in my life there is no one to whom I live near who is willing to listen.

Verbal harassment can also produce a major setback. Small children can be cruel to one another in the way that they may tease and taunt. Teens tend to be similar. The person who seems to be out of place is always the simplest target for disrespectful comments. My peers feel no sympathy toward me when they hurt my feelings because they have no strings attached to my life. They painfully cut my self-esteem down to the last inch, while their social lives remain unharmed. I have no power in the social status of this school. Therefore, my life, in a sense, has no meaning.

In addition, within the roller coaster of making an effort to gain the acceptance of new friends, there lies the difficulty of preserving old friendships. The expenses of phone calls and visits are overwhelmingly high. Consequently, months may pass before I see or talk to friends who were once my living shadows. I kept nothing from these people. All my problems immediately became their problems, as theirs became mine. These people are the ones with whom I've shared all of my life experiences, the people who really know what I'm about, my truest and dearest friends.

As the time I spend here lengthens and drags on, the friends I left behind are beginning to notice a slight acculturation in my lifestyle. I never meant to change the person I had already become, but interacting with a dramatically different group of peers will shift anyone's personality. Being hurt piece by piece in both worlds only doubles the pressure on my part. Rejection is not easily dealt with by teenagers, and when it hits you in all directions you have no safe place to turn. Keeping your mind in the books, instead of on the aspects of a social life, may be one way to escape depression.

In my particular case, a switch in the educational system I am accustomed to has gradually added to my stress. As a matter of fact, adjusting to a different type of schooling may be my most difficult challenge yet. Being taught in the same school district from grades 3 to 11, you acquire a certain learning and studying style that will vary from other locations. Attempting to learn the skills of another district is extremely tough when you are almost brainwashed to think in another style.

Anyone in this same difficult situation should simply reverse the negativism to a positive challenge. Think of the new skills a student is capable of learning as an insightful experience. Although I will go through high school with the same amount of credits as other students, I will have the knowledge of two educational systems. Realizing and accepting their differences is part of adapting to the real world. Conquering the challenge of functioning in a new society is an important step you can always refer back to for guidance. Being able to cope with change prepares you for a workforce that has many ups and downs. Taking the worst and producing something of great value is the true work of a mature adult.

Knowing when the time has come to stop accepting whatever is handed down to you and strive for the best is a critical period of change. Here is where you learn what type of person you'd like to become, and which goals are worth putting forth the effort for. Transfer students experience many hardships, but these hardships may simplify the process of reaching adulthood. Being comfortable with adjusting to change is a large step toward independence. Accomplishing this advancement during senior year may be difficult, but later on in life, success will be the outcome. Being able to alter your relationships and learning abilities will extend your knowledge to unlimited growth. This growth is the birth of my freedom and independence.

The Stress of Senior Year
by Nicole Owen

"The desire to win can sometimes be overwhelming."

Nicole Owen is a senior at Weberville High School, where she has been on the speech team for 4 years. When not writing papers, Nicole is listening to R.E.M., Depeche Mode, or U2 or out having fun with her friends. Nicole plans to attend the University of Illinois at Champaign—Urbana.

It is important for students to be involved in school activities. A student's involvement in sports, clubs, or other activities, however, should not inhibit his or her academic life. It would be easy to balance life and time if these were the only factors in a high school senior's life, but they are not. For most seniors, including myself, friends, family, and college selection and preparation are very important. Therefore it is essential to manage time effectively and set priorities; effective time management and setting priorities are crucial in order for a senior to minimize stress.

As a senior at Weberville High School, I have needed to balance my time among my classes, involvement in the speech team and other activities, and whatever else I want to do. Because I am a part of the accelerated and Advanced Placement track at school, I have experienced a great deal of stress and homework. Involvement in speech team requires a lot of time. Practice is necessary during the season, which runs from October through February. The competitions take place on Saturdays at various schools from approximately 7:00 a.m. to 4:00 or 5:00 p.m. practically every week. I am also a member of the National Honor Society, which holds meetings the first Monday evening of each month. National Honor Society requires that I take part in various service activities. I enjoy spending time with my friends and by myself, reading or pursuing other interests. As a senior, I must choose which colleges I will apply to, and this requires a lot of time. I feel that achieving a balance of school, activities, friends, and the like is a very important part of the school experience.

The level of stress placed upon students at Weberville High School can sometimes be quite high. The stress placed on accelerated seniors is higher than that placed on those in the average level. Weberville is also a very fast-paced and competitive school. Students are competitive with each other, and this adds to the stress on the individual who wishes to excel.

Senior year involves several important and stressful choices that require a lot of time and thought.

One, and for some the most important, decision is where to apply to college. Counselors recommend that interested students begin visiting universities early in the senior year or as early as the summer before. Applications must be acquired and filled out. Some require more time than others. For example, one application I had required two essays, had a long main section asking for general information, and a chart listing all activities. One application asking for only the basics took 45 minutes to complete. Completed applications are sent out and the student anxiously awaits a response. However, the process does not end there; many more decisions must be made.

Parents add to the stress felt by students making the college decision. They tend to remind their son or daughter constantly of the impending application deadlines and ask how close he or she is to being done. This often adds stress because the student feels overwhelmed by all that must be done.

Another form of stress related to college is the fear of leaving the security and familiarity of high school and moving to a completely new lifestyle. Although this change is exciting, it stresses out the senior who worries about such new experiences.

Many colleges give class credit to students who take the AP exam and do well. Weberville offers AP classes in several areas including physics, calculus, American history, and literature. Not only are these classes stressful because of the greater difficulty of a college course, but also because of the student's desire to do well on the May AP exams.

A good score is desired because it will save time and money in college. Therefore, students often stress themselves studying and preparing for the test. Because the test is more than 3 hours long and covers the entire year, excellent preparation is necessary.

By planning and balancing workloads, students can reduce their stress. Students need not wait until the night before the test to study. Many teachers often help the students prepare for the AP test throughout the year by giving sample problems on tests, for homework, or for class discussion. This can greatly lower the level of stress because the students learn what to expect.

For many seniors, extracurricular activities are a very important part of life. They give a break from homework and are a chance to have fun with friends. However, they also add stress.

In most team activities, the desire to win can sometimes be overwhelming. For seniors, the stress is greater because they are the oldest members of the group. They are expected to be the leaders of the team and help the younger members. On speech team, seniors are usually called upon to compete at regionals. This is especially stressful because it is a difficult meet and a team victory here is a major goal of the season. The National Honor Society adds stress because of the many rules members must follow. Members must also maintain a certain grade-point average and take part in service activities in the community.

These stresses can be lessened by using practice time effectively to develop increased confidence and make competitions less scary. Strong team unity can also help.

Although stress has some positive effects, such as motivation, it can be very damaging if not handled properly. Many seniors who improperly deal with stress develop "senioritis," an attitude that is characterized by lack of motivation and an "I don't care" philosophy. Many sufferers of senioritis do not complete homework assignments or study for tests, and they do not enjoy school as they once did. Falling grades are often a result of senioritis due to the lower effort put forth by the student.

A person unable to deal with stress in high school will definitely be unable to cope with college. College lacks the guidance and structure of high school. This can cause a person to drop out, ending his or her education.

Stress is a big part of every student's life. Therefore, managing stress is very important. Students must let their own intelligence guide their actions and not let stress take over. Although stress management is not easy, it is possible and necessary. If someone lets stress build throughout his or her life, major health problems can result.

A White Teen's View of Minorities in School
by Derek Blume

"Weberville High School offers a high-pressure atmosphere with much intensity and some quality. The effects of this environment are that students are more competitive. They are forced to handle more stressful situations but they may be better prepared to accept the outside world."

Derek Blume is a senior at Weberville High School, where he excels on the cross-country and track teams and in the classroom. Derek is sports editor for the school newspaper and a member of the National Honor Society. He plans on attending Grinnell College in the fall. When not writing, he is working on the computer, running, or trying to create new and impractical inventions.

This paper is based on a topic that has generated an increase in interest in the last few years. Racial tensions have increased due to many problems facing the country. Minorities in this country have had to go through a lot. Many people believe that the whites in this country have hated the minorities and have not given them the opportunities that they deserve. This paper was written to show my perspective of the way minorities are treated and their response at this school.

The reason I feel that I have to write this paper is that I have very strong feelings about this subject. I see this country coming apart because of racial tensions everywhere. What happened to the peace that we had during the 1980s; where did it go? I do not know, but I wish to find out. Through thinking about people and events at this school I hope to understand why we have so much hatred in the larger society. Why does it happen? What is the cause? We have to ask these questions. I hope to answer them, or at least help.

Weberville High School offers a high-pressure atmosphere with much intensity and some quality. The effects of this environment are that students are more competitive. They are forced to handle more stressful situations, but they may be better prepared to accept the outside world.

I come from German ancestry. I am white and therefore am in the majority. Most of my friends are also white. I've noticed that in this community most people look down upon minorities. I feel the blacks and the Hispanics in this area have a negative reputation put on them. These two minorities are viewed as crooks and gang-bangers. I guess it is the way I was taught, but whenever I see groups of them walking down the street, I think to myself, "They are up to no good." Many people believe this. Many of my friends feel the same way. I do not have any friends who are African American or Hispanic. About 90% of my friends are white. One friend of mine, who I think is racist, sees a group of black guys walking down the hall and starts to tell me what immature losers they are and that they are all stupid morons. Many people in this school believe along the same lines as my friend. He sees a group of Hispanic kids walking down the hall (actually, they usually run down the hall) speaking Spanish and says something along the lines of, "Those dumb Mexicans; why the hell don't they stay in their own country?"

I have another friend who, in my opinion, is part of the minority of whites who says absolutely nothing against the minorities at school. When the same circumstances exist as above, he thinks or says that they had a different upbringing or that they do not really know any better. He is one of the most caring kids in this school. Unfortunately, when he goes up to support one of these minority kids, they "spit" right back in his face and make fun of him by calling him a nerd or a loser.

My friends also include Asian people (one of whom is Chinese) and an Indian. The guy with an Indian background is a kid of very strong determination. He must have his way. Most people think he is a good guy and he has a lot of friends. Other Indians in this school are not as popular. They seem to be outcast from everyone. Many of them are only friends with kids from Asian or Muslim backgrounds. Many people do not want to be seen around them because they wear their native clothes or because of the way they talk.

The Asian kids are also picked on because of their strong motivation to learn. They seem to have an ability to want to achieve a lot and they do not fit in with the rest of the white people in the school. This group therefore is rather isolated. My friend who is Chinese is also very popular. He is also strongly determined to do well in school, but he does get picked on a lot. What makes him popular, though, is his ability to fight back.

Most people in this school believe that the blacks and Hispanics are not serious about learning. It is believed all they do is goof around and cause distraction. There is some evidence to support this. There is not a single person in any of my accelerated classes who is black or Hispanic. Most of the white kids begin to classify people by their race. "The Chinese are nerds." Then you have, "The blacks are dumb." These racist sayings are not uncommon to hear around here, but it is not always the white people who say them. Despite the fact that many white people in this school occasionally think these types of things, it is usually the African Americans who come out in public and say things like that.

How do the minorities feel about other minorities? In this school, the black and Hispanic kids seem to get along rather well. But when it comes to the Asian kids, the blacks and Hispanics are rather rude to them. They do not usually say anything about their race, or the color of their skin, but something like, "Get outta my way, you ugly fool." Many of the Asian kids fear the Hispanics and blacks. You almost never see them hanging even close to one another.

The minorities at WHS often overreact to whatever happens in their surroundings. They try to claim that everything that goes wrong for them is caused by racism. I am on the track team at this school. I recall one time during a meet that one of the white members of my team was talking about one of the other members of the team. The boy he was talking about was black. Another black kid on the team overheard the white kid and got very angry. The white kid was talking about the kid's intelligence (and he was not talking very nicely about it). The kid that overheard him got so angry that he went over to the white kid and pushed him over. The African American boy started to shout things like, "Stop pickin' on us," and, "You rich little white boy, I'm going to kick your —-." Then one of the coaches came on the bus and broke up the struggle. If you knew the boy who was talking, you would believe as I do that he would never say anything bad about any race or any other thing. He was a very kind person. The boy he was talking about was not very intelligent. This was rather well known and even the black athlete who became angry must have known this. In any case, the comments were not racial. Why do some blacks have to see everything as racial?

For 4 years I have seen the way students from minorities have acted and behaved. My junior high school was an all-white private school. I came to WHS and was a little concerned. I never really hung around any blacks or Hispanics. I saw them walking down the street, living around my house, and on television. I feel that television was what really scared me. The negative connotations given to these minorities was just unbelievable. All the news was about was black gangs and black people killing each other. I came to Weberville and saw what they really were like. It seems they are expected to act this way. I never could understand why so many of the minorities do not try to take their chances and work at being the best person they can possibly be. The few who have tried are really successful. Some of the smartest minority students are the ones that are on sports teams like football and track.

The people who are on teams such as track and football are able to concentrate on things other than hatred. In football, everyone must work together in order to win. Our football team is very successful because it is able to unite the team, no matter what the color of a person's skin. I feel that white people in this school are able to put aside prejudices (even though they do have them) and are able to make a good environment for everyone who works, learns, and visits Weberville High School.

I cannot compare this school with other schools in this area because I do not know what their situation is. I do know this: Even though prejudice does exist at Weberville, the people put aside their feelings and we live together. There are those few skirmishes that happen and, well, they happen everywhere. The world is not perfect and neither is this school. Weberville does promote unity.

I have tried to express the way many feel and act at Weberville. Many white students do act and think in racist ways, but they learn not to let it interfere with making a rational judgment. There is no difference except in the ways we were brought up and the color of our skin. Many people do believe this and try to live by this creed. It is those few who do not follow this rule who promote division.

When I look and see what is happening, I am saddened. We need to respond to the needs of every social group in this country. I feel proper schooling is one of the most important of all of these. We just need to be more concerned for everyone. I wish that one day everyone will be able to walk on the street and be able to think not in terms of race but in terms of the personality of the individual.

Becoming Legal
by Antonio Navarro

"Please listen to what I have to tell. Getting a job, getting paid, going out and having a great time, and having no worries may seem like easy, everyday-type things, but I couldn't do them. I spent countless hours at home waiting to see if my case number would come up at the Immigration and Naturalization Service. My parents wouldn't let me go out much because of fear that I would get picked up by the Immigration officials."

Tony has been involved with Junior Achievement for the past 4 years. The J.A. company of which he is the president was runner-up for company of the year. He plans to attend college and major in finance, marketing, and real estate. Tony's main goal is to become a U.S. citizen. Only at age 15 did he learn he was not.

Last year was the happiest year of my life.

What I am about to explain may not be significant for you, and you may not give a darn, but because I am a former illegal immigrant what I had to go through to live here is permanently engraved in my mind. I went through a mental hell and distress just to be free, to be able to work, to be able to drive (with a license), to be able to go outside and not worry about immigration picking me up and treating me like an animal. The right to live here is something you American gringos (only kidding) take for granted.

Please listen to what I have to tell. Getting a job, getting paid, going out and having a great time, and having no worries may seem like easy everyday-type things, but I couldn't do them. I spent countless hours at home waiting to see if my case number would come up at the Immigration and Naturalization Service. My parents wouldn't let me go out much because of fear that I would get picked up by the immigration officials.

During my freshman year my father told me that I was an illegal; I was shocked. He explained that he would talk to a respectable lawyer who had worked with Hispanic people through similar matters. Although I was relieved at first, the lawyer explained that it would take about 1 year for the whole process. Yeah, right; 2 years passed by. The lawyer hid and stole about $1,600 of my dad's hard-earned money. I was ready to do something crazy. That lawyer wasted 2 precious years of my high school life. I was ready to give up.

I'd feel so depressed at times that I thought nothing would ever get done. I was always in a bad mood. None of my friends knew what I was going through. At times I wanted to end it all. I didn't know what to do, who to talk to, who to turn to. I was lost, I didn't have many close friends. People wondered why I wouldn't go out. I felt like I wasn't accepted here. However, there was never a time I felt jealous of people having all those things I saw.

I always felt that things would work out. Time was the issue, but how long would it take? This is how it was for me freshman through junior year. People say the high school years are the best years of your life. For me, that was bullshit. It could take years for the I.N.S. to hear my case.

There was a point when all I did was sit around and watch TV, feeling sorry for myself. My self-esteem sank to rock bottom. I couldn't get along with anyone. I bitched about every little thing. I was disrespectful to my parents, calling them things I wouldn't normally say. I didn't know what to do. Life was passing me by. I slept most of the time. Sometimes I'd sneak out and just hang around the railroad tracks, always thinking about it, thinking about ending it. I started to smoke. From time to time, I'd drink and smoke a few of those special roll-ups. I just didn't give a damn. If I died, it would be no big deal.

During my junior year, my father finally talked to someone who really helped us out. To this social worker, I owe a lot: my life, possibly. Within 9 months everything worked out.

The actual process took only 2 days. I left for Mexico on September 19th. I was to take my physical examination and receive results from a blood test. I had gotten up around 5:00 a.m. and left with my parents for the medical exam. The lines were blocks long. There was only one nurse and two doctors. It took about 5 hours until the doctor examined me. He asked so many questions, I thought I was being questioned by a lawyer. First they drew blood, then I was examined from head to toe. The whole process took about 13 hours. I was also required to see a psychologist. This alone took 5 hours. I was interviewed and given four psychological tests. I was also given a test of logical thinking and a test in American history. Although I enjoyed talking to the psychologist, this was the longest day of my life. By the end I was dead tired.

The next and final day, we got up at 5:00 a.m. for an interview at the U.S. Consulate, after which final determination of my application for resident status would be made. Oh man! There were lines of people as long as two football fields. There were people selling coffee and beggars asking for money. I was shocked; so many people! Many were waiting to be interviewed. After patiently waiting, eventually I reached the front of the line and was seated. After I had waited about 2 hours, my name was called. I, along with several hundred others, was seated in a different building, where we waited 3 additional hours. At that time I showed my birth certificate, passport, and several other IDs, and was diverted to the previous building to pay $200. After an additional hour, I was again interviewed. To my surprise I was asked only three questions. One: Was I involved in gangs? Answer: No. Two: Do I have a problem with the police? Answer: No. Three: Have I been picked up by immigration? Answer: No. Next thing I knew, at this time, he gave me a white sheet of paper that stated: "You are now a 'Legal Resident,' Congratulations!" Within 1 hour I was able to pick up a packet and my passport, at which time I immediately left for the United States, the happiest man in the world. Although I was not born there, the United States was the only country I ever knew as "home." At the U. S. border, I waited 5 hours until my name was called. I presented my packet and passport. My passport was my temporary "green card." I don't know why they call it a "green card." In reality the card is pink. The passport was then sealed with the date of legal residency. I was free at last!

I'm happier. I understand and appreciate the true meaning of freedom. It doesn't come cheap. It's a long struggle.

The Effects of Size: Bordertown Versus Weberville
by Amity Carrubba

"To realize the truth in a student's life, one must travel outside the school's limits and experience something new for comparison."

Amity Carrubba is a senior at Weberville High School, a member of the National Honor Society, and on the soccer team. Amity plans to attend the University of Illinois at Champaign—Urbana.

The purpose of this paper is to compare the total student experience in two different high schools located in two distinct communities. As may be expected, the schools and their effects are as dissimilar as the communities in which they are located.

Bordertown Central School (BCS) is located in upstate New York. My father was assigned to the local military installation for a term of 3 years; consequently, I attended BCS those 3 years. I attended Weberville High School (WHS) when my father decided to separate from the U.S. Air Force and fly for American Airlines out of Chicago's O'Hare Airport. My parents and I decided to live in a suburb of Chicago with quality schools, and Weberville was our choice. I attended WHS my junior year and am now completing my senior year.

A unique aspect of BCS is the building. It accommodates students from grades kindergarten to 12. Most of the students attending the high school in the building have known most of their classmates since early grade school. The high school is small in number, with only approximately

125 students in each class. This small size accounts for many effects on a student's life. The low number of students enables a person to know almost everyone in the high school personally, but it limits the choice of friends. For example, when a new student comes to the school, classmates immediately recognize this student and a certain group befriends the person. Having these new friends and participating in athletics and clubs, a new student is able to meet virtually everyone in the school quickly. Most students stay with the same friends throughout their high school careers because of the small number of students at the school.

WHS is a typical suburban high school with a large student body and very diverse students. The considerable size and varied types of students have a profound impact upon a student's life. A typical student does not know nearly everyone in the school personally, yet that student is acquainted with many different types of people. When a new student begins at WHS it is more difficult to be noticed than at BCS. Classmates are friendly but may not realize that a peer is new at the school; consequently, the only way to meet a lot of people is to participate in extracurricular activities.

BCS is in a community that contains many farms and lower-middle-class families. Most students live in the town their entire lives, and few travel or experience life outside of town. In the school two "classes" are formed within the student body, the "in" crowd and the "out" crowd. The "in" crowd participates in sports or other clubs, and they are generally in a slightly higher economic bracket than their counterparts. The "out" group does not participate in school activities outside the regular school day. The two groups in the school barely mix and there is virtually no middle ground. This aspect of BCS contrasts greatly with WHS. The size of WHS does not enable students to create such defined "classes"; however, less-defined "classes" do exist, with many more middle grounds and fewer "in" and "out" extremes. At BCS, the limited number of active students enables a student to be in sports and clubs at the same time. A student will attend school, go to a club meeting until 3:15, then go to practice at 3:30.

At WHS the abundance of active students allows students to specialize in athletics or clubs, but not both. Time allotment for sports practices and club meetings are the same, so it is impossible for a student to be involved with both. The ability of a student to concentrate all time on a sport or a club results in better teams and clubs but less well-rounded individuals. At WHS different groups are defined by the students' activities, rather than BCS's definition by activeness. Different "classes" also have different courses at BCS. The students who are involved in school activities seem to most often be in the higher tracks; therefore, the same students spend time together during school, after school, and away from school. The only accelerated classes at BCS are in the math and science departments; all other areas are either average or lower. This also is very different at WHS. Weberville has different tracks for nearly every subject offered. One student at Weberville could possibly have some accelerated, some average, and some lower-level classes the same semester. This mix of classes enables the student to interact with a greater number of peers, yet it also increases the need for acceptance within a defined group.

The curriculums at the two schools are considerably different. At BCS the accelerated and average classes are not extremely difficult or challenging. The subject matter studied is most often dull, and unusual material is rarely introduced. Year after year the material seems to remain the same, and the homework assignments are simple yet almost never completed. The WHS curriculum for accelerated tracks is mostly challenging and time-consuming. Various nonaccelerated courses are not difficult, but they also demand some type of attention. To be in an "average" accelerated class means that the student is intelligent but most of all willing to work diligently for that class. In an accelerated class, the instructor pushes students to excel by introducing new material in large quantities, and each year classes have new challenging material. The courses at BCS are unimaginative, whereas those at WHS are difficult yet interesting.

Social events at the two schools have some noticeable differences. At Bordertown, a football game is viewed with slight interest and little school spirit is shown. A basketball half-time show consists of 10 cheerleaders yelling bad cheers. Weberville's sports events have excitable fans, 50 cheerleaders, and a pep band. Formal dances at BCS are rare. The only one each year is prom, which is looked upon as the best evening of the year. Being chosen by your peers in a vote for the Prom Court is considered a great honor and the crowning of the king and queen is the highlight of the night. Weberville's prom is not as special because the school has a total of three formal dances per year. Prom is not considered the best evening, but a fun weekend. The Prom Court is not a focal point of the dance, and the king and queen are not considered royalty of the school. The differences between social events reflect the overall sentiments of students attending both schools.

The class size, different groups, clubs and sports, curriculum, and social events all contribute significantly to a student's experience at a high school. At BCS the outcome is student life in a small, poor upstate New York community. The WHS experience is that of a large suburban Midwest high school.

The general atmosphere at BCS is that of a slightly run-down small community school. A student can excel but only to a certain point, at which nothing more is then attainable. A student can know almost everyone in the school, have good grades in the highest classes, and participate on teams and clubs. The active students at Bordertown tend to be very proud—some might even say overly proud—of their accomplishments. They have little with which to compare themselves, so they may believe they are better than they actually are. To realize the truth in a student's life, one must travel outside the school's limits and experience something new for comparison.

The experience WHS offers is an intense yet effective one. The school does not allow students to believe they are the best, but it does recognize the work and effort that students put into academics, sports teams, or clubs. Students are forced to cope with intensity in school and after school; this intensity creates much stress in a student's life, but that helps students keep things in perspective. A typical accelerated student at BCS will find school effortless, activities subdued, and social life easy. At WHS the student will discover school to be challenging, activities intense and time-consuming, and social life elaborate.

The size of a school can have significant effects. Bordertown Central School is a small school that offers a student a relaxed high school career with little pressure—or quality. This type of schooling gives students a relaxed high school career with possible involvement in many different areas. It also does not put stress upon teens to cope with extreme homework loads and intense practices. Weberville High School offers a high-pressure atmosphere with much intensity and some quality. The effects of this environment are that students are more competitive. They are forced to handle more stressful situations but they may be better prepared to accept the outside world.

Inner-City Schools Versus Suburban Schools
by Terrell Watson

"Growing up in Chicago, moving here, moving back, and moving here again, I have had firsthand experience with different inner-city and suburban schools."

Terrell Watson is active in Cultural Awareness Club, PEER (a peer counseling program), and gospel choir. He plans to attend college in West Virginia.

I have gone to black schools and I have gone to white schools. The education at the white schools I have attended is outstanding.

Through the years at Weberville, I have had to cope with prejudice and discrimination. This has motivated me to make a serious effort here to bring black students together. Through this effort, I think I have reached at least half of them.

Growing up in Chicago, moving here, moving back, and moving here again, I have had firsthand experience with different inner-city and suburban schools. The peer pressure in city schools is like putting a gun to a person's head and pulling the trigger. If you don't believe me, think "drive by." There is more violence in the city and its schools. Not only are the rooms overcrowded, but the city schools have fewer programs to interest students. Therefore students interest themselves in gangs and drug distribution. The majority of the students come from low-income families and high-risk areas.

The dropout rate is appalling. The staff should be more in contact with the students. If the teachers were, they could encourage the students more. Most students do not get much attention at home. Maybe if there were more support, there would be more graduates.

Last year I attended a Chicago high school. The library is so small it could fit into a corner of Weberville's Media and Technology Center. This is a problem that people should be aware of. Why is this? I believe it's due to funding. Weberville High School has numerous programs. All schools should have these. Weberville has so much high-tech equipment, the city schools could share and be satisfied. Is this a funding problem, or is it a racial problem? It is just one high school. There are many other schools I have visited with this same problem. Weberville Grade School has more equipment than Chicago grade schools. If city high schools and grade schools cannot compete with suburban schools, how are we going to compete in the world?

Why is the black unemployment rate higher than that for any other race? Why is there so much crime in the black community? Education, or rather the lack of it, is the answer. Black people have been oppressed for hundreds of years, and it's still happening today. The government expects us to hurt ourselves. They make damn sure of it when they make unequal the opportunity of education.

I moved to Weberville, Illinois to obtain the same education as the white children. I attended Weberville Junior High School. Moving from Chicago was a big step. I had a great challenge with the white students here. I had not been as well prepared as they. The white children were more serious. I was used to easier subjects than science and algebra. The eighth-grade level in the suburbs was like the tenth-grade level in the city. The one subject in which white kids could not touch bases with me was history. History was my favorite subject.

I felt good about attending the white junior high and about being able to compete with different races. After graduating , I went to Weberville High School. The environment is much cleaner, and the people are more friendly. I have had my few problems with racism here at Weberville, but I would rather deal with that than not obtain the same education as white kids. I left Weberville for a semester and returned to the Chicago high school I had attended. There was a city teacher's strike, just like most of the years I attended Chicago schools. It is a shame. I was glad to come back to Weberville.

There is a big problem in the Chicagoland school system and its funding. Almost every year, the teachers go on strike. That's a shame! If there is not an equal amount of funding for all schools, there will be no future. Everyone is worrying about other things besides education; I guess no one will see their children prosper.

If the dominant race doesn't look out for the others, there will be a war, a gigantic war, between the races. I wonder who would win in the end. We as a people must come together and help one another, instead of fighting and discrimination.

Blacks have come very far and there is no turning back now. People of all races, creeds, and ethnic backgrounds should come together. We must look beyond the color of one's skin and concentrate on character. The African American has contributed in numerous ways. We can contribute more. We can raise this nation to the true meaning of its creed. Let us come together.

From One Country to Another
by Urooj Arshad

"Moving from one country to another leaves an indelible mark on a person, especially when the two countries are worlds apart."

Urooj Arshad is a senior at Weberville High School, where she is a member of Amnesty International. She also helps the local 4-H Chapter. Urooj plans to attend the University of Illinois in Champaign—Urbana. When not in school, Urooj is either reading books or being Americanized by the TV.

Moving from one country to another leaves an indelible mark on a person, especially when the two countries are worlds apart. This is exactly what has happened to me. Moving from Pakistan, a Third World developing country, to America, an advanced nation, has given me insight and understanding of the vast differences possible between nations.

Apart from my own firsthand experiences, I have come to know those of many others at this school who, like me, have moved from the Third World and have had to adjust to new surroundings. Their experiences and mine have made me realize that every Third World dweller has the same kinds of problems in adjusting to the life in America. This paper expresses not only my feelings but those of others.

Until Weberville, Illinois, I had lived my entire life and gone to schools in Karachi, a major city in Pakistan. The differences in high schools have affected me the most.

In Karachi, the school I attended for 11 years was situated in a major residential area. The school is a small one-story building with a small garden and a small playground. The school's name is P.E.C. High School.

Weberville is a small suburban township near Chicago. Weberville High School is an excellent school. The campus covers a large area of land including fields and space for many recreational activities.

When I left Karachi, I knew I was going to a different world. Despite this, nothing could have prepared me for the alien and foreign atmosphere I encountered as I proceeded from the airport to the house in which I was to stay. As visions of high buildings, cars, trees, etc. rushed by me, the fact registered that I was really in America.

As time went by, the differences became more apparent. For example, Weberville has a very organized system of house planning. Anyone living here would take it for granted, but compared to a city like Karachi, this is heaven. In Karachi, there is no specific planning for any building to be constructed. Apartment buildings stand between houses and industrial areas loom dangerously into the residential blocks of the city.

Karachi also happens to be an extremely dirty city. Air, land, and sea pollution has become a major problem for the city authorities. Air is polluted by countless vehicles and industries that throw out smoke unchecked. Land and sea pollution has occurred due to the problem of human waste disposal, which has already filled up land dumps and is constantly growing at an alarming rate. In Weberville, there are no visible signs of air pollution. The people's drive to preserve, keep pure, use wisely, and recycle the materials has led to a cleaner, more healthy environment. One can see natural forest preserves.

Utilities like streets, school systems, roads, police protection, the traffic system, and public transportation are extremely organized, and any problems or complaints are immediately attended to and corrected. In Karachi, these utilities are scarce. For example, many people do not get clean water for drinking. The transportation system is in shambles. There is almost no police protection and crime is rampant. The people of the city are surrounded by numerous health and other problems due to the lack of any organized system for the management of such basic utilities.

The differences in school systems are immense. In America, apparently each district has its own school system and students attend according to the district they live in. In Karachi, the system works differently. You go to schools according to your financial position. Government or public schools are not preferred by the majority of middle- and upper-class families because the schools do not offer a high standard of education. Private schools are much better, but the degree of quality also depends on how much you can afford. I went to an average private high school for 11 years.

As one approaches Weberville High School for the first time, it seems large, even gigantic. I was surprised to find that many things were handled separately in different offices. My previous school had nothing like this. It consisted of a small building with only one office to deal with paperwork. This sometimes led to confusion.

At Weberville High School, every student had access to his or her own counselor who could help with any academic problem. At P.E.C. High School, no such counseling was available. As a matter of fact, students didn't have any choices that might have required a counselor. For example, at Weberville, students are offered an incredible range of subjects to choose from. At P.E.C. High School, this was hardly the case. Students took subjects without being given any choices. When I came to Weberville for admission, I was completely baffled by the amazing number of subjects I was offered.

Moving on to other things, there is so much one can do at Weberville. The subjects available for us to choose from allow the kind of mental stimulation needed to be successful at college. Besides that, there is a range of extracurricular activities in which students can be involved. For every Weberville student, the sky is the limit, so to speak. Unfortunately, at P.E.C. High School, most of the work involves emphasis on book reading and more book reading. The students are cooped up in their own make-believe worlds and do not taste the real world until much later. Similarly, no worthwhile extracurricular activities are offered and students are pretty much on their own after school.

As can be expected of Third World schools, students work hard; however, students do not have the technologies that can make them as productive as they could be. Computer labs, sophisticated computer word processing and layout, CD-ROM information searches, informative video programs, and good school libraries are not available in the Third World.

The differences do not end here. There is also a wide chasm in the teachers' attitudes. Over here, teachers are more friendly and treat students more as their equals than in Pakistan. In Pakistan, you are required to refer to the teachers prefixed as "Sir" or "Miss" to show reverence to them. They are also regarded with fear as a source of immense authority.

I reacted to this sudden change in a strange sort of way. When I was in Pakistan, I desperately wanted to come to America; however, when I arrived, I did not jump or anything. Perhaps the surroundings were quite familiar to me from the numerous films I had watched on television. Nevertheless, I can definitely say that no single day passes without my learning something new about this country. I am thoroughly enjoying this learning process.

Perhaps because everything is so new and so much more advanced, I have undergone some kind of an inferiority complex. I suspect it has happened to many who come here. At first I was afraid of people laughing at me because of my origins. To tell the truth, from experience I can tell you certain people do discriminate against you just because you are a foreigner.

After arriving at Chicago's O'Hare Airport this past September, it took me some time to settle in. I am sure I would not have made it without the help my friends and the sense of my achievement I experienced. I am glad to say that I have come a long way.

Vast cultural and technological differences lie between Pakistan and America. There is no doubt about that. Despite this fact, a lot of people from Pakistan have come over here and have been successful. I believe that anyone who can adapt himself or herself to the new environment can be successful. With typical Third World hard work, no differences can be too high to climb and overcome.

7

Listening to Student Voices

School administrators and teachers have consistently devalued participation of students in educational reform on the assumption that students were poorly positioned to offer input and inadequately aware of the reality in which they operate. This book argues the contrary. Students, as recipients of policy, are well positioned to provide input and feedback as to the potential impact and effects.

First, students are not deaf. They have the ability to listen attentively and to assess intelligently the importance of information available to them. However, they also possess the ability to tune out information they find irrelevant.

Second, students are not dumb. They have the need and desire to express themselves creatively. Because the locus of learning resides within each individual student, only through their words and voices can their reality be understood. Students, however, also reserve the right to say nothing if they feel their ideas will go unexplored.

Third, students are not blind. Their eyes remain acutely aware of everything that goes on around them. They may, however, turn their eyes away if they feel issues important to them are being ignored.

As introduced in Chapter 1, a gap exists between the reality of to-day's student and the reality of the school as an institution. Because the concentration of power—for example, community support and fund-ing—belongs to the institution, the school can consistently choose to not listen, not see, and not respond to students, and to act without tak-ing responsibility for the consequences. In other words, they can re-main deaf, dumb, and blind to the student reality.

If education can be defined as the process by which students develop, challenge, and strengthen their ability to think critically in a variety of situations, then there is little doubt that today's schools are failing. Interestingly, upper-middle-class students do learn to take objective, standardized tests well. They do learn to join more activities and teams than their schedules can handle. They do recognize the importance of quality over quantity in their extracurricular efforts. Unfortunately, athletic and extracurricular skills alone are not an adequate replace-ment for the critical-thinking skills needed to equip young people ef-fectively to combat the economic, political, and social dilemmas certain to be part of our future.

Standardized curriculums fail to develop the critical-thinking skills necessary for students intelligently to contemplate answers to non-standardized questions. Students are told not to question whether ma-terial is relevant but simply to do well on the test. ACTs, SATs, GPAs, APs, and the number of extracurricular activities, rather than the qual-ity of lessons learned, determine college acceptance. Students are told that their ideas about the curriculum are unimportant and that every-one knows what is best for them. Many students view the system as a game and simply play along. Many feel overpowered and out-maneuvered. Today's students become victims twice—first by their schools and then by the society. This book has tried to demonstrate that students do not want this to be their future.

Together we must reform our schools to include students as vested partners in school reform. School is a dynamic set of human resources of which students are a fundamental and invaluable part. Like other resources, students must be cultivated and developed to their fullest potential. This means treating students as thinking, feeling human be-ings. It means we must both encourage and seriously consider student ideas about schooling and curriculum and their relation to the reality within which young people operate. The current system has severe deficits in design. The time has come for the school system to seek stu-dent input and accept redesign rather than continue to force-fit stu-dents to an unfit system.

As a result, we propose that an understanding of the student perspective become a sincere contributing factor in the creation of the curriculum. This change would include student input in class selection, level of courses, and issues dealt with within each course. Although basic skills such as reading and writing should continue to be maintained, students, teachers, and administrators must daily reinvent the classroom to make it relevant. Curriculum issues should not only include "What *should* students learn?" but also "What do students say they *need* to learn?" and "What do students *want* to learn?" Again, we do not propose that students write the curriculum. We are simply arguing that by understanding the student perspective, policymakers can make better policy and that it logically follows that student input is the best means toward this end.

The benefits of the approach to the curriculum described above are far-reaching. A more inclusive approach will cultivate a classroom of students with ownership and a stake in the learning process. Resulting student enthusiasm can only lead to greater intellectual development and sense of personal accomplishment. Similarly, teachers should not be reduced to small cogs in a big machine handing out standardized lessons. A more inclusive approach to students implies that teachers also will have more room for creativity and personal expression.

For parents, the inclusion of the student perspective will provide their children with a sense of pride in and ownership of their educations. With ownership comes individual initiative and responsibility. A relevant classroom will allow parents to feel that school is doing more than babysitting. In addition, because their children are the ones who will take care of them as they get older, it is to the parents' advantage that their children develop the skills necessary to inherit the future.

For society, educational reform ensures that social, political, and economic crises can be dealt with in a peaceful, nonviolent framework. Quality education empowers people with the skills needed to deal with societal dilemmas intelligently.

Finally, and most significantly, progressive educational reform through the inclusion of student input enhances student lives. A positive educational experience may curb the deep cynicism characteristic of many of today's students.

As the student pieces in this book clearly demonstrate, young people today are on to the game. They know how to play the current school system. They recognize that much of their schoolwork is irrelevant to their lives and contributes little to their preparation for the future. Although this recognition can be empowering, it also has led to a cynical outlook about our nation as a whole. Unfortunately, the cynicism is not unfounded. Students are frequently told that they will make less money than their parents. They are told that Social Security will most likely "run out" before they reach retirement age. They are told that many of their peers will die from AIDS before a cure can be found. However, at the same time, the tools of progress—critical-thinking skills—are kept from them. Instead, they are told to play the game. It is no surprise that voter turnout in presidential elections is lowest among younger age groups. The young feel powerless within the political process, for no one has given them the skills to make major decisions. Indeed, students leave the school system without even the critical-thinking skills needed to vote! Cynicism naturally follows. However, it is not the cynicism that we must attack but the situation that created it.

We must teach students that the school system is not a game. We can do this only by creating in each school a productive and progressive environment that encourages intellectual stimulation and fulfillment. In addition, we must show today's young people that alternatives to the current educational model do exist and are possible. We must destroy cynicism and replace it with optimism. We need to show students that we feel their ideas, development, and success are our nation's top priorities. This book is an attempt to begin that process. We hope other such attempts will follow. The prosperity of an entire generation, and of our nation as a whole, weighs in the balance.

References

Bloom, A. (1987). *The closing of the American mind: How higher education has failed democracy and impoverished the souls of today's students.* New York: Simon & Schuster.

Center for Critical Thinking and Moral Critique and Foundation for Critical Thinking. (1993). *Critical thinking 2000 workshop handbook.* Sonoma, CA: Author.

Elkind, D. (1988). *The hurried child.* New York: Addison-Wesley.

Gardner, D. P., & Larsen, Y. W. (1983). *A nation at risk: The imperative of educational reform.* National Commission on Excellence in Education. Washington, DC: U.S. Department of Education.

Glasser, W. (1990). *The quality school.* New York: HarperPerennial.

Herdt, G., & Boxer, A. (1993). *Children of horizons.* Boston: Beacon.

Hirsch, E. D. (1987). *Cultural literacy: What every American needs to know.* Boston: Houghton Mifflin.

Holtz, G. T. (1995). *Welcome to the jungle.* New York: St. Martin's Griffin.

Howe, N., & Strauss, B. (1993). *13th GEN.* New York: Vintage.

National Commission on Excellence in Education. (1984). *A nation at risk: The full account.* Cambridge, MA: U.S.A. Research.

Rai, M. (1995). *Chomsky's politics.* New York: Verso.

Ritzer, G. (1993). *The McDonaldization of society.* Thousand Oaks, CA: Pine Forge.